The Life
and Times of
Horatio Hornblower

Portrait of Sir Horatio Hornblower, K.B., painted by Sir William
Beechey, R.A., in 1811 and now in the possession of the present
Viscount Hornblower.

The Life
and Times of
Horatio Hornblower

by C. Northcote Parkinson

Little, Brown and Company · Boston · Toronto

LIBRARY OF CONGRESS CATALOG CARD NO. 73-149465

T06/71

FIRST AMERICAN EDITION

PRINTED IN THE UNITED STATES OF AMERICA

To the memory of C. S. Forester

CONTENTS

PREFACE   11

CHAPTER ONE   *Schoolboy*   17

CHAPTER TWO   *Midshipman*   38

CHAPTER THREE   *Lieutenant*   57

CHAPTER FOUR   *Master and Commander*   79

CHAPTER FIVE   *Secret Agent*   100

CHAPTER SIX   *Frigate Captain*   124

CHAPTER SEVEN   *Senior Captain*   141

CHAPTER EIGHT   *Commodore*   167

CHAPTER NINE   *Peerage*   188

CHAPTER TEN   *Rear-Admiral*   207

CHAPTER ELEVEN   *Admiral*   226

CHAPTER TWELVE   *Admiral of the Fleet*   246

APPENDICES   267

INDEX   289

ACKNOWLEDGEMENTS

My thanks are due to the following for permission to use illustrations in which they hold the copyright: The Trustees of the British Museum, for Plates 8, 27, 28 and 29; Mr Brian Kennett, for Plate 3; The National Maritime Museum, Greenwich, for Plates 11, 15, 19, 23 and 25; and the West India Committee Library, for Plate 21.

ILLUSTRATIONS

Frontispiece Portrait of Sir Horatio Hornblower, K.B.

2   Title page of Pennant's SYNOPSIS with Hornblower's schoolboy signature *facing* 32

3   Title page of Pellow's book on the Barbary States 33

4   Sir Roger Manwood's School, Sandwich 48

5   Illustration from a book entitled THEATRE OF THE PRESENT WAR 49

6   The Blue Posts Inn, Portsmouth 64

7   Title page of HISTOIRE DES AVENTURIERS FLIBUSTIERS (1775) with Hornblower's adult signature 65

8   Jamaica and Haiti, from a French map 80

9   *Swan V*, Revenue Cutter, in action with a smuggler 81

10   Hornblower's first Gazette letter 96

11   The funeral of Vice-Admiral Viscount Nelson 97

12   Chart of the Harbour at Brest in 1801 112

13   Lady Barbara Leighton 113

14   Notice of the marriage of Rear-Admiral Sir Percy Leighton to Lady Barbara Wellesley 128

15   H.M. Cutter *Witch of Endor* 129

16   Smallbridge Manor 129

17   The Château of Graçay, near Nevers 144

18   Page from Hornblower's copy of the GUNNERY MANUAL 145

19   The Battle of Algiers 192

20 Boxley House   193

21 Admiralty House, Kingston, Jamaica, often called
    'Admiral's Pen'   193

22 Map of Kent showing the relative positions of
    Boxley House and the Royal Naval Dockyard at
    Chatham   208

23 The *Comet* steamship as seen on the River Clyde   209

24 The Castaway   224

25 The Battle of Navarino   225

26 Singapore in 1851   240

27 The Harbour at Balaclava   241

28 The storming of the Great Redan   250

29 The fall of Sebastopol   251

LINE DRAWINGS

Section of H.M. Ship *Renown* of 74 guns   67

Map of Samaná Peninsula, Haiti, with detail of fort   70

The capture of H.M. Ship *Sutherland* in 1810   158

The Battle of Rosas in 1810   163

Chart of the Frisches Haff   177

Map of Kent showing Smallbridge Manor and its
    relation to Paddock Wood and Maidstone   252

Preface

The life of Admiral of the Fleet the Viscount Hornblower, G.C.B., has been vividly described by the late Mr C. S. Forester, to whose memory the present work is dedicated. He wrote twelve Hornblower books over thirty years and they would have sufficed, in themselves, to place him among the leading writers of his day. He was the author, in fact, of many other volumes, all good of their kind and some of them incomparable; but to lovers of the sea the books in which Hornblower is the hero have an enduring magic of their own. They have given pleasure and inspiration to readers throughout the world.

For the basic facts about the Admiral's career Mr Forester relied, it is known, upon the letter-books and collected correspondence which the 4th Viscount handed over to the Royal Naval College, Greenwich, in 1927. This material, now in the National Maritime Museum, had all been stored in the attic of Lord Hornblower's town house, 129 Bond Street, from which it was after transferred to the family's later town house in Wilton Street, Knightsbridge. There can be no doubt that Mr Forester, like the 4th Viscount, regarded this collection as complete. Unknown to them both, however, the old Admiral had lodged a letter with the County Bank, Maidstone, addressed to his most direct descendant and not to be opened until a hundred years after the date of his death. The County Bank was eventually absorbed by the Westminster Bank Ltd, 3 and 4 High Street, and it is much to the Manager's credit that he actually produced this letter on January 12th, 1957, notifying the 5th Viscount of the document's existence. The late Lord Hornblower was superstitious in his later years and recoiled from the idea of discovering what his famous ancestor had to say to him. He spoke about the letter, however, to several naval historians, including the present author. On his death, therefore, in 1968, I wrote to his successor in the title and asked leave to see the unopened letter. To this the 6th Viscount did not agree. Writing from Braamfontein in the

Transvaal, he authorised me, however, to collect the letter on his behalf. I did so and found that there was also a covering note, unsealed, which referred to three other boxes of documentary material, deposited with Mr Hodge, a Maidstone attorney. The sealed letter went by registered post to South Africa and I set out to discover which firm of solicitors had taken over Mr Hodge's business. This was the easiest part of my search for I soon discovered that Hodge, Winthrop, Knightley and Hay are still practising in the High Street, although no one of the original names is represented among the present partners in the firm. Their senior clerk, however, searched the attic and finally produced two iron deed boxes, one marked 'Smallbridge Manor' and the other one marked 'Boxley House'. I assumed at first that these boxes would contain only correspondence relating to property; interesting in itself, no doubt, but unrelated to the Admiral's naval career. I soon realised, however, that the papers formed a haphazard collection, grouped neither by chronology or subject, and that many were written or received at sea. I had there a mine of information to which Mr Forester had never had access. New light was shed on stories we knew and the gaps were filled in between events already covered. With these newly discovered sources of information available, I decided to write a biography of Hornblower; something which Mr Forester, lacking this material, would never have dared attempt. This book is the result and it is written to supplement, not to contradict, the Hornblower books already published. For the first time it is possible to cover with a continuous narrative the whole of the Admiral's epic career.

Where I have been so far disappointed is in my search for the third deed box to which the Admiral's note refers. There can be no doubt that all three boxes were stored together in the dusty attic where two of them were found. The likelihood is that one of the Hornblowers, and even possibly the Admiral himself, sent for one of the boxes, perhaps to check on the wording of a conveyance or lease, and forgot to return it. In that case the third box may eventually be found, revealing more details of a remarkable career. With this possibility in mind, I might well have hesitated over the publication of this biography, hoping that the discovery of this further material might make the story more complete. But as a thorough search had revealed nothing more,

I reminded myself that no collection of material is ever complete. If we were to wait for complete information we might never publish anything. Should more information come to light, however, a second and enlarged edition may have to replace the first.

Only after the book had been finished did I hear, finally, from the present Lord Hornblower. He had readily allowed me access to the new documentary material but he had not mentioned the letter which his distinguished ancestor had addressed to him. I had asked him for a copy, undertaking to make no use of it unless authorised, but he was reluctant to do this and still more reluctant, evidently, to see the letter in print. He finally sought the advice of a professor of history at the University of Cape Town, who assured him that the letter is of historical and not merely family interest. Thus advised, Lord Hornblower sent me a photostat copy which I transcribed and which is included in its proper place, but added nevertheless, at the last moment. It gives the final solution to a problem which I stated but did not pretend to solve in an earlier part of the book. I make no pretence of having guessed the answer in advance.

I must not end this preface without a word of thanks to all who have given me encouragement and help. First of these is Mrs Forester who has made the enterprise possible. Neither I nor the publishers would have dreamt of undertaking this work without her approval, which was most kindly given. My thanks must go in the second place to a host of willing informants, beginning with the Librarian of the Central Public Library at Maidstone and ending with the present owners of Boxley House and Mr Teesdale, chief clerk to the solicitors in whose attic the new material was found. My thanks go finally to my helpful publishers, to Mrs Kate Green who so efficiently typed the manuscript, and to my chief collaborator in this and every other venture, without whom all my efforts would be pointless, without whose aid no book of mine would be begun or continued or brought to an end.

C. NORTHCOTE PARKINSON

Guernsey
12 January, 1970

The Life
and Times of
Horatio Hornblower

CHAPTER ONE

Schoolboy

When asked in later life about his place of origin, Horatio Hornblower would mention, modestly, a village in Kent where his father had been the physician, playing a weekly game of whist with the Vicar, and where he himself as a boy would have to touch his hat to the squire. The actual circumstances were even more modest than he cared to admit for the place was hardly a village, his father scarcely a physician, the clergyman was not the vicar and the local dignatory was not really the squire.

Worth, in 1776–93 was so insignificant as to border on the actually disreputable. It lies on the flat land between Sandwich and Deal and is about a mile from the sea. On the seaward side the land was waterlogged and sour, giving the farmers good excuse to make their living from contraband. A farm called the Blue Pigeons was central to the smuggling business, being placed on the track that led down to the shore, opposite which is the anchorage known as the Little Downs. Inland, at a road junction, a score or so of cottages clustered around a chapel of ease, a building which the present church has replaced. Worth is now well populated with church and school (dated 1873), Inn and cricket ground. This was not so in the 18th Century when the place was hardly important enough to be shown on the map, its name, when indicated, varying from Word or Worde to Worth.

If the village was not a village, still less was its medical man a physician; to understand which fact we need to go back in history. For when Horatio himself died in 1857 *The Times* obituary stated that his father, Dr Hornblower, had come of 'an ancient family in Kent'. There is a sense, of course, in which this is true for the word 'ancient' can apply to any family provided at least that no more than antiquity is meant. Ancient the Hornblower family may have been; important it certainly was not. Whether Men of Kent or merely Kentish Men, the Hornblowers all seem to derive from forbears who lived either in Maidstone or in villages adjacent. Early in the 15th Century one Nicolas

Horneblowe held land enough in Aylesford to justify his application for a coat-of-arms. The escutcheon he was granted bore 'Sable, on a chevron argent, between three horns proper, a mullet azure.' He could claim no other achievement, however, and his descendants, as undistinguished, were not even freeholders. The first Hornblower to make any sort of name for himself was Jeremiah (1692–1754) Corn Merchant of Maidstone, whose will provided a local charity under the terms of which poor orphans might be apprenticed to a trade. We hear no more of this bequest after 1760, perhaps because funds were lacking to execute the will as intended. We know, however, that he had five children including two daughters. The eldest son, James, was an apothecary and herbalist who was born in 1714, practised in Maidstone and died without issue in 1769. The second, Jonathan (1717–1780) was an engineer of some note, and the third, Josiah (1729–1809) emigrated in early life to the American Colonies where he made himself Speaker of the New Jersey Assembly. From him are descended the American Hornblowers; from Jonathan the family with which we are concerned.

Jonathan had three sons in his turn, Jacob the eldest (born 1738) and his two younger brothers, Jonathan Carter (1753–1815) and Jabez Carter (1744–1814) who were both engineers; the latter being the inventor, it is said, of a machine for glazing calicoes. The former was employed by James Watt but quarrelled with him over a patent. Jacob was apprenticed to his Uncle James, the Maidstone apothecary. When qualified to practise he soon realised that there was no room for another apothecary at Maidstone. He married Margaret Rawson in 1759, she being the daughter of a fairly successful boat-builder in Deal, and it was this alliance which brought him to that neighbourhood. He practised as an apothecary in the village of Worth and it was there, on the 4th July, 1776, that their only son was born; on the very day, as it happened, when the American Colonies chose to declare their independence. In naming the boy Horatio, the apothecary was showing his own independence, for the family custom had been to give all male offspring some name beginning with the letter J. Whatever the origin may have been of this slightly unreasonable tradition, Jacob would have none of it. Nor can we doubt that he named his son after Horatio (or Horace) Walpole, the fourth son of the famous Prime Minister. His claim to any patronage from that quarter was slight indeed but is just worth recording. It would appear that Jacob was enough of an engraver to have illustrated his own (and only) published work, *A Kent Herbal* (Canterbury, 1761) and to have thus earned a two-line mention in Walpole's *Engravers in England* (1763). When the *Herbal* came to be reprinted, therefore, in 1771, it carried a dedication to Horace Walpole; one we could fairly describe as fulsome even by the standards of the day. There was no response to this overture, either then or at any time, and the choice of a name for his only son thus represented Jacob's last flicker of hope so far as Walpole was concerned; a plea for a patronage that never materialised.

If the medical man was not a physician, neither was his opponent at whist the vicar. Worth was not a parish at this time, its chapel being served by a series of curates, few of them actually resident. We thus find mention in the register of the Rev. William Thomas in 1773, the Rev. John Atkins in 1776, the Rev. M. Nisbett in 1779, the Rev. Mr Thomas Pennington in 1781 and the Rev. M. Garrett in 1789. Of these the one who actually lived at Worth was Pennington and it was he and his wife who played whist with the apothecary and his wife, as seems very right and proper. According to Hasted (1799) the Church of St Peter and Paul was 'a small mean building, having a low pointed wooden turret at west and in which are two bells'. With this damning summary, Hasted turns to some other topic, leaving us to conclude that a pilgrimage to Worth should at least be postponed until the weather is fine.

What, finally, of the squire? The only house of consequence in the present parish is Upton House, which existed as early as 1736. It is on the better land, inland of the village, and was the residence of Charles Matson, Esq, who died in 1791 and was commemorated by a tablet. He is clearly the great man to whom Horatio touched his cap. He was certainly the only squire the place could boast. But here again there is disillusion, for Upton House was also called Upton Farm. Nor did it even belong to Mr Matson but to an absentee Earl Cowper who had probably never even seen the place, where he was rivalled in land owner-ship by an equally absentee Earl of Guilford. So the squire turns out to be little more than a tenant farmer, cultivating a hundred and twenty acres of the better soil. Had he been a Justice of the

Peace his tablet would have dwelt on the fact. We can assume, therefore, that he was not, which must at least have saved him from the embarrassment of seeing, while studiously ignoring, the activities which centred upon Blue Pigeons Farm.

The first significant event in Horatio's life was the death of his mother, who was buried in the churchyard on January 18th, 1782. It was a hard winter that year and we can fairly assume that the snow-covered burial ground was swept by a bitter east wind. On that sort of day few neighbours would have cared to appear and the relatives of the dead woman numbered no more than four. There was the bereaved husband, more bewildered perhaps than sorrowful. There was Uncle Thomas, well wrapped up no doubt but shivering. There was Uncle George, the scarlet of his uniform just showing beneath his cloak. There was, finally, the dead woman's only living child, a six-year-old boy whose hand was held by a maidservant called Janet. It was Janet's appointed task to take him home should he be overcome by grief. He gave Janet no trouble, however, remaining silent at the graveside until the last words had been said. (The tears came later that night but were not prolonged even then.) Horatio Hornblower had begun a period of loneliness which was to last for nearly thirty years.

With young Horatio and his father accounted for, it remains to explain the presence and the appearance of Uncle Thomas and Uncle George. In marrying Jacob, Margaret Rawson might have been thought to have married below her station in life. Her father, after all, was a man of substance who had himself married Elizabeth Maynard, youngest daughter of the Rev. Samuel Maynard, Vicar of Brandsby in Essex. His elder son, Thomas (1736–1799) was connected in some way with the Honourable East India Company or at any rate with its 'Shipping Interest', and Thomas's father-in-law was a friend and neighbour of Robert Keene, then a Master and Commander in the Navy. His younger son, George (1742–1787) was a Lieutenant in the 77th Regiment of Foot, at this time stationed in Dover. It would not seem that either brother had taken much notice of Margaret since her marriage, but her death, from a fever, found them both, as it happened, in the neighbourhood; Thomas with some business to be transacted with an Indiaman in the Downs, George in garrison not more than ten miles away. They could not, in decency, absent themselves from the funeral. There they were and this

was probably the first occasion on which young Horatio saw
either of them. Where so much is surmise, it is satisfactory to
feel confident, as we may, of the words used in the funeral service.
The clergy of today have no hesitation in improving on the
Book of Common Prayer but their predecessors of 1782 were
humbler and more literate men whose duties were defined by
law. Though shivering with cold, the Vicar of Worth must have
begun:

> 'I am the resurrection and the life, saith the Lord; he that
> believeth in me, though he were dead, yet shall he live; and
> whosoever liveth and believeth in me shall never die. . . . The
> Lord gave, and the Lord hath taken away; blessed be the name
> of the Lord.'

It would have continued to the point where earth is thrown
over the coffin:

> '. . . we therefore commit her body to the ground; earth to
> earth, ashes to ashes, dust to dust; in sure and certain hope of
> the Resurrection. . .'

The sorrowful husband may be supposed to have realised his
loss and given all proper expression to his grief. He erected no
tombstone, however, and it is only from the parish records that
we know her age at death, which was forty-one. No letter of hers
has survived and she remains a shadowy figure. What she had
meant to Horatio we have no means of knowing but such reference as he ever made to her would suggest a feeling of guilt that
he missed her as little as he did. Of Jacob we know rather more
and our picture is of an unsuccessful and dissatisfied dreamer,
with some of the aptitudes but none of the ambition which
characterised his father and brothers. His *Herbal* is regarded
by experts as a mediocre work, largely borrowed from other
authors. As for his engraving, that was only one of a dozen
hobbies, none of them profitable and each of them a distraction
from his proper trade. What attention he paid to Horatio was
absent-minded and spasmodic and the boy's early upbringing
was practically entrusted to Janet; who married, however, a year
or so after the funeral. Of her successor Horatio could not even
remember the name.

With the concluding words:

'The grace of our Lord Jesus Christ, and the love of God, and the fellowship of the Holy Ghost, be with us all evermore. Amen.'

the funeral came to an end. The little group broke up and headed for home, stamping in the snow and eager to find shelter. Jacob Hornblower led his two brothers-in-law back to the house where he lived and practised and from which the procession had set forth an hour before. There would be mulled claret, one is confident, and his guests would have needed it.

Our problem is to decide now on the vexed question of Horatio's exact birthplace. Local tradition on this point is emphatic but divided. The historians of Sandwich and Deal have argued the point before learned societies, some pointing to Farrier's Cottage and others as insistent that Jacob's house was the building more recently used as the village shop. The dispute might have been settled, in theory, by reference to the title deeds, but Jacob was clearly a tenant, owning no property at all. In the time of the late Mr. John Laker there was a tedious correspondence in the *Deal Mercury* between those who accepted Pritchard's word for it and those who sided with Laker.[1] It came to be called the Battle of the Pig Trough because much of the argument seemed to depend upon the presence or absence of a pig trough. It is known that the young Horatio used to play with such a trough, pretending that he was a castaway in an open boat. There is evidence enough that he could have done this at Farrier's Cottage but we cannot prove that it would have been impossible at the other house. The fact is that a stone trough is not as stable a feature of the landscape as some people choose to assume. It can be moved or sold or broken up at will. If we had to depend upon such an object we should argue for ever about the Admiral's birthplace. There exists, however, a neglected piece of evidence which clinches the matter in a way to satisfy everyone. The parish register records the death of Samuel Hewson, apothecary, in 1764. This proves that Jacob came to Worth as Hewson's assistant and took over the practice when Hewson died. He and Margaret lived, therefore, at Farrier's Cottage (built in 1723) from 1759 to 1764 and then moved into the larger house. That Horatio was born at the latter address is thus virtually

[1] See *History of Deal* by John Laker. Deal, 1917, appendix VII.

certain but those who maintain that Jacob lived at Farrier's Cottage have not been misled. He was there for five years but this was before the birth of his only surviving son. The parish registers show, incidentally, that there had been two daughters born to Margaret, one of them in 1762, but both died in infancy. Horatio never mentioned these and may not have known that they ever existed.

Horatio described himself as a 'Doctor's son' and with only a slight exaggeration of his father's status. The 18th Century apothecary stood somewhere between the modern chemist and the general practitioner. The London Society of Apothecaries had existed from 1617, with a qualifying examination to restrict its membership. Outside London the Society had no authority, however, and entry for a druggist like Jacob Hornblower was by local apprenticeship. The physician ranked higher in society than the apothecary and especially so if he were a university graduate. Then as now, moreover, the physician assumed (without usually earning) the title of 'Doctor', which implied a marginal status of 'gentleman'. But physicians were relatively few and expensive and most people went to the apothecary with their minor complaints. An apothecary with a good bedside manner might sometimes be called 'Doctor', perhaps in jest; and that was as near to a doctorate as Jacob would ever aspire. Where he differed from the modern chemist was in the fact that his more prosperous clients sent for him. He thus spent more of his life on horseback than behind a counter. Poorer patients would admittedly come to his door but they would often have to content themselves with the advice of an apprentice. In comparing the status of the apothecary and the physician in 18th Century England we should remember, finally, that neither would be invited to dine with the squire and both might be sent to have lunch in the housekeeper's room.

So far as the village of Worth was concerned, the squire at the time of the funeral would have been Charles Matson, as we have seen, a man of no great consequence. We know that Horatio, like the other village boys, was expected nevertheless to touch his hat to him. He was no more, after all, than the son of a tradesman and should behave accordingly. If he began to think of himself in a different light, he owed this to Uncle Thomas and Uncle George. That is why the funeral of Mrs Hornblower marks the beginning of the story. It was the occasion on which he first glimpsed the foot of the ladder. He began from this moment to regard himself, potentially, as a gentleman. He was the nephew, after all of George Rawson, Esq. He would eventually come to realise that the 77th Foot came low on the list, that a wartime commission was not very hard to obtain and that a Lieutenant aged forty would be unlikely to achieve much higher rank. At the time it would have been enough for him, perhaps, that his uncle wore a sword. His other uncle had no sword but his clothes and manners were even more impressive in a different way. He at least reflected, if he could not exactly represent, the world of wealth and fashion. Without any great fortune or position of his own, he could refer casually to his acquaintances, Sir Lionel and Sir Fergus. That they referred as often to *him* may be doubtful but both were aware of his existence. Whether as slop-chandler, dunnage merchant or assistant ship's husband, he had made himself useful to the circle in which he moved.

The two uncles vanished after the funeral, going their several ways, and young Horatio settled down to the life of the village. He saw little of his father during the day and not much more in the evening. Jacob Hornblower had a workshop to which he would retire, a place where he did etching or wood inlay, taxidermy or mechanical invention. He never patented anything so far as is known but he was always on the verge of making some important discovery. Once a week he used to play whist with the curate (Mr Pennington) and the curate's wife. While she lived, Margaret had been the fourth player but her death nearly deprived Jacob of his weekly indulgence in cards. It is significant that the village provided no other adult whist-player, making it inevitable that Horatio should be brought in to make a fourth. He thus learnt the game from an early age and from players who must have taken it very seriously indeed. He presumably attended the village school for he could read and write at an early age. There would have been books in the house, for Jacob was a man of some learning, and more books to be borrowed perhaps from the curate. What books Horatio read we do not know. What books he possessed we do know to the extent that he kept them. Several tattered volumes were to be found in his library when he died and one or two with a schoolboy signature in the fly-leaf.

The first book he is known to have possessed was the *Synopsis of Quadrupeds* compiled by Thomas Pennant and published at Chester in 1771. The signature on the title page is perhaps the earliest writing of his which remains, the year being 1783. One may imagine that the book must represent Jacob's taste for he was, we know, something of a naturalist. The other works young Horatio possessed included *The Historical and Chronological Theatre* of Christopher Helvicus, London, 1687; and an odd volume of Camden's *Britannia*, 1701 (which includes the chapter on Kent); *The History of the Long Captivity and Adventures of Thomas Pellow, in South-Barbary*, 2nd edition, circa 1740; *The Theatre of the Present War in the Netherlands*, by J. Brindley, London, 1746; *The Shipwreck and Merciful Preservation of Zachary Peacock* told by himself, Bristol, 1759; *A Voyage to New Guinea and the Moluccas from Balambangan*, by Captain Thomas Forrest, Dublin, 1779; and *A Journal of the late and important Blockade and Siege of Gibraltar*, Samuel Ancell, Edinburgh, 1786. Included in Brindley's *Theatre of the Present War* is an Introduction to the Art of Fortification. This section is marked by a slip of paper in Hornblower's schoolboy handwriting and he has sidelined the sentence which reads, 'Fortification is defined (as) the art of applying the Doctrine of Plain Trigonometry to the Calculation of the Lines, Sides and Angles of a Fort. . .' He took no comparable notice of Christopher Helvicus and the splendid opening of his Chronology with the words 'The Creation of the World, which is suppos'd to be made the Autumn preceding, was finish'd in seven days.' He evidently preferred, even then, the application of trigonometry to the Art of War.

If there is a significant title among these it would be Zachary Peacock's *Shipwreck* for this helps to account for the castaway game which Horatio is known to have played with the pig-trough for a boat. From the same early period of his life dates a small oil painting of a damaged ship and a boy apparently awaiting rescue. He must have been given this to decorate his bedroom. The story suggested by the artist is far from obvious but a boy will amuse himself by imagining the series of events which could lead up to the situation depicted. We should, however, avoid attaching too much significance to his choice of books. He had some of maritime interest, it is true, and these are among the works he decided to keep. It is probable, however, that he had another score of books which he later decided to jettison or give away. We cannot finally dismiss the subject of his tastes in literature without remarking that Thomas Pennant, author of the first book in which Horatio's signature appears, had the good fortune to be praised by Dr Samuel Johnson. Boswell described the scene where a group of Johnson's friends, deep in conversation, were momentarily interrupted by his saying, 'Pennant talks of Bears.' They continued their discussion about something else and he persisted in his talk about Bears, the word 'Bear' providing a background noise to all else that was said. Pennant's chapters on Bears can be found in his *Synopsis*, the book which Horatio possessed as a child.

The only one of the books named which Horatio may have had new from the printer was Ancell's *Siege of Gibraltar*, very much a best seller of the day. His other books were not so much those he had chosen from a library as those which had turned up on a bookstall in Sandwich market place. Sandwich is about two miles from Worth and Horatio found his way there at an early age. Its great days as a seaport were in the remote past and it had little to offer except a sense of history. Less than four miles in the other direction, however, is the town of Deal, placed opposite the Downs. Here, between the coast and the Goodwin Sands is a well sheltered anchorage with eight to ten fathoms of water. It was a place where sailing ships used to collect for convoy or wait for a favourable wind. There was and is no actual harbour and access from the shore was obtained with the aid of the Deal boatmen. These used either a Deal Lugger or the smaller Galley Punt, both launched down wooden rails laid on the steep beach and so crashed through the surf. The Deal boatmen had a reputation, on the one hand, for driving a hard bargain with passengers whose business depended on going ashore or on board in a hurry. They were as famous, on the other hand, for their courage and seamanship in going to the rescue of vessels wrecked on the Goodwins. Writes H. Warrington Smyth on this subject:[1]

No more dangerous work exists in the world than the rescue of men from a ship which has once beaten in on the surface of such shallows as the Goodwin. The true power and horror of a

[1] *Mast and Sail in Europe and Asia*, London, 1929, p. 190.

long line of heavy breakers, rising up in foaming cataracts twenty feet high and thundering forward at thirty miles an hour as their momentum is checked by the sand beneath, can only be realised by those who have once been among them and have survived. Huge seas breaking and roaring in across the wind, their tops blowing away in sheets of solid water to leeward, and anon leaping forty feet into the air as they meet the big line of breakers, add to the terrible danger of any lifeboat or other which dares among them. A cross tide-stream running at four or five knots, the dense drift of sea-spume, the stinging rain, the gripping, shrieking wind, and the thunder in the canvas, all add to the appalling confusion.

There were no lifeboats in those days and it was the Deal, Walmer and Ramsgate boatmen who did what rescuing was done. They were also alert, no doubt, with their claims for salvage, but of their heroism there can be no question. It is one thing to run for shelter when caught in a gale at sea. It is quite another to put out deliberately into a gale already blowing, and that is what the Deal boatmen habitually did. They had plenty to talk about while ashore and there was plenty of gossip to which a small boy could listen.

Boatmen and sailors are not, strictly speaking, in the same line of business. Some men from Deal found their way to sea, nevertheless, and some of them spent their old age in their place of origin. One of these, Tom Gammon (father of one of the pilots listed in *The Kentish Companion* of 1780) had served so he said, under Admiral Vernon. As Vernon was last at sea in 1745, this was quite possible, and Tom could even have been at the capture of Porto Bello. Whether all his stories were true is another matter, for several he told about Vernon had been previously told about Benbow. He was evidently good value, however, and willing to talk for as long as anyone was willing to listen. He told of Vernon the story of the Captain who wanted to visit London but was told by the Admiral that he could go no further from his ship than his barge would take him. It was Vernon, by his account, who had his barge lifted on to a wagon and went to London in his barge but by road. The Captain who actually threatened to do this was Mad Montague while serving under Sir Edward Hawke. Another story told by Tom Gammon, and this time correctly attributed to the Hon. William Montague, concerned a Dutch ship lost in Portsmouth harbour. Coming ashore, Montague saw a dozen Dutch corpses laid on the beach. He told his men to put the Dutchmen's hands in their pockets. That done, he found the Dutch Captain in the Prospect Coffee House, the centre of sympathy. Going up to him, Montague blamed the disaster on the Dutch crew: 'Damn their eyes for a set of lubberly bastards who wouldn't take their hands out of their pockets even to save their lives.' He bet six dozen of wine that any cast ashore would *still* have their hands in their pockets. When the irate Dutchman took the bet, the waiter was sent out and returned to say that Captain Montague was right. 'There,' said the Hon. William, 'didn't I tell you that they were too lazy to save themselves?'

There were other stories, no doubt, about shipwreck and desert islands, about piracy and buried treasure. And stories apart, there were dramatic scenes of which young Horatio might have been a witness. A Dutch East Indiaman was wrecked off Deal in July, 1783. In September of the same year the *Swift* transport came into the Downs with a hundred and fifty convicts aboard, bound for Nova Scotia. The convicts mutinied, overpowering the officers and crew, and about fifty of them escaped ashore in the boats. They were all captured again, however, and taken back to the ship. More important, if more remote, were the closing phases of the War of American Independence. News came of the Battle of the Saints and of the relief of Gibraltar. News came finally that peace had been made. As ships were paid off, more tales were told of Admiral Howe and Admiral Rodney. Clever as they might think themselves, with their manoeuvres at long range and their firing on the upward roll, the French had been defeated in the end. Horatio was brought up on the Kent coast, with daily talk about the recent war. How often he heard gunfire in the distance we are not to know but Worth is little over a mile from the sea. He had only to walk or run down to Blue Pigeons Farm and so down to the shore opposite the Small Downs, the anchorage for smaller merchantmen. There was always activity there and sometimes there were ships at anchor for as far as the eye could see.

In 1785 Horatio went as a day boy to Sir Roger Manwood's School in Sandwich. This school was founded by an eminent citizen of Sandwich in the year 1563. It had begun with a flourish, well housed and well endowed, and was even visited once by Queen Elizabeth. Unfortunately, the English Grammar Schools went out of fashion in the 17th Century and the prosperity of Sandwich itself declined over the same period. Ships had grown larger and the older seaports, placed well inland on navigable rivers—places like York and Exeter, Chester and Ipswich—were giving place to the deep-water harbours of Hull and Plymouth, Liverpool and Harwich. Sandwich declined as Deal expanded, the local authorities repeatedly asking the King to do something about it. There was nothing he could do, even supposing that he had been interested, and Sandwich by the middle of the 18th Century was all but dead. So was the Grammar School, to which the Rev. John Conant was appointed in 1758. The salary attached to this post, £30 a year, which had been princely in 1563, was by this time unattractive. It was, for example, the pay allowed to each boatman of the Customs Collector's launch; and far less than was paid to the Riding Officers. John Conant added to his income, however, by becoming Vicar of St Peter's in 1766, holding the two offices until he died in 1811. When Horatio became a pupil the boys taught by Conant may have numbered a dozen. Conant taught them Latin and mathematics and the older boys went on to study Greek; that is if they stayed long enough at the school, which few of them seem to have done. Numbers in the school were slowly declining and there were no boys at all by 1804, the year in which Conant vacated the school and went to live elsewhere. He was over seventy by then and the local authorities could fairly complain, as they did, that he had been idle for years. His neglect of his duties was at least less obvious in 1785 and his pupils plodded on from Caesar to Tacitus, and some from Virgil to Xenophon. If Horatio had a gift, however, it was for mathematics, and Conant took him as far as plain trigonometry, which was probably the limit of his own accomplishment.

Sir Roger Manwood's School was revived in 1895 and is today a flourishing place of learning, combining ancient tradition with modern facilities. What it lacks is the school register for the period of its decline. No list is in existence, therefore, of the pupils who attended the school between 1785 and 1792 and there is only one name known among Horatio's schoolfellows, that of Peter

Holbrook. Of him we know a great deal because he wrote and published his memoirs.[1] His own life was almost totally devoid of incident and he never held any higher office than Deputy Postmaster of Deal. He has relatively little to say about his schooldays but the following passage (page 27) is of interest so far as it goes:

'I was a private pupil in those days of the late Mr John Conant, Master of the Sandwich Grammar School. The school had fallen on evil ways and Mr Conant lacked the energy afterwards displayed by the Rev. William Wodsworth. He was a good teacher of those who were willing to be taught and several of his boys went afterwards to the university, being proficient latinists and not without some knowledge of Greek. Only one, however, can be said to have achieved fame and that was the present Admiral Lord Hornblower. He was my junior by two years and I remember him as a silent and self-possessed little boy, backward in his grammar but good at sums. He had been christened Horace, about which we teased him unmercifully as boys will, but he preferred even then to be called Horatio. He was somewhat ungainly and took little pleasure, I thought, in the games which took place after class ended. Although ordinarily well behaved, he was one of those accused of disorderly behaviour on "Guy Fawkes night". The youngest of those questioned, he took the lead in their defence and managed, for a wonder, to establish their innocence.

We all asked each other afterwards whether they had not been lucky to be acquitted. Looking back on those years spent in the old schoolhouse on the Canterbury Road, I reflect on God's mercy in bringing me at that time to a knowledge of His scripture, without which I should never have asked myself that solemn question "What must I do to be saved?" The fear of the Lord is the beginning of wisdom but those who truly fear God have a secret guidance . . . etc. etc.'

That is all we learn from Peter Holbrook whose book is otherwise filled with pages of moralising and platitude. What little he says of Horatio is consistent, however, with what we know from other sources. It is quite true, incidentally, that the young Hornblower had been christened Horace. The theory, however, that

[1] *The Autobiography of Peter Holbrook*, Canterbury, 1838.

his preference for the name Horatio was due to his admiration for Lord Nelson is plainly incorrect, the change having been made before Nelson had become famous. The picture we have formed is of a lonely boy living his own secret life, dreaming of some future success and set apart from his schoolfellows by his own deliberate choice. It is perhaps significant that he never referred in later life to anyone whose friendship dated from boyhood. As against that, a real crisis suddenly revealed in him the natural leader. We should give much to know what actually happened on that 5th November and more to know how Horatio talked himself out of it on the morning of the 6th. One is tempted to conclude that he had already decided upon a career in the Royal Navy, inspired by Tom Gammon and other old seamen, encouraged by the news of Rodney's victory and given confidence by his own success in mathematics. It may be doubted, however, whether the choice was made at this time. A boy's intentions are apt to vary from week to week but the likelihood is that Horatio thought more at this period of a possible career with the East India Company. If he had ever thought about the army he might have decided against it in the year 1787, when news came of Uncle George's death. The 77th had been sent out to the West Indies, where George Rawson died of yellow fever. Any hopes which remained must have centred, therefore, upon Uncle Thomas. Quite apart from that, the Navy offered only the poorest prospects in time of peace. It required influence to gain a first nomination, more influence to achieve a commission and a lifetime's patience to obtain a first command. There were few ships in commission and most of the officers posted to them came of naval families, being the sons of men who had served under Anson or Hawke. There was no future in the peacetime Navy for an apothecary's son from an obscure village in Kent.

In 1789 came news of the Revolution in France. Events on the continent may have had no great impact on many an English county but Kent differs from the rest in having a coast from which France is (sometimes) visible. French noblemen began to appear at Calais just as Huguenots had appeared a century before. First to arrive were the farseeing and astute, with their fortunes converted into negotiable securities. Next came those whose exit had been unplanned but who carried what valuables they could pack. Last of all came folk who had escaped arrest in the clothes they happened to be wearing at the time. In subsequent fiction all the refugees appear as aristocrats or priests but many, in fact, were neither. Some were merely loyal to their king and church and a few were quite humble folk who had no taste for bloodshed and riot. Of the arrivals at Dover and Deal a majority found their way to London. A few, however, remained in Kent, perhaps hoping for a reversal of fortune which would allow them to return home. Among the first and most apprehensive of these was Monsieur Gustave Laporte, a bachelor lawyer's clerk who had collected rents for some of the nobility round Abbeville. A nervous man, he had reached Ramsgate even before the Bastille had fallen, moving thence to Sandwich in search of cheaper lodging. He set up there as a teacher of French, music and dancing and made a scanty living out of it, being careful to remain on good terms with Mr Conant who luckily taught no one of the subjects which Laporte had to offer. Gustave seems to have fallen sick in the autumn of 1791 and called in Mr Jacob Hornblower as his medical adviser. Being unable to pay the apothecary for his attendance (for his income ceased when the illness began), M. Laporte offered to pay him in kind when he was well again. Unable to recover his fees in any other way, Jacob sent Horatio to him as a pupil. It must have been obvious even on the first day that Horatio was tone-deaf and unable to tell one note from another. In dancing he was awkward, learning little more than the ceremonious bow with which a gentleman salutes his partner in the minuet. As a student of the French language he was more promising. By the end of 1792—his last year at the Sandwich Grammar School—he had a good vocabulary and syntax, spoilt only by a dreadful accent. He could read the language better than he could speak it and some books he acquired at this period were still in his library when he died. One work was entitled '*Nouvelle Description des Châteaux et Parcs de Versailles et de Marly* . . . Par M. Piganiol de la Force.' It was published at Paris 'Chez Aumont, Libraire, Place du College Mazarin' in 1764, but Hornblower had only the first volume and that without its binding. Another book acquired at this period was the '*Histoire des Aventuriers Flibustiers qui se sont signalés dans les Indes* par Alexandre-Olivier Oexmelin', published in 1775. Of this he had evidently studied both volumes; adding some

Synopsis

of

Quadrupeds

BYDDUW HEBIDDIM · A DUW A DIGON

Chester
Printed by J. Monk
MDCCLXXI.

M. Griffith Del.ᵗ   R. Murray Sc.ᵗ

Horace Hornblower
His Book

Title page of Pennant's Synopsis with Hornblower's schoolboy signature

T H E
H I S T O R Y
OF THE
Long Captivity
A N D
ADVENTURES
O F
Thomas Pellow,
In SOUTH-BARBARY.

Giving an Account of his being taken by two *Sallee Rovers,* and carry'd a Slave to MEQUINEZ, at Eleven Years of Age : His various *Adventures* in that Country for the Space of Twenty-three Years : Efcape, and Return Home.

In which is introduced,

A particular Account of the *Manners* and *Cuftoms* of the MOORS ; the aftonifhing *Tyranny* and *Cruelty* of their EMPERORS, and a Relation of all thofe great *Revolutions* and *Bloody Wars* which happen'd in the Kingdoms of *Fez* and *Morocco,* between the Years 1720 and 1736.

Together with a Defcription of the Cities, Towns, and Pub-lick Buildings in thofe Kingdoms ; *Mifcries of the Chriftian Slaves ;* and many other *Curious Particulars.*

Written by HIMSELF.

The Second EDITION.

Printed for R. GOADBY, and fold by W. OWEN, Bookfeller, at *Temple-Bar,* LONDON.

Title page of Pellow's book on the Barbary States, in Hornblower's possession as a schoolboy notes in the fly-leaf on the meaning of some technical words. He had by this time some (but not all) of the habits which mark the scholar.

Horatio's father died suddenly on January 11th, 1793. The cause of his death is unknown but it would seem to have been from illness rather than accident. Horatio Hornblower was now an orphan and left to organise the funeral as well he might. He wrote at the same time to Thomas Rawson. Rawson arrived within a matter of days and assumed the duties of executor.[1] The estate he had to administer comprised no more than some furniture and books; an old horse, complete with saddle and bridle; the drugs and bottles which had comprised the apothecary's stock-in-trade; and the goodwill of what had never been a particularly lucrative practice. Having thus raised just over two hundred pounds, he had to decide what to do with Horatio. A kinder man, married to a more sympathetic wife, would have taken the boy into his London home. Thomas had no such intention but he was concerned, for his own credit, that his nephew should not be seen to starve. He almost certainly meant to secure for the boy a berth as midshipman in one of the East India Company's ships. For this, however, Horatio, at sixteen, was twelve months too young. He needed another year at school with some further coaching in mathematics. Sir Roger Manwood's School was now out of the question, for it catered only for day boys. The best idea would be to enter him for a year's schooling at the King's School, Canterbury, and this was the plan which Mr Rawson decided to adopt. The necessary letters were exchanged and Horatio was packed off to Canterbury in John Sneller's stage waggon, which went there each Monday and Friday. His duty done, though not perhaps exceeded, Mr Rawson returned to his home in Portman Square. For any shortcomings in his care for the bereaved he had the possible excuse that there were other things on his mind. George III was on the point of going to war with France.

We are accustomed by now to the procedure by which an ultimatum is delivered stating that a failure to reply in satisfac-

---

[1] In point of fact, Jacob's two engineer brothers were both alive and were nearer relatives, but contact had been lost and Horatio had met neither of them.

tory terms will mean the commencement of hostilities as from
such an hour (Greenwich Mean Time) on such a date. The 18th
Century process lacked, of necessity, this sort of precision.
Mr Rawson's return to London coincided with a message from
the King to Parliament calling for an augmentation of forces by
sea and land. Mr Pitt, presenting the message, told the Commons
that war was probable. Louis XVI was executed on January 21st
and news of this crime reached London on the 23rd. The French
ambassador was ordered next day to leave the Kingdom. He
replied that this would be regarded in France as a declaration of
war. The French Embassy was in Portman Square and it is
almost certain that Mr and Mrs Rawson watched the loading of
the coaches as the Marquis de Chauvelin prepared to leave. The
same coaches might have been glimpsed in Canterbury by the
young Horatio and Citizen Chauvelin (as we must now call him)
was in Dover on the 29th. His return to France was the signal for
the French government to declare war on February 1st. Parliament was officially informed about this in a message from the
King on the 11th. The war by then had fairly begun. It was not
until March 13th, however, that the *Scourge* brig (of 18 guns)
captured the French privateer *Sansculotte* (12) off the Scilly
Isles. It was later still in the year when the frigate *Nymphe* (36)
commanded by Edward Pellew, fought and took the French
frigate *Cleopatre* of equal force. Pellew, the hero of the hour, was
knighted almost as soon as he came ashore.

The immediate problem for the Lords Commissioners of the
Admiralty was to man the ships they had to commission on war
establishment. The process had begun in December, the flag-
ships were being fitted out in January and their Lordships
appointed Captain Horatio Nelson to the *Agamemnon* on the 31st.
The Rt Honourable Richard Earl Howe (aged 67) was to command in the Channel, Lord Hood in the Mediterranean, and
there was an Order in Council for empowering the Board to issue
press warrants. There was no shortage of captains and Thomas
Rawson thought that his wife's cousin, Robert Keene, was lucky
to secure the command of the *Justinian* (74). Mrs Rawson herself
thought that Robert's health was too uncertain and that he would
have done better to apply for a dockyard appointment. He and
fifty more were at their wit's end to man their ships and even
midshipmen were momentarily in short supply. It took twelve

months of effort to place eighty-five sail of the line in commission and the frigates, numbering over a hundred, were even more urgently needed for the protection of trade. The French, luckily, were in worse difficulties and unlikely to give battle before the summer of 1794.

The idea of placing young Hornblower on the quarterdeck of the *Justinian* was so obvious that one wonders why the move was so long delayed. An appointment to an East Indiaman was, after all, a favour; not difficult to obtain for a man in Mr Rawson's position but still a favour and one which would have to be repaid. To obtain a similar berth in the wartime Navy was relatively easy, for the Navy was expanding and the Company was not. The difficulty and delay in this instance was over the exact rating he should have. Captain Keene offered the Rawsons a vacancy as captain's servant or first-class volunteer, for which the Navy's allowance was £9 a year, less £5 for the schoolmaster, supposing the ship carried one. A midshipman, on the other hand, was paid £2 8s. a month in a third-rate, not enough for his needs but quite as much as he was worth. Harriet Rawson held out for a midshipman's rating and finally obtained it by dint of persistence. The *Justinian* was not actually in commission until the autumn of 1793 and Horatio, told of the change in plan, was urged to concentrate upon mathematics in general and upon spherical trigonometry in particular. What else happened at the King's School we do not know, but life there cannot have been easy for a boy of his age, thrown among youngsters who had grown up together. All we do know is that he was a tolerable mathematician but a mediocre 'Grecian' by the time he left the school in December. He went up to London by coach and spent Christmas in Portman Square.

This, his first visit to London, was mainly spent by young Hornblower in being equipped for the service. Mr Rawson was familiar with a tailor and outfitter in Leadenhall Street who would provide what was necessary at a minimum cost. A midshipman's best uniform had to be of blue cloth, a tail-coat lined with white silk and adorned with gold anchor buttons. The collar had a white patch known as a 'weekly account'. This outfit was completed by breeches and waistcoat of white nankeen, with stockings to match and a three-cornered hat. For daily use he would need a short working jacket and trousers with a glazed hat and a boat cloak. For cold weather he had to be provided with a frieze watchcoat as well. To this essential clothing there had to be added a proper proportion of white-frilled shirts and stockings, with books on seamanship and navigation, a sextant and (for sidearm) a midshipman's dirk with a sharkskin covered hilt. All had to be packed neatly into a midshipman's chest, with the name painted clearly on the lid. It then remained to pay the Captain's agent the sum of seventy pounds in advance so that the youth could be given pocket money from time to time out of which would be paid his contribution to the gunroom mess. All this more than exhausted all the Hornblower money and Horatio's uncle had reluctantly to pay the remainder himself. It was only after Horatio had gone to sea that Mr Rawson discovered the existence of the other two uncles, Jonathan and Jabez Hornblower. He eventually made contact with them and procured from Jonathan, at any rate, a proportion of Horatio's annual allowance. This would be needed for the next four years and it came from a relative that Horatio had never seen. He very fully repaid this debt, however, in later years.

Once these preparations were complete Mr Thomas Rawson saw Horatio to the Portsmouth coach and gave him a letter of introduction to Captain Keene. Wishing him luck, he said goodbye and saw the coach start on its journey. He was seriously concerned about the total of his expenditure on this occasion and there was Harriet suggesting that the uniform coat was hardly good enough! Thomas was, of course, a patriot and concerned for the good of the Navy. He had just made a substantial contribution to the country's defence. Whether he could maintain the boy's allowance was another matter. It was quite possible, however, that the young man would be killed in a year or two, as often happened in the wartime Navy, and without even the expense of a funeral. It was an arduous service and the boy did not look particularly strong. As against that, there was always the possibility of prize-money. It might be true that a midshipman's share was rather small but there was also the chance of promotion, especially in the West Indies. Sent to that station, a youngster might soon be provided for, one way or another. One thing certain, however, was that this appointment as midshipman marked the furthest limit of the Rawsons' influence. . . . These are the thoughts which probably passed through Thomas Rawson's mind as he made his way back (on foot) to Portman Square. He could do nothing whatever to obtain for Horatio his commission as lieutenant. As from this moment the young man was definitely —yes definitely—on his own.

CHAPTER TWO

Midshipman

The arrival of the London Coach was always a moment in the life of Portsmouth. Even if the last miles had gone slowly, the coach picked up speed as it neared the town and the horses fairly galloped through the arched gateway. With a cracking of the whip and a blowing of the horn the coach pulled up at the George, dropped the mail and the civilian passengers, passed through High Street and so out through another archway and over a drawbridge on to the Parade. Swerving to the right it came to the Point, passing a narrow street before stopping at the Star and Garter and pulling up, finally, at the Inn called the Blue Posts. This was where young Hornblower alighted and where his sea chest was dumped in the entrance. The coach wheeled about and went back into the town and Horatio rather timidly entered the coffee room. There would be no officers present—it was the midshipman's place—and no civilians either. Such youngsters as might be there that afternoon would each be consuming tea for two and toast for six. Of Hornblower, an obvious novice, they would take no notice whatever. Drinking his tea and placed far from the fireside round which the others were grouped, Hornblower would have listened for the first time to the language spoken in the Navy of 1794. He had heard the yarns told by old seamen on the foreshore at Deal. But this was Portsmouth in time of war. This was a world of which he could know nothing.

Wherever men are banded together for a purpose, sharing the technicalities of a trade and with a daily background of danger, they create their own language. It is not merely the language of war—as it was here at Portsmouth Point—but of that particular war. Everyone in the Britain of World War II shared a certain slang but each Service had its own; the language of, say, '*Flare Path*' or '*The Cruel Sea*'. Official and technical terms are duplicated by slang words known only to members of the group and used indeed as a barrier against the uninitiated. Men set apart by the wearing of a uniform can sense at once whether another man

—even wearing the same uniform—is a member of the same fraternity. These different types of atmosphere and vocabulary were fully developed in the French Wars of 1793–1815, and the more developed in that the wars were so prolonged. In the Portsmouth of Nelson's day the youngster's desperate need was to learn the language and gain acceptance among men who had already been under fire. The danger in the background was very real and it gave an edge to life, a keen sense of urgency. What we enjoy today may not be there tomorrow or we may not be there to have it. We live more intensely when there is peril in the offing and the flash of gunfire on the horizon. That life for Hornblower began at the Blue Posts on that blustering day in 1794.

Hornblower found his way out to the *Justinian* in a shore boat and reported to the lieutenant of the watch. The *Justinian* was a third-rate ship of the line, built to the same design as the *Thunderer*. Sir Thomas Slade, the naval architect, was so well pleased with his *Thunderer*, launched in the Thames in 1783, that she had a whole series of sister ships, the *Theseus, Ramillies, Hannibal* and others, all built just too late for the previous war. The *Justinian* was one of these, launched on the Thames in 1786, measuring 1,685 tons with a length of 170′ 10″ on the gun-deck. She mounted twenty-eight 32-pounders, as many 18-pounders on the upper deck, with fourteen 9-pounders on the quarterdeck and four more on the forecastle. She was established for a crew of 590, including twelve midshipmen. These, with Master's Mates, the Assistant Surgeon and Captain's Clerk, made up the membership of the Gunroom. She was an unhappy ship at this time with Captain Keene a sick man and several of the lieutenants far too old for active service. Robert Keene had been a good officer in his day, one who had been commissioned in 1771, served under Admiral Hughes in the East Indies and was promoted from First Lieutenant after the Battle of Negapatam. He was invalided home with hepatitis, the liver complaint, in 1783 and had never really recovered. He actually resigned his command in 1795 and died soon afterwards. His first lieutenant was invalided at about the same time, a victim of dysentery and boredom. The *Justinian* herself was badly damaged by grounding in 1797 and ended as a sheer hulk at Plymouth.

From inability to complete her crew the *Justinian* remained at Spithead until Lord Howe put to sea on May 2nd. For nearly four months Hornblower thus learnt his seamanship in a ship at anchor. It was a period for him of acute misery, the result of bullying. His mess was ruled by the senior midshipman, John Simpson, a powerfully built man aged thirty-three who had repeatedly failed the examination for lieutenant. As the junior midshipman, awkwardly adolescent and naturally shy, he was the inevitable butt for the sadistic Simpson who was further embittered by his own failure. The crisis came in their relationship when they were both ashore on duty. Hornblower managed to provoke Simpson into fighting a duel and in circumstances which allowed to Hornblower the choice of weapons. He chose pistols at one yard range, the one to be loaded and the other empty, the combatants not to know which had the cartridge and bullet. It was an extraordinary proposal which the seconds might well have refused to accept, but it gave him what he wanted—an even chance—and the other midshipmen thought that it might free them from Simpson's tyranny. The meeting actually took place and both pistols miss-fired, at which point the seconds intervened and stopped the fight. It afterwards transpired that neither pistol had been loaded—this was by the Captain's order—and that the duel had thus been frustrated. The result might have been a further challenge but Captain Keene forestalled this by having Hornblower transferred to another ship. John Simpson remained in the *Justinian*, which was one of the ships detached under Rear-Admiral Montagu—so missing the Battle of the Glorious First of June—but he did not live much longer to terrorise his messmates. In early July he fell overboard as the result of the footrope breaking on the foretopsail yard. The accident happened in daylight with only a moderate breeze and sea but the boat lowered to pick him up would seem to have searched the wrong area. Mistakes like this are not unusual and they sometimes seem, in retrospect, inevitable.

Hornblower was not at this time posted to the *Indefatigable*, as an earlier biographer had reason to believe, but to the *Modeste* receiving ship at Portsmouth, a ship taken from the French in 1759 and now used merely as a floating barracks in Portsmouth Harbour. When ships in commission were taken into dock for urgent repair, their men might be accommodated in *Modeste* (or *Essex* or *Grafton* or *Warspite*) for a few weeks. The receiving ship also accommodated men collected by the pressgang and not yet entered on board a ship in commission. Other temporary guests were officers unemployed for the time being or otherwise 'spare', including some just out of hospital whose ship was at sea. Commander of *Modeste* was an old officer called William Finch who had lost his right leg in battle and who spent much of his time ashore. So did the First Lieutenant, another veteran, almost totally deaf. The daily routine was more or less observed but there was little to do except to keep the ship clean. That *Modeste* and the other ships permanently in harbour were properly maintained was the responsibility at this time of Commodore James McTaggart, who was answerable in turn to the Port Admiral. The Commodore was a conscientious officer but his task was as dispiriting as it was endless. He had a mission in life which no one else would take seriously, not even his superiors. His boats were on constant patrol and his messages of reproof were issued daily but with all too little result. The one point of discipline upon which he could effectively insist was that a proper watch should be kept. Everyone could see that this was vital and a failure in this respect could lead to serious trouble, not excluding a court-martial. So long, however, as there was an answering hail from every ship and hulk, the niceties of appearance could be largely ignored. For a midshipman a prolonged period on board a receiving ship could only be regarded as disastrous.

It had not been Captain Keene's intention to punish Hornblower. He had spoken, rather, of transferring him to a frigate. There was no immediate vacancy, however, and Keene's first care had been to separate the two duellists. The unintended effect of the transfer was very much as if Hornblower had been sent ashore as useless or insubordinate. Without a friend in the service, he must have thought, for a time, that his career had finished before it had even begun. If he did not despair at this time as he might have done, he owed something to the *Modeste*'s elderly carpenter, Mr Timothy Blackett. Alone of the warrant officers on board, he had a real day's work to do. There were admittedly no shot-holes to plug but the maintenances of so old a ship was a lifework in itself. For Blackett was an artist, a man who loved his work, and the *Modeste* had been a fine ship in her day. French ships were generally better designed than ships built in England, though not always as well constructed. Hornblower

accompanied Blackett on his daily rounds and learnt all about the
points in which *Modeste* differed from ships which came from an
English dockyard. More than that, the carpenter had seen
service under Captain John Schank, R.N., the inventor of the
centre-board. Schank was not in England at this time, having
gone to the West Indies with Vice-Admiral Sir John Jervis, but
Hornblower heard all about him and his ideas, gaining at the
same time his first knowledge of naval architecture. He also
learnt a great deal from the Boatswain, Mr Josiah Smedley, who
showed him the purpose of every rope in the ship. *Modeste* had
only her standing rigging, of course, but the Boatswain had the
leisure to go over it with him as he could never have done at sea.
In a situation which might have driven many a young man out
of the service, Hornblower made the best of it, quietly learning
the rudiments of his profession. Although not naturally agile, he
came to know his way aloft and overcome the first feelings of
panic with which he looked down on the deck so far beneath.

There were three lieutenants in the *Modeste*, the First included, and their only real duty was to stand their watch and
keep order on board. There were two Master's Mates to assist
them and just the one Midshipman, and it was to these that much
of the duty was delegated. The First Lieutenant, Knox, had a
home ashore and a demanding wife. The other two, Watterton
and Bailey, were interested respectively in fishing and chess. As
the junior petty officer on board, Hornblower had much more
than his share of the duty, the others doing as little as they could.
He made no complaint about this and was seldom ashore
until April, when the *Indefatigable* (64) was taken into dock. She
was one of the survivors of an obsolete class and the decision
had been taken to cut her down by a deck, thus converting her
into a frigate. Mr Blackett took Hornblower to see the work in
progress and listen to some of the talk in the dockyard. It was all
very well to make her into a frigate but what about her centre of
gravity? Experienced shipwrights examined the ship and shook
their heads, talking about problems of flotation and ballast.
Hornblower was a born technologist and took the greatest
interest in the problem being discussed. As from this time he too
was often out of the ship and was sometimes an evening visitor
at Mr Blackett's house, where a scale model of the *Indefatigable*
(as reconstructed) was being tested in water.

The inevitable happened. The night came when there was nobody on watch and the ship's bell was missing in the morning. Mr Watterton had *meant* to ask Mr Bailey to take his place and Mr Cook had *meant* to make a similar arrangement with Mr Hornblower. Each had taken the thought for the deed and had gone ashore without being relieved on the quarterdeck. So slack was the discipline that this sort of thing could easily happen and had probably happened before. Captain Finch was hastily informed and came on board with all the cold fury to be expected of someone who was plainly responsible. Mr Watterton was certain by then that he *had* spoken to Mr Bailey and Mr Cook was nearly as positive that Mr Hornblower *had* agreed to take his place. These excuses were, of course, futile. The point was that Mr Walker (First Lieutenant) had gone ashore without handing over the duty to anyone. His watch was not over until he had been relieved. There was some little difficulty in making the situation clear to him but he was finally as alarmed as the others and with even better reason. Central to the whole nightmare was the disappearance of the ship's bell. For the bell, as everyone realised, had not been stolen. It had been taken by seamen from the guard-boat, as proof that there had been no one on deck. Nor had there been, for the harbour watch had gone below as soon as they realised that there was no officer on board. The Commodore had the bell and would probably send for Captain Finch and ask him whether he had seen it before. With the name MODESTE cast in solid brass, there was no real scope for argument but plenty for sarcasm on the Commodore's part. Neither need that be the end of it, for McTaggart might well want to make an example for the benefit of others. There might be a court-martial with Mr Walker the probable victim.

The Commodore had his broad pennant hoisted in the old *Royal William*, a three-decker built in 1719, but he was ashore that day holding a Court of Inquiry at the Dockyard. It was not until the afternoon, therefore, that a letter was delivered by the grinning coxswain of the guard boat, summoning Captain Finch to appear next morning, together with the officer who had the second dog watch on what we might fairly call the night of the crime. Hornblower knew enough of the service by now to realise that all blame must fall, eventually, on the junior midshipman. He was not surprised, therefore, when the Captain told him to

appear next morning in his best uniform and ready to make his
best excuses. For one whose naval career had begun at Spithead
and had continued in Portsmouth harbour, the next logical step
would be to the beach. Even more depressing was the thought
that he was not, in fact, entirely blameless. Cook had not asked
Hornblower to keep his watch for him but he *had* talked of going
ashore, from which the inference was that *someone* would have to
take his place—and who else could that be? The ship's whole
routine was slipshod and Hornblower (as he realised) had not
been immune to bad example. He could plead that he had never
yet served under an officer whose example was good, but that was
not enough for his own conscience. He had to share in the
responsibility for the general slackness of discipline and he made
an inward resolve that this should never be said of him again. In
the meanwhile he was in a tight corner and had to make some sort
of a plan. Once at sea he must expect to be in tight corners and it
would be his task to show that a good officer knows how to
wriggle out of them. For him the test had come almost at the
outset and failure in it might prevent him even becoming an
officer at all. His first glimmerings of tactical instinct told him
that excuses made before the Commodore—even if he were given
the chance to utter them—would be futile. What mattered was
the action he must take in the meanwhile. How would it be if he
were to save the ship from disaster or save a man from drowning?
We may be certain that Hornblower considered a score of such
futilities before he asked himself, as he finally did, what was the
essence of the thing he had to do? Once the right question had
been asked, the right answer was obvious. To prove that *Modeste*
was efficiently commanded was impossible. Nothing could be
done in that direction. All that he could hope to demonstrate—
without any show of argument—was that other ships were as bad
or worse. Before nightfall he had thought of a desperate plan for
use in a desperate situation. People might say afterwards that his
action was lunacy but no one would be able to say that he had
done nothing.

Hornblower's scheme involved an accomplice and a small boat.
There was no problem about the boat because Mr Watterton had
one that he used for fishing. He made no difficulty over lending
it when Hornblower approached him, explaining that he and
Blackett wanted to visit a friend. As accomplice he chose a boy

called Dick Charlesworth who worked in the sick bay. The boy
readily accepted both a bribe and the explanation that Hornblower's object was to win a wager. On board but not on duty
during the first dog watch, Hornblower made good use of a
telescope, climbing to the maintop so as to have a better view
round the harbour. He had a talk with the boatswain about the
sort of routine observed by the guard boat. At what hour would
the bell have been removed? Mr Smedley said that the guard boat
went the rounds before and after midnight, once during the
second dog watch and once again during the first watch. If the
bell had been removed at (say) 10.0 p.m., there would be no
further patrol until after the watch had been changed. Thanking
the boatswain, Hornblower spent another hour aloft but this
time up the foremast. He was watched idly by Mr Bailey, in
charge of the deck, and he explained afterwards that he was still
learning the ropes. He was himself on duty during the second dog
watch, keeping careful lookout for signals. He also observed the
guard boat just before the church clocks ashore were striking
eleven. At midnight Mr Bailey was relieved by Mr Walker and
he himself by Mr Cook. He went below to the midshipman's
berth and changed into the working clothes he had bought from
the *Justinian*'s slop-chest. Coming barefoot on deck at 1.0 a.m.,
having fetched Charlesworth from his hammock, he found the
night moonless (as he knew) and cloudy (as he had expected).
He and his accomplice managed to reach the entry port without
being seen or heard, slipped silently down the ladder and undid
the painter on Mr Watterton's gig. A minute later the boat was
gliding away on the flood tide, the oars motionless until they were
out of earshot. With rowlocks muffled, Charlesworth now rowed
very quietly and Hornblower steered for the *Royal William*,
aiming as if to collide with her stem to stem. There should, in
theory, have been a lookout-man on the forecastle but Hornblower guessed that he would have joined the other lookout at
the ship's entry port. There was no challenge, anyway, and Hornblower managed to find the rope he had noticed, trailing as it
should not have done from the port cat-head. Telling Charlesworth to hang on and wait, he managed to scramble on to the
forecastle. Without pausing for a second, he made for the fore-
stay and began to walk up it, just as during the evening's rehear-
sal. He arrived gasping in the foretop and rested for a minute or

two. Seeing nothing of the deck below, which had made the climb easier, he concluded hopefully that he was himself invisible from the deck. Finding the main topmast stay, he swung himself along it hand to hand. Somewhere ahead of him was the topmast head, the point he had sworn to reach.

To Dick Charlesworth the period of waiting seemed endless. He was obsessed with a fear that he might sneeze, with consequences too horrible to think about. He was not cold, however and he stopped his nostrils, moreover, to lessen the danger. The church clock struck two and he guessed that this crazy midshipman—a lad of his own age—had been gone for a quarter of an hour. Perhaps he had been caught? But there would have been a noise in that case, footsteps and voices raised. No, all was quiet except for the lapping of the flood tide against the ship's stem. . . The things these young men would do for a wager! . . Suddenly there was a slight noise overhead and a tense whisper 'Catch!' A bundle of cloth dropped into the boat and he managed to break its fall. By the feel he judged it must be something wrapped in cloth for the sake of quiet handling. A minute later Hornblower slid down the rope, not too handily, and dropped on the floorboards with a bump. It sounded to young Charlesworth like the crack of doom and he waited, breathless, to hear some reaction on board. All was quiet, however, and he heard Hornblower hiss the words, 'Shove off!' This was not too easy with the tide tending to carry the boat into the ship's bow but Hornblower took one oar from him and they began to make headway by a combined effort. Pulling hard and still in silence, they headed back for the *Modeste*. As they neared her, Charlesworth had a fresh moment of panic. 'What if Mr Walker hears us?' he managed to whisper. 'He can't,' snapped Hornblower, 'He's stone deaf!' Charlesworth felt happier when reminded of this, but his heart nearly stopped when he heard a challenge from the *Grafton*. 'That's the guard boat being challenged.' Hornblower reassured him, 'She's passing *Grafton* on the shoreward side.' Ten minutes later the gig was tied up again and Hornblower with his bundle of cloth, was silently climbing the ladder. A minute later he vanished below and Charlesworth tip-toed back to his berth. He heard five bells made on board the *Warspite* as he turned in, wondering why there was no similar sound in the *Modeste*. Then he remembered—there *was* no bell! Someone would catch it for that in the morning. As he snuggled under his blanket he was happy to think that he, of all people, was free from blame.

The Captain's barge was ready at the appointed hour and the First Lieutenant and Hornblower were at the entry port, properly uniformed. Captain Finch looked at them sourly as he returned their salutes and was piped to the barge. The other two took their places and they were presently alongside the *Royal William*. Pipes twittered again and Captain Finch saluted Captain Hargreaves, who led him below to the Commodore's quarters. The other two waited outside, pacing the deck for what must have seemed a long time. Then Mr Walker was sent for and there was a still longer pause. We have no means of knowing what was said to the Captain and First Lieutenant but the interview with Hornblower became a legend at Portsmouth and was exactly or at any rate fully described in the memoirs of Josiah Houghton, the Port Admiral at this time.[1] He was not present, of course, and repeats only what McTaggart told him, but we may believe that his story is not wildly incorrect.

'The receiving ships, hospital ship and other hulks in Portsmouth Harbour were placed immediately under the supervision of Commodore James McTaggart, who did his best to ensure that these old warships should be properly maintained and guarded. A guard boat used to go the rounds so as to test the vigilance of the harbour watch. When there was no challenge from one of these old men-of-war the guard boat's Petty Officer was instructed to remove some piece of equipment that could be readily identified as proof of inattention to duty. So badly guarded was one ship that the guard boat's crew were actually able to remove the ship's bell. Glad to have such indisputable evidence, old McTaggart sent for the "Master and Commander", the officer whose watch it was at the time and the midshipman who should have been assisting him. Had they been summoned immediately the consequences might have been serious for all those concerned but some other duty prevented McTaggart from taking action until after another night had passed, a night which the midshipman had put to good use. It so happened that this

[1] *Reminiscences of Vice-Admiral Sir Josiah Houghton.* Edited by his nephew, the Rev. Mark Houghton, M.A., of Oriel College, Oxford. London, 1843 (page 229).

midshipman was none other than Horatio Hornblower, then aged seventeen or eighteen and quite new to the service. When his turn came to face the Commodore it was evident that the First Lieutenant had tried to fix the blame on his young assistant. After some five minutes of official rebuke he was asked for his explanation. There was the ship's bell on the cabin table, the damning proof of a negligence beyond all previous example in the Navy's history. What had he to say for himself? The Commodore probably expected some plea on the grounds of youth and inexperience but the midshipman made no excuses. He replied in one sentence as follows:

' "You will find, sir, that your broad pennant is missing."

'There was an awful silence and the Commodore turned to his ship's First Lieutenant with a look of inquiry.

' "The pennant *was* missing this morning, sir," that officer had to admit. "I think it must have blown overboard during the night. I have asked the dockyard to provide another. I beg pardon, sir, for not having reported it." The Commodore looked again at the midshipman with eyebrows raised still higher. He considered him in silence for a minute and then barked out the order, "Go and fetch it!" Hornblower said "Aye, aye, sir!" and fled. The story was round Portsmouth before nightfall and the ship's bell was restored without further comment to the place where it usually hung.'

All this is probably true but Houghton fails to finish the story, perhaps because he never heard what the finish was. The *Arethusa* (38 guns) came into Portsmouth a few days later, a famous frigate commanded by an already famous seaman, Sir Edward Pellew. The *Arethusa* was ordinarily stationed at Falmouth but Pellew wanted to look at the *Indefatigable* for which he thought of applying when she was ready again for sea. He was asked to dine with McTaggart, with whom he had served at one time during the previous war. Over their wine McTaggart told his tale of the bell and the pennant, a story against himself. Pellew was interested and asked who the midshipman was. The name Hornblower meant nothing to him but he knew about the *Modeste*. What was an active young man doing in a mere hulk at permanent moorings? McTaggart remembered, perhaps with an effort, that Hornblower had fought a duel with another midshipman as a result of which the two had to be separated. Still more

Sir Roger Manwood's School, Sandwich, from an 18th Century print

Illustration from a book entitled The Theatre of the Present War in the Netherlands which was in Hornblower's possession as a boy

intrigued, Sir Edward asked Captain Finch to send Hornblower out to the *Arethusa*. The interview which followed was a turning-point in Hornblower's career and he described it years after-wards to a friend:

Pellew: I have heard about you from the Commodore, Ports-mouth. What puzzles me is what you are doing in the *Modeste*. That is not the active service in which a young man can learn seamanship. You are wasting your time!

Hornblower: Yes, sir. But I have used my opportunity to study shipbuilding, chiefly on board the *Indefatigable*.

Pellew: You have? And what do you think of her?

Hornblower: With the masts and spars ordered there is danger that her centre of gravity will be too low.

Pellew: Just entered and you already know better than the Navy Board!

Hornblower: I think, sir, that Captain Schank, were he here, would advise reducing the amount of ballast.

Pellew: You are known to John Schank, my old shipmate? Good god! You don't also happen to play whist, by any chance?

Hornblower: Yes, sir.

Pellew: Then that settles it. We need a fourth player aboard. I have great pleasure, therefore, in offering you a midship-man's vacancy in the *Arethusa*. I think that Captain Finch will agree to the transfer. Tell him, however, that we sail at noon to-morrow and that you should be on the hard by the Sally Port at nine.

Hornblower: Aye, aye, sir—and thank you, sir!

This is one of the rare instances in which we know (more or less) what actual words were said. The scene which follows is invented but one is morally certain that it must have taken place. We can safely assume that Hornblower kept away from the Blue Posts for the whole of the period he was in a receiving ship. He was too proud to risk an encounter with other youngsters who would ask 'What ship?' and then smile pityingly when he had to admit that he was in the *Modeste*. On that magic morning, how-ever, in April, 1794, he would certainly have appeared, however, briefly, in the coffee room. Someone would have asked 'What ship?' and nothing could have been more casual than his laconic reply '*Arethusa*'. There would have been a roomful of people looking at him with a new respect. But we cannot be sure that things happened the way they ought. It is quite possible that the question was never asked, the other midshipmen being merely interested in themselves. It is even possible, worse still, that there was nobody there at all. What we do know is that Hornblower was delighted to find himself in a frigate; more than that, in a crack frigate and more than that again, in the frigate commanded by Sir Edward Pellew. It must have been a great moment when he reported for duty and felt, for the first time, that he was (or would anyway soon become) a member of the team.

Pellew's was a name to conjure with in those days. He was the ideal frigate captain, a born leader, quick, active, intelligent and brave. There was nobody in his ship whose work Pellew could not have done as well or better and he could race any midshipman to the masthead. Not yet forty, he was the subject of ballads and engraved portraits, a man to be recognised in the streets. To gain a place on the *Arethusa*'s quarterdeck must have been the ambition of a hundred young men, some of them well-connected in the Navy, some with influential families ashore, some already experienced at sea and in action. What so many wanted, however, was given to Hornblower on impulse, partly because he had shown initiative, partly because he could play whist. If he was lucky it was in his mention of Captain Schank when ignorant that Pellew and Schank were old friends who had served together on the American Lakes. If questioned he would have to admit that he had only heard of Schank from the *Modeste*'s carpenter but Pellew had given him no time to say anything further. It now rested with him to prove that Pellew had been justified in his choice. Finding himself among messmates who were picked men, keen, high-spirited and confident, he quickly became a practical seaman. Sailing at once, the *Arethusa* joined her frigate squadron at Falmouth. This comprised the *Flora* (36 guns), flying the broad pennant of Sir John Borlase Warren, the *Arethusa* herself (38), the *Melampus* (36) commanded by Captain Wells, the *Concorde* (32) commanded by Sir Richard Strachan and the *Nymphe* (36), Pellew's old ship now commanded by Captain Murray. Sir John put to sea on April 15th, 1794 and fell in with the *Minerva* frigate on the 22nd. The *Minerva* bore the flag of Rear-Admiral the Hon. William Cornwallis, on passage back from the East Indies. *Minerva* had sighted four frigates the

previous day—which could only be French—and this information allowed Sir John to intercept the French squadron off
Guernsey on the 23rd (St George's Day). The French Commodore, Desgareaux, had with him the *Engageante* (36 guns),
Pomone (44), *Resolue* (36) and the corvette *Babet* (20). He was
out-gunned by his British opponents but did not realise the fact
until the engagement began. It was then a running fight with the
French trying to escape. The *Flora* lost her main-topmast in
action with the *Pomone* and the *Arethusa* came up to take her
place in the battle. Pellew put the *Babet* out of action and then
closed to pistol-shot range with the *Pomone*. This was at 8.30.
By 8.55 the *Pomone*'s main and mizzen masts were over the side
and her poop on fire. At 9.5 she struck her colours and the
Concorde went on to capture the *Engageante*. The *Resolue* escaped,
mainly because the *Melampus* failed to close with her, and the
Nymphe, a slow ship, was never in action.

This was the first occasion when Hornblower came under fire
and we know all too little about the exact part he played in the
action. Letters written by midshipmen are apt to be thrown away
and Hornblower was peculiar, moreover, in having practically
no one in the world to whom he could write. There were the
Rawsons, to be sure, and he probably sent them the news, but
their interest in him was slight. He would not, therefore, have
written at length and they would not have preserved the letter.
The story goes, however, that he was stationed in the maintop
and received a slight wound from a splinter which flew down
from the main topsail yard when it was hit. The result was a
slight but permanent scar to the left of his left eyebrow, too
small to show in his portraits but visible, say, to any future
partner at a ball. The squadron returned to Portsmouth after the
St George's Day action and we can assume that his next entry at
the Blue Posts was with something of a swagger. His share of
prize-money for the capture of the *Pomone* was no vast sum but
it sufficed for a new uniform from a better tailor. That and a
visible scar made him begin to look the part. He had been in
battle, as anyone could see at a glance. He was not, however, to
enjoy this admiration for long. The squadron put to sea again
almost immediately and the *Arethusa* was soon detached from
the rest in pursuit of French merchantmen in the Bay of Biscay.
As each ship was captured a prize crew was sent on board, the

fifth victim being the *Marie Galante* brig of Bordeaux with a cargo of rice from New Orleans. Hornblower was given four hands and told to take her into an English port. This was his first independent command and he was proud to have been given the responsibility. Unfortunately the brig had not surrendered until after being fired on and one shot had holed her between wind and water. The cargo of rice expanded when wet and so forced open the planks of the brig that she began to sink. Hornblower had to abandon ship, crowding the French prisoners and their British captors into one crowded small boat. The boat was picked up by a French privateer, the *Pique*, and Hornblower was taken prisoner for the first time. His eighteenth birthday (4th July, 1794) was thus spent on board the *Pique*, trying to read a French textbook on navigation. Luckily for him the *Arethusa* captured the *Pique* on the following day, assisted by a fire which broke out in the privateer; a fire which Hornblower had lit.

Soon afterwards Hornblower appeared in the Channel Islands, where he was given temporary command of a cutter, the *Royalist*, and saw some service on the French coast. The officer commanding the cutter was killed, it would seem, and it fell to Hornblower to bring the cutter away from a situation of great danger. He was soon, however, relieved by another lieutenant and sent back to the *Arethusa*. Once more in his proper ship, he played a part in cutting out the French corvette *Papillon* which had been chased into the estuary of the Gironde. The boats from the frigate took her by surprise and Hornblower, with the gig's crew, loosed the *Papillon*'s main topsail and so enabled Mr Eccles to get the ship under way. That was in early September (4th–5th) and the *Arethusa* was next in action against a smaller French frigate, *Eugenia* (28), which was taken on October 17th. For this action Hornblower was stationed in the mizzen-top and had rather a narrow escape when the mast was shot away. The *Eugenia* put up a good fight for a ship of her size and the damage she did before her capture by boarding was enough to justify an extensive refit. The *Arethusa* and *Eugenia* returned to Portsmouth in company and were docked for repair in November, the crew being sent on board the *Grafton* receiving ship. The officers and midshipmen went on leave but Hornblower stayed in the *Grafton*, having nowhere to go. He was promptly appointed A.D.C. to Sir Edward and attended him on his visits to the dockyard. Pellew had already applied for the *Indefatigable* and he now began his final skirmish with the Navy Board. It was too late to do anything about the masts and yards, for she was masted already, but a shifting of the ballast was still possible. Pellew was a fine practical seaman but the dockyard officials were prompt to remind him that he was not a qualified shipwright. He was, however, a founder member of the Society for the Improvement of Naval Architecture, formed in 1791 with the Duke of Clarence as President. More important still, Captain Schank returned in December from the West Indies and was quickly in action on Pellew's side. There was an awkward moment for Hornblower when he was bidden to dine at the George with Pellew and the Port Admiral and knew that Schank was to be there. He could foresee the moment when Sir Edward would make the intro-ductions, adding 'Mr Hornblower you already know.' When Schank replied (as he might) that he had never met Hornblower or even heard of him, Pellew could conclude that his present A.D.C. was a liar. Hornblower had the presence of mind to call on Schank, therefore, and explain the misunderstanding. He was shown into the presence of a large, fat man in Captain's uniform who spoke with a broad Devonshire accent. Hornblower began to make his apologies but they were brushed aside as soon as Hornblower mentioned the name Timothy Blackett. 'What, is old Tim here?' Schank roared. 'And he's made a model of *Indefatigable*? Let's go and see him at once!' There followed a session at Blackett's house with the model floating in a wooden trough and the two enthusiasts deep in a technical discussion about her centre of gravity. They agreed between them to take the model and its trough to the George and demonstrate their contention to the Port Admiral after dinner.

It is once more to Sir Josiah's *Reminiscences* that we are in-debted for an account of what transpired:

'The dockyard officials maintained that the *Indefatigable*, as cut down by a deck, would answer well with a frigate's masts and guns and the same ballast as when she was ship of the line. Sir Edward Pellew argued that a ship so balanced would be too stiff and would lose her mast overboard in the first full gale she should encounter. The dispute came to a head at a dinner given by Sir Edward to the Dockyard Commissioner, to me as Port Admiral, to Captain Schank and several other gentlemen whose names I cannot now recall. After the dinner itself at the George, Sir Edward invited all present to witness a scientific experiment in a stable or outhouse at the back of the Inn. There his guests found an exact model of the *Indefatigable* floating in water, masted and armed as a frigate. Weighted strings were led to the model's mastheads and it was shown by the ship's carpenter of the *Modeste*, with the assistance of a midshipman, that a certain weight would be necessary to lay the ship on her beam ends—the weight representing a gale-force wind. Sir Edward then produced a calculation to show that this force would exceed the breaking strain of the weather shrouds. There was no denying that his point was proved and several of the civilians present appeared to resent being made to look foolish. It was Captain Schank who came to their rescue, pointing out that the ship's centre of gravity might be effectually raised by giving her back the 18-pounders on the quarterdeck for which the ports were originally designed. These would replace the 12-pounders as established and those on the forecastle should be replaced by 42-pounder carronades. This was finally agreed, although not before the Navy Board was overruled by the Admiralty. The final result was a frigate of great speed, armed with 24-pounders on her main deck, and able to fire an exceptionally heavy broadside. She recovered her original masts and yards within a few months' time and was then, as everyone had to concede, a worthy instrument for her distinguished captain, who transferred to the *Indefatigable* the whole complement of the *Arethusa*.'[1]

The midshipman of the experiment was, of course, Horatio Hornblower. His first service in the new ship arose from a landing in France; an attempt by M. de Charette to raise all Brittany against the Republic. His knowledge of French gained for Hornblower the doubtful privilege of going ashore with the troops and of re-embarking with them under heavy fire. The expedition (June, 1795) was a failure and left the Republicans in complete control of the region which the landing was to have liberated. There followed an uneventful autumn cruise on the French coast, ending abruptly when the *Indefatigable* was badly damaged on a submerged and uncharted rock. Pellew brought

[1] *Reminiscences of Vice-Admiral Sir Josiah Houghton*, 1843, (page 269).

her back to Plymouth with all hands at the pumps, and it was not until February, 1796 that he was able to sail again. The *Indefatigable* was now under orders to join the Mediterranean Fleet, which was using Cadiz as its base. This was no longer possible after 19th August, 1796, the day on which Spain changed sides, concluding a treaty of alliance with France. The surprising sequel was an attack on a convoy by two Spanish rowing galleys. The *Indefatigable* was the escort but a dead calm made it almost impossible for her to afford any protection except by means of her boats. Hornblower took the jolly boat with her crew of six and was largely instrumental in capturing one of the galleys. As one of the lieutenants had been killed in the action, Hornblower was given the acting rank. At Gibraltar two months later he presented himself for examination along with other candidates for promotion. Before the examining Board could reach its verdict in his case the harbour was attacked by Spanish fireships. He was still only an acting lieutenant, therefore, when he was appointed prize-master of the captured sloop *Le Rêve* and ordered to take her to Plymouth. This was in January 1797 and Hornblower ran into fog soon after he sailed. When it cleared he found himself in the middle of the Spanish fleet and so forced to surrender. The Spaniards were brought to action on February 14th and defeated in the Battle of Cape St Vincent, but this did nothing for Hornblower and his men who were taken as prisoners to Ferrol. He was a prisoner of war for nearly two years, during which period (August, 1797) he was confirmed as lieutenant. This was to give him the privileges of an officer, which included the right to give his parole. He spent his enforced leisure and greater freedom in learning Spanish.

His release was due to the shipwreck of a Spanish privateer, chased on to a lee shore by H.M. Frigate *Syrtis*. She was wrecked on the Devil's Teeth and Hornblower was instrumental in saving some of the crew. The boat which he took to the rescue reached the *Syrtis* but Hornblower, being on parole, had to go back to Corunna under a flag of truce. He was prisoner again but not for very long. News of his life-saving feat had reached Madrid, where the First Minister ordered his release. He was sent to Gibraltar and from there obtained passage in a transport to Portsmouth. He came ashore there on March 9th, 1799, after a three year absence. He was posted almost at once to the *Renown*

(74) under Captain Sawyer, serving in the Channel Fleet, then commanded by Lord Bridport. After a week's leave, during which he bought officer's uniform and cabin chest, cocked hat and sword, he joined the *Renown* in Torbay. He was now aged twenty-two, an experienced leader and navigator and a master of his profession. He had seen active service both afloat and ashore and had been highly regarded by Sir Edward Pellew. He was fluent in French and Spanish and had, temporarily at least, held independent command. Above all, he was now a sailor who could hold his own in any company, speaking the language of the sea and sure of himself as one who has risked his life and who would always know exactly what to do. He could regard himself, and be sure that he was regarded on the lower deck, as an officer, a seaman and a man.

CHAPTER THREE

Lieutenant

The *Renown* was a typical 74-gun ship but almost new, being completed in the Thames in 1798. She had been copied from a French prize, the *Impetueux*, and measured 1,888 tons. With an established crew of 590, she mounted thirty 32-pounders on her gun-deck, as many 18-pounders on her upper deck and a dozen 32-pounder carronades distributed between quarterdeck and forecastle. She was a good ship of her class, roomier than many, and Captain David Sawyer was lucky to have the command. He was an ex-collier skipper from South Shields aged about 47, whose naval service had begun in the rank of Master. He distinguished himself at the Battle of Ushant in 1778 and was promoted Lieutenant by Sir Charles Hardy. He was Captain before the war ended but was ashore on half-pay from then until 1793, when he was given the command of the frigate *Orpheus* (32). As luck would have it, the other officers of the *Orpheus* were all of a higher social rank, the First Lieutenant being the nephew of a Baronet, the Second a Scottish Honourable and the Third the youngest son of a Rear-Admiral (retired). Even the midshipmen were well-connected, some of them, the most junior being grandson of a Bishop. It is just possible that this arrangement was deliberate, their Lordships deciding that these young officers should learn their trade under a practical seaman of the old school. If that was the plan it was ill-conceived for Sawyer thought himself the butt of the wardroom. The worst possible relationship developed between him and his officers, culminating in the indecisive action between *Orpheus* and the French frigate *Entreprenante* (36).

How the French frigate came to escape is not to our present purpose. The two ships engaged at fairly long range and their gunnery would seem to have been indifferent. When the *Orpheus* came into Falmouth the lieutenants all but accused Sawyer of cowardice and he, for his part, reported them for neglect of duty. There was no court-martial but the Commander-in-Chief, advised by Sir John Borlase Warren, split up the aggrieved parties and secured for Sawyer his posting to the *Renown*. It was promotion but it also brought him more immediately under the Admiral's eye. Posted to the *Renown* were officers of more humble origins: Buckland (First), Roberts (Second), Huggins (Third), Smith (Fourth), and now—completing the list—came Hornblower (Fifth). There was not an aristocrat among them and Smith had once served in a West Indiaman. Sawyer was being given another chance, as he must have been told, and success with *Renown* would ensure that people forgot about the *Orpheus*. No one doubted that he was a good practical seaman who had done well at the Battle of Ushant. It only remained for him to show that he was and had always been a born leader of men.

Sawyer was never to prove his gift for leadership but he was making, at this time, an effort to seem at once thoughtful and decisive, resolute and kind. He welcomed Hornblower aboard and asked him some questions about his past service. He spoke of his intention to make *Renown* the smartest ship in the fleet. He expressed his loyalty to Lord Bridport, under whom he had the good fortune to serve. He reminded Hornblower that he had much to learn, that service in a frigate was not the same thing as service in a ship of the line. He spoke at some length of the importance of loyalty. He told Hornblower that his duties as junior and signal lieutenant would include the care of the ship's small arms and regular instruction of the crew in musketry. He hoped, finally, that *Renown* would be a happy ship and that all hands would be *loyal*. Dismissed from the Captain's presence, Hornblower made himself known to the wardroom officers, who were all rather similar to each other in type; experienced, worthy and middle-aged. He was the youngest as well as the most junior and he realised that he had indeed much to learn, especially in signals and fleet evolutions. Sailing as part of a fleet, a ship of the line was always under critical eyes, not only of the Admiral but of the other ships. To gain the wrong sort of reputation could land a captain on the beach and ruin his officers' chance of promotion.

Hornblower's first significant task had nothing to do with fleet evolutions, however. A French prize, the *Esperance*, had been found to contain Barry McCool, a leader in the Irish rebellion of 1797, who had escaped from Ireland by joining the Navy. He had served in the *Renown* but had managed to desert on the French coast. He wore the uniform, when recaptured, of a French infantry officer but was treated merely as a deserter. Landed in Britain he would have had to stand trial for treason but the Admiral's decision was to have him tried by court-martial for desertion. Hornblower was put in charge of the prisoner, confined in a storeroom on board the *Renown*, and told to guard against the prisoner's escape or suicide. He was also to supervise the execution, which the Court took about fifteen minutes to decide upon. He was, finally, to ensure that the con-demned man should make no speech before he was hanged, for the *Renown*'s crew included a high proportion of Irishmen—of men, therefore, to whom McCool might appeal. This was an unpleasant task, given inevitably to the most junior officer, but Hornblower carried out his orders to the letter. McCool was helpful to the extent that he promised to be silent at his execution if Hornblower would send a letter and his sea chest to his wife (now to be a widow) in Dublin. When he discovered that McCool was unmarried he threw the chest overboard, and with it—hidden in the lid—the names of McCool's fellow conspirators in Ireland. It was an odd decision for an aspiring officer but he knew something by now about Ireland and concluded that the hangman there had already had work enough.

McCool was hardly dead before the Channel Fleet resumed the blockade of Brest, from which it had been temporarily driven by westerly gales. No work could be more monotonous and the only hope of improvement lay in the approach of spring and better weather. It is to the credit of Lord Bridport that he blockaded Brest more closely than any predecessor in his com-mand. He was always off Ushant and often took the fleet close in to the Black Rock, his flagship, the *Royal George*, even passing it on the landward side. As against that, Bridport had failed to intercept the French expedition to Bantry Bay in 1796–97 and this fact was remembered against him. By this period (1799–1800) he was too old, at seventy-two, for the service expected of him. As Captain of the Fleet (or Chief of Staff, as he would now be called) he had Captain Sir Andrew Macfarlane, efficient, pedantic and unpopular. Sir Andrew, like Bridport, believed in the close blockade for several reasons, one being that the French fleet would have no opportunity for training. They had begun the war by removing all their senior officers as aristocrats and politically unreliable. These had been replaced by their suddenly promoted juniors and by good republicans taken from the merchant service. It was hoped that revolutionary enthusiasm would make up for lack of experience but the Battle of the Glorious First of June had disproved this theory. The French Navy was strong again in numbers but blockaded in port. It was always assumed in the British service that a newly commissioned ship would need about three months at sea to become efficient. For all that time the crew would be exercised in sail drill, gunnery and small arms. To be in action within that three month period would be thought unfortunate. One effect of the close blockade was to ensure that the French, on putting to sea, would be in battle within three hours. This would ordinarily mean an ignominious and disastrous defeat.

For the blockading fleet the chief enemy was boredom, relieved only by such tactical exercises as the Commander-in-Chief might care to organise. In the Channel Fleet of 1800 morale had suffered because recent fleet actions, from the Battle of St Vincent to the Battle of the Nile, had been in or near the Mediterranean. Macfarlane's remedy lay in fleet evolutions based upon an inspired book. John Clerk, a civilian theorist, had published his *Essay on Naval Tactics* in 1782 and his admirers had since claimed that Rodney had won the Battle of the Saints with this work in his pocket. This claim was baseless but the enlarged edition of 1790 had Rodney's approval and the weight of his legend. Some naval officers, and Macfarlane among them, saw in Clerk's *Essay* the secret of tactical success; others pointed with scorn at Clerk's ignorance of both seamanship and gunnery. Lord Bridport had his own reservations on this subject but it suited him to encourage tactical discussion among his captains. Corks were pushed around the table as senior officers argued about the curve of pursuit from to windward. With better weather in April, 1800, Macfarlane obtained his Admiral's consent to a day of fleet evolutions in the course of which one of Clerk's theories would be put to a practical test. For our present purpose it is enough to record that one manoeuvre involved the whole line of battle tacking together, the line ahead thus becoming, for the moment, a line abreast. The Commander-in-Chief's flagship was in the centre and two other flag officers, Sir Charles Cotton and the Hon. G. Craven Berkeley were with their respective divisions in the van and rear. The *Renown* was next astern of Berkeley's flagship *Mars* and Sawyer paced his quarterdeck in a fever of anxiety. At last the moment came when the expected signal was made. Hornblower, as signal lieutenant, reported the signal 'Tack together'. The rule was (and is) that the signal should be obeyed when the flags are hauled down, only preparatory action being taken while the flagship's signal is being acknowledged. But Sawyer forgot this basic rule and gave orders for tacking ship. Mr Buckland immediately pointed out that this would be incorrect and Hornblower repeated the warning. Ignoring both of them, Sawyer shouted his orders through the speaking trumpet and the ship came close to the wind. Five minutes later the ship astern, the *Dragon* (74) just missed the *Renown*'s stern, carrying away her spanker boom and wrecking her own bowsprit. There was a scene of horrid confusion and bad language and the evolution then took place with two ships out of line and hopelessly entangled. An hour passed before they were back in station and *Dragon* then signalled her request for permission to leave the fleet. Her captain, George Campbell, said that his ship needed to go into Plymouth for repair. Soon afterwards there came a similar request from the *Renown* and Bridport signalled to each his reluctant consent.

There was remarkably little reaction to this unfortunate exhibition, Bridport being about to haul down his flag and Campbell being frankly delighted at the prospect of a few weeks in harbour. It was rumoured, however, that Bridport's successor would be Lord St Vincent, whose ideas on discipline were sufficiently known and whose opinion on the subject of excuses for a return to port might be foreseen. The collision between *Renown* and *Dragon* had more immediate repercussions on board *Renown* where Sawyer now saw himself as the victim of a conspiracy. His officers had planned the whole incident in an effort to discredit their captain. It was Buckland who urged him to tack ship when he did and it was Hornblower who aided and abetted the first lieutenant in his diabolical plot. Relationships were tense on the voyage back to Plymouth but there was a sudden improvement when harbour was reached. Other captains thought that Sawyer had been rather astute in escaping from the drudgery of the blockade. For a few days he basked in a glow of self-congratulation, looking upon his officers with a tolerance which bordered upon affection. Their feelings of relief were reflected upon the crew and for a week it might almost have seemed that *Renown* was becoming a happy ship. The atmosphere changed abruptly again, however, when the newspapers announced Lord St Vincent's appointment to the Channel Fleet. Soon afterwards there was a story going the rounds that a certain Captain had exclaimed, 'God forbid the Mediterranean discipline should ever be introduced into the Channel Fleet!' What was significant about the story was that the incident took place at Lord Bridport's table aboard the flagship and that there had been no reproof. Captain Sawyer had been fortunate, arguably, in that he was not present on that occasion. As against that the story would have reached Lord St Vincent, who would see in it the proof that the Channel Fleet was on the point of mutiny. He might come down heavily on a captain who had damaged his ship and made the damage an excuse for three weeks' leave ashore. Realising this, Captain Sawyer came round again to his theory that the collision had been the result of a plot. The atmosphere in *Renown* now worsened rapidly and her wardroom, on the voyage back to Ushant, was a scene of despondency and gloom.

Lord St Vincent hoisted his flag at Spithead on 2nd May and shifted it to the *Ville de Paris* off Ushant on May 5th. Sir Thomas Troubridge was his Captain of the Fleet and Sir George Grey his Flag-Captain. The fleet was driven off station on 17th May, the ships making their way individually to the fleet anchorage at Torbay. On this occasion the *Renown* lost her fore-topmast, the incident adding nothing to Sawyer's reputation for seamanship. On 9th June the Commander-in-Chief wrote to the First Lord of the Admiralty, Earl Spencer, requesting that the *Renown* should be stationed elsewhere. The letter is worth quoting in full:

H.M.S. *Ville de Paris*
near the Black Rocks
9th June, 1800

My dear Lord,

I believe I may without vanity say that I am fully informed as to the calibre of the officers who serve under me. Some here off

Ushant are as good as might be found in the Mediterranean Fleet. Others show a want of discipline and activity and are just the sort of people my predecessor might be expected to favour. Few men are qualified to command ships-of-the-line as they ought to be. Some whose talents are rated very high were never able, at any period of their lives, to regulate and govern six or seven hundred men of the description our crews are composed of, even though some of these officers were distinguished as frigate captains. The total dereliction of discipline in some few of the ships in the Channel Fleet has long been a matter of notoriety. There is now some improvement and the fleet which was recently at the lowest ebb, is now above mediocrity and some captains who were fit only for Greenwich Hospital have been replaced. Others remain, however, who are unfit to command a sloop, let alone a ship of the line. Such a one is Captain Sawyer of the *Renown*, who cannot govern his ship's company, is continually making frivolous excuses for non-performance of his duty, and appears at all times in a wretched state of imbecility, convinced that his officers are plotting against him. The licentious conversation of wardroom officers has indeed occasioned infinite mischief on board other ships but I am satisfied that the *Renown*'s lieutenants have tried at least to do their duty. The wretched performance of this ship in colliding with the *Dragon* is something for which Sawyer himself must be held responsible. If this faulty manoeuvre was due to bad seamanship I must conclude that Sawyer is as much of an old woman as Bridport himself. If it arose, as Troubridge believes, from an effort to cripple his ship and so make occasion for a stay in harbour, his conduct is infamous and worthy of exposure before a court martial. It is now too late for an inquiry into this wretched mishap but I must ask your Lordship to direct that the *Renown* should be removed from this fleet and sent on some service for which Captain Sawyer's meagre talents may be thought sufficient. I judge it absolutely necessary to dispense with this ship as one unfit to serve in the line of battle and I question whether her captain should remain for long in command.

I have the honour to be
Your Lordship's very faithful
and obedient servant
St Vincent

Lord Spencer might have relieved Sawyer there and then but receipt of St Vincent's letter chanced to coincide with a despatch from Sir Richard Lambert, Vice-Admiral at Jamaica. His request was for a new ship-of-the-line to replace the *Elizabeth* (74), built in 1769 and now condemned by survey. He also suggested that the replacement ship should be ordered to make her landfall at Bahia de Escosesa in Santo Domingo (or Haiti) and attack the fort on the Samaná Peninsula. This covered the anchorage used by Spanish privateers operating in the Mona Passage. It was impossible to make a surprise attack from Jamaica because all ship movements there could be seen and reported and because the beat to windward must be slow. A new ship arriving on the station would be unseen before her appearance off Haiti, would approach from the windward, and might have a better chance, therefore, of catching the privateers at their anchorage. The First Lord decided to send out the *Renown* as a replacement for the *Elizabeth*. He probably reasoned that Sawyer might do better on his own than in a fleet. The raid on Samaná should be his last chance, anyway, and Lambert would be told to send him home if the attack failed. Apart from that, the *Renown* was a new ship, which was advisable on the West Indies station, and Lord St Vincent had evidently come to hate the sight of her. Orders were drawn up accordingly, one to the Channel Fleet with a direction to send *Renown* into Plymouth, one to the Dockyard and Victualling Board to have her supplied and provisioned for six months and one finally to Captain Sawyer ordering him to Kingston, Jamaica, via Samaná Bay. These last and secret orders were under seal, to be opened in a certain latitude. That she was bound for the West Indies might be obvious but her immediate task was concealed even from Sawyer until long after he had sailed.

At anchor in Hamoaze, the *Renown* was soon buzzing with rumours about her destination. Most people preferred the West Indies to the blockade of Brest but the Third Lieutenant, Mr Huggins, had already had his fill of the *Renown*. He applied for a medical survey and managed to convince the Board that his health was seriously undermined. The trick, he explained afterwards, was to make oneself sick by swallowing tobacco an hour or so before the Board assembled. His replacement was Lieutenant William Bush, a year senior to Hornblower. Bush's last ship had

The Blue Posts Inn, Portsmouth, from a drawing by Martin Snape. The Inn itself was destroyed by fire in 1870

HISTOIRE

DES

AVENTURIERS

FLIBUSTIERS

QUI SE SONT SIGNALÉS DANS LES INDES;

CONTENANT ce qu'ils y ont fait de remarquable, avec la vie, les mœurs & les coutumes des Boucaniers, & des habitans de St. Domingue & de la Tortue ; une description exacte de ces lieux, & un état des Offices, tant Ecclésiastiques que Séculiers, & ce que les grands Princès de l'Europe y possedent.

Le tout enrichi de Cartes Géographiques & de Figures en taille-douce.

Par ALEXANDRE-OLIVIER OEXMELIN.

NOUVELLE ÉDITION,

Corrigée & augmentée de l'Histoire des Pirates Anglois, depuis leur établissement dans l'Isle de la Providence jusqu'à présent.

TOME SECOND.

A TREVOUX,

PAR LA COMPAGNIE.

M. DCC. LXXV.

Horatio Hornblower

Title page of HISTOIRE DES AVENTURIERS FLIBUSTIERS (1775) with Hornblower's adult signature

been the *Dolphin* sloop, employed on convoy duty between the Humber and the North Foreland, and he saw in the West Indies his chance of promotion. What he did not foresee was that the captain should be virtually insane. We are not to know what Lord St Vincent said to him in his final interview but it had the effect of unhinging a mind which had all along been unequal to command. Many captains would have welcomed a transference to the West Indies but Sawyer knew that his present orders were the sequel to his failure in the Channel Fleet. For the second time he had been given officers who were incapable of loyalty, men who sneered at him behind his back; men, moreover, whose stories about their captain must have reached the flagship. But for them he would have had the smartest ship in the fleet. For a brief period he regarded Bush with favour as one not (so far) involved in the plot, but he soon thought him as bad as the rest. His only consolation was in the belief that the lower deck was on his side. He had begun his career in the forecastle and he was convinced that the real tars knew a seaman from a dandified upstart. His policy was thus to tyrannise over the officers and midshipmen and to aim at popularity among the foremast hands.

The *Renown* sailed from Plymouth on July 14th, 1800, and the situation on board deteriorated from week to week. Unless he were actually certified insane the captain had almost unlimited power; enough for all practical purposes to break his officers. The mere hint of mutiny would be enough to sway a court-martial in the captain's favour. The officers were in the most difficult position, unable to prevent the irregularities which were taking place and afraid even to address each other on the subject which was uppermost in their minds. Knowledge that the captain had his spies was enough to reduce the wardroom to an uneasy silence. Regulations did provide for the first lieutenant taking command in the event of the captain's illness but to invoke that provision would be a desperate step and one likely to be the ruin of all concerned. It depended above all on the surgeon's courage and Mr Clive was as terrified as the rest. On August 6th the *Renown* was on a course, it would seem, for Antigua, where she might be expected to make landfall in ten days. So tense by then was the atmosphere that the lieutenants (barring Mr Smith who was officer of the watch) met that night in the hold. Such a secret meeting was in itself little short of an act of mutiny for which the penalty was death. They were there warned by one of the young gentlemen, Mr Wellard, that the Captain was coming. The officers quickly scattered, Buckland and Roberts reaching the maindeck by the forward hatchway, Bush going aft on the lower gun-deck and Hornblower, with Wellard, up the main hatchway to the upper deck. Apprised somehow of what had been brewing, the captain had summoned a corporal's guard of marines and sent Mr Hobbs (Acting Gunner) with two hands, to arrest the mutineers in the hold. The marines went down the after hatch, directed by the captain, but the corporal had not gone ten yards from the foot of the ladder when he heard a crash. Hurrying back, he found the captain at the foot of the ladder having fallen down the hatchway. Besides concussion, his injuries included a broken nose, two fractured ribs and a cracked collar-bone. He later became delirious and Mr Buckland formally assumed command of the ship.

The bare outline of these events can be extracted, not without difficulty, from the report rendered to Vice-Admiral Sir Richard Lambert at Jamaica, with the various depositions attached; from the findings of the Court of Inquiry; and from the Admiral's despatch to the Admiralty. The historian is left at the end with the impression that the statements taken and witnessed may have been accurate but that much remained unsaid. A desperate situation would seem to have been saved by a rather surprising accident. But was it not too much of a godsend to be so entirely accidental? We might guess that it was not. But even then there were questions which no one chose to answer. The attached diagram (see page 67) may serve to explain the situation as it appeared to the officers of the *Renown*. Their formal conclusion was that Captain Sawyer was leaning over the after hatchway in a state of excitement, shouting to the corporal as he went down the ladder from the lower gun-deck. He overbalanced as the ship pitched, fell over the hatch coaming and crashed into the hold, receiving injuries from which he was never to recover. Of the officers who most wanted to see the captain dead only one, Hornblower, was on the upper deck when the accident happened. He was admittedly accompanied by Wellard (1st Class Volunteer) but that youngster had been the chief victim of the captain's sadistic impulses, having been unjustly beaten for imagined offences on six recent occasions. Had Hornblower thrown the captain down the hatchway, Wellard was the very witness to keep quiet about it. There was no proof, however, that Hornblower was present when the incident occurred. By his own account, he and Wellard were at that time making their way aft from the main hatchway with insufficient light to see what happened. No other witnesses came forward, nor was this a matter for surprise, for it was the middle watch when all below might be supposed to be asleep. With some relief Mr Buckland logged the captain's fall as an accident and drew up a report which pointed to the same conclusion, one which those in authority were glad to accept.

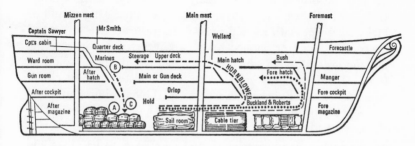

Section of the Renown

A Meeting place
   Lieuts Buckland
      Roberts
      Bush
      Hornblower

B After Hatch

C Where Captain Sawyer
   fell into the hold

Having assumed acting command, Mr Buckland read the orders which Sawyer had opened and altered course for the Bahia de Escosesa. Arriving there at daylight on August 18th he cleared for action and rounded Samaná Point. Up the Bay were the privateers at anchor but they were defenced by the fort on the headland and by a battery opposite, the two together providing a crossfire. Buckland took *Renown* into the bay but accidentally ran her aground, presenting a sitting target to the enemy, whose guns were firing red-hot shot. As this was done on a rising tide it seemed possible to kedge off, taking out an anchor to a point astern and then hauling on the cable. This eventually succeeded and the ship was warped out of the bay and out of range. Nine men had been killed, however, including Mr Roberts, twenty had been wounded and the ship herself damaged. Buckland had failed in the first operation he had attempted in his first acting command. What made matters worse was the prolonged existence of Captain Sawyer. He had been manifestly insane since his fall down the hatchway, a mindless and pitiable object, terrified and friendless, a prey to nameless fears and a sense of inexorable and eternal persecution. The fact remained, however, that he might recover, for all the surgeon could tell, becoming again the more plausible kind of maniac, able to bring his officers to trial before a court composed of other senior officers. Buckland would have to defend his action in superseding his captain. More than that, he and the others would be charged by Sawyer with mutiny, with disobedience, with subversion of discipline. They would be lucky to escape with mere dismissal from the service—men had been imprisoned or hanged for less. Given success in carrying out the orders under which Sawyer had sailed, there would be less likelihood of the Admiral being too interested in the accident which had given Buckland the command. Given failure, however, there would be more questions to answer; and failure was all that Buckland had achieved. His mistake, as he realised, had been to enter Samaná Bay in daylight. Had he arrived in darkness and landed at dawn, the fort might have been captured before the Spaniards were even awake. All chance of surprise had now been thrown away.

But was that entirely true? It was at this grim moment, with *Renown* once more at sea, that Hornblower came up with a proposal to attack again. He pointed out that the garrison would be more relaxed after their victory than they had been before danger threatened. He observed that the wind was fair for Bahia de Escosesa and that a return after dark would allow Buckland to put a landing party ashore on the seaward side of the Samaná Peninsula. The fort might be captured at dawn and its guns would prevent the escape of the privateers. All this could be accomplished by a hundred seamen and the eighty marines. To Buckland this plan seemed extremely hazardous but it was still his only chance of avoiding ruin. He agreed, with painful reluctance, wore ship and set a course once more for the Bahia de Escosesa. Mr Bush was put in command of the landing party and Hornblower made his second-in-command. Men were told off, organised and armed, the boats made ready. It was dark when they landed unseen, dark when they made the painful climb up from the beach and dark (save for the rising moon) when they sighted the fort, two hours before sunrise. They rested after the march and deployed and then, with the first glimmering of light, Bush gave the order to attack. (See plan facing p. 71.) In a matter of minutes the fort had been stormed with a hundred men and twenty women taken prisoner. It would need time for the *Renown* to reach Samaná Bay but the battery which had foiled her the day before was now in British hands and so was the furnace in which the shot could be heated. When the privateers made their attempt to leave the anchorage the first schooner was driven aground and blew up. Three more craft turned back and crept out of range. Soon afterwards on August 19th, a boat appeared under a flag of truce. The Spanish commandant asked for the return of the women and the wounded and indeed for all prisoners, the combatants to be released on parole. By the time the preliminary negotiations were over they had established a truce and the *Renown* had worked up the Bay and dropped anchor just out of range of the other battery. While she remained there, the other privateers were trapped. It was Hornblower's knowledge of Spanish that made the negotiation possible and it soon became clear that Villanueve, the commandant, was prepared to capitulate. Faced with a negro rising in the interior, and cut off from the sea, he preferred to surrender to the British.

Mr Buckland was in a difficult position. He had won a victory which would give him some prestige at Kingston. There would now be fewer questions about the process by which he had assumed command. He might well be considered for promotion. As against that, he was now compelled to grapple with a complex problem in international relations. All that he had gained might now be lost by a single mistake in diplomacy. He knew all too little about the situation in Haiti and his orders, while full of warnings against error, did not extend to the situation in which he now found himself. He was a good practical seaman and disciplinarian; fit (as he had thought) for command. What he had never considered was that a Captain in the Royal Navy needed to have a general grasp of strategy and indeed of foreign policy. Did Britain want to occupy a fort in Haiti? Was it of concern to the British if the Spaniards there should be massacred by the

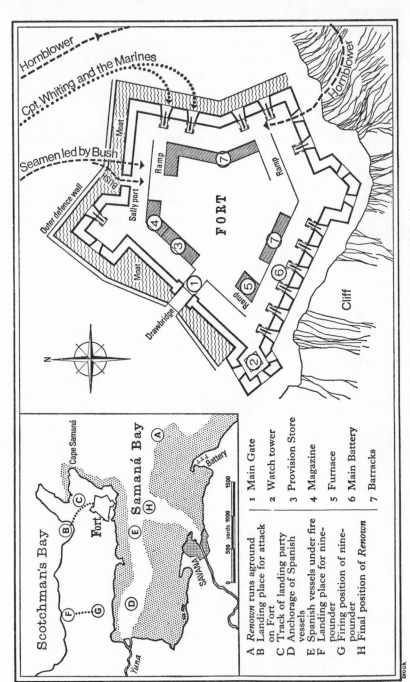

Map of Samaná Peninsula, Haiti, with details of fort

Hornblower

Cpt. Whiting and the Marines

Seamen led by Bush

Hornblower

Moat

Bush

Outer defence wall

Sally port

Ramp

Ramp

Ramp

FORT

Drawbridge

Moat

N

1 Main Gate
2 Watch tower
3 Provision Store
4 Magazine
5 Furnace
6 Main Battery
7 Barracks

Scotchman's Bay

Cape Samaná

Fort

Samaná Bay

Battery

SAVANA

Yuna

0   500   1000   1500
          yards

A Renown runs aground
B Landing place for attack on Fort
C Track of landing party
D Anchorage of Spanish vessels
E Spanish vessels under fire
F Landing place for nine-pounder
G Firing position of nine-pounder
H Final position of Renown

brook

negroes? What was the British policy towards Toussaint L'Ouverture, the negro leader? Was it thought useful to maintain Spanish influence in the island so as to exclude the French? Amidst all these doubts he knew that any prolonged stay in Samaná Bay would expose his crew to yellow fever. He would have to decide soon, and here was Villanueve demanding a free passage for his troops and vessels to Cuba or Puerto Rico. Would he be blamed for conceding this? Should he insist upon an unconditional surrender? But then there would be renewed fighting— and yellow fever. What was he to do?

It was Hornblower who suggested the next move, which was to hoist a nine-pounder cannon up to a position (see plan opposite) from which its shot could reach the schooner anchorage. This was a considerable effort but Mr Bush organised the move with forethought and drive. After a few rounds had been fired, proving that the craft in the Bay were helpless and doomed, the Spaniards surrendered unconditionally on August 21st. After they had laid down their arms, some thirty officers, fifty women and four hundred soldiers were brought on board the *Renown*. The three prizes, including a ship *La Gaditana*, were put under Hornblower's command with a small prize-crew in each. The forts at Samaná were then blown up and their guns, rendered useless, were rolled into the Bay. With a fair wind it would take less than a week to reach Kingston but it would seem longer before they could drop anchor there. The *Renown*, sailing on August 24th, was horribly overcrowded and there were appalling difficulties over water and food as well as space. Special problems were created by the women and children, who had to be given some consideration, and even the men could not be perpetually confined to the hold but had to have a turn on deck for exercise and air. Casualties in the recent operations (twenty-nine) and sixty men detached on board the prizes, had left the *Renown* with a barely adequate crew, inferior in numbers to the people they had to guard. For a few days, nevertheless, all went well and some of the routine precautions were slightly relaxed.

On the morning of August 27th the surgeon, Mr Clive, reported to Mr Buckland that Captain Sawyer was showing signs of recovery. He had been kept under opiates for a fortnight and was now calm enough to be released from the canvas straitjacket in which he had been confined. His terrors were less and

the various fractures had begun to knit up. He startled the lob-
lolly boy that day by suddenly asking whether the crew were on
make and mend. When he spoke again, hours later, he seemed to
be repeating some of the excuses he had made to Lord St
Vincent. 'A mistake, my Lord, of the signal lieutenant. . . They
are all against me. . . I could call witnesses, my Lord, who have
heard them plotting. . .' Much of what he said was incoherent
nonsense but he was no longer screeching with terror. If he
continued to recover, said Mr Clive, he might be well enough to
give evidence before a Court of Inquiry. He might even shed
some light on the accident which had deprived him, for the time
being, of his reason. Here was a final complication and danger
in a situation already complex and dangerous enough. That
evening Mr Buckland signalled for Mr Hornblower to come
aboard and report. There is no means of knowing what was said
but it is probable that Buckland asked Hornblower, not for the
first time, whether he had anything further to say about Sawyer's
accident. It is as probable that Hornblower again denied any
knowledge of it. He went back to *La Gaditana* and the voyage
continued. They might expect to reach Kingston on the 29th.

On the night of the 27th/28th the prisoners in the *Renown* rose
against their captors and overran the upper deck of the ship.
It would seem that some of the women gained their liberty by
pretending to offer their favours to two sentries posted outside
their quarters in the midshipmen's berth. A few male prisoners
also escaped, enough to liberate the officers, but the actual leader
at this stage was a mulatto woman married to one of the privateer
officers. In the course of some confused fighting, some but not
all the prisoners managed to arm themselves. Mr Buckland was
surprised in his cabin and taken prisoner at the outset. Mr Smith
was killed at his post on the quarterdeck. Mr Bush tried to rally
the *Renown*'s crew but was repeatedly wounded and left for dead
on the upper deck. Fortunately the shots fired were heard in the
Gaditana, where Hornblower also noticed that *Renown* had come
up into the wind. He did the same, sending boats to collect the
prize-crew from each of the other vessels. Each prize-master was
ordered to cut all sheets and halliards before coming away. With
sixty men, half of them marines, Hornblower now put the
Gaditana alongside the *Renown* and boarded her at the head of
them. The Spaniards were surprised before they could organise

any defence and Hornblower was able to retake the ship, clearing the decks and driving the prisoners back to the hold. In the course of the fighting, before or after the counter-attack, some Spaniard must have broken into the captain's cabin and cut Sawyer's throat with a sword. He was found dead, anyway, the irony being that Buckland should have been spared by men who were merciless towards the wretched lunatic they had equally found in his bed. Strange things happen in the heat of battle. That the prizes were afterwards retaken was not so surprising—they had not had time to repair their running rigging.

The *Renown* and her prizes came into Kingston on August 30th and Buckland made his report to the Admiral. Much to his relief he was not questioned closely on the subject of Sawyer's lunacy. Sir Richard Lambert knew more indeed about Sawyer than Buckland realised, having heard from Lord St Vincent as well as from Lord Spencer. The fact on which the Admiral fastened was the capture of Buckland in his cot. Of the other lieutenants on board, one had been killed, the other so badly wounded as to require fifty-three stitches. Captain Whiting of the Royal Marines had also been killed, and so had Merrick, his ensign, while Carberry, the Master, was in hospital and with only a doubtful chance of recovery. The acting captain, by contrast, was unharmed, his ship recaptured for him by Hornblower. He had admittedly done well at Samaná Bay—and the *Gaditana* was fit to take into the Navy as an 18-gun sloop—but he had very nearly lost the *Renown* afterwards. He finally told Buckland that there would have to be a Court of Inquiry, delayed if necessary until Mr Bush had sufficiently recovered to give his evidence. In the meanwhile a new captain would be posted to the *Renown*. That ended Buckland's ordeal for the moment but Captain James Cogshill of H.M. Ship *Buckler* (28) appeared next day on the *Renown*'s quarterdeck and read his acting commission. With two more lieutenants to be appointed, Hornblower knew that he should now rank as third; a great improvement on being fifth.

The Court of Inquiry assembled on September 7th aboard the *Renown*, the president being Captain Armitage of the flagship. Mr Buckland was the first witness and he was soon in trouble over the prisoners' attempt to capture the *Renown*. So far as his career was concerned, the following questions and answers were decisive:

The Court: What happened after you turned in on the evening
of August 27th?

Mr Buckland: I was woken in the middle watch by a confused
noise outside my cabin. An instant later the door burst open
and four or five men entered. From their appearance I knew
them to be enemy prisoners of war.

The Court: Were they armed?

Mr Buckland: One had a cutlass, which I saw was bloodstained.
Another had a belaying pin.

The Court: Where were your own weapons?

Mr Buckland: My sword and pistols were slung from a nail in
the bulkhead.

The Court: Were they within your reach?

Mr Buckland: Yes, sir, but I had no time to snatch them. The
man with the cutlass held its point at my throat. The others
then tied me helpless with strips of my bedding and so left the
cabin.

The Court: Can you account for the fact that you were spared
while Captain Sawyer, lying ill, was killed?

Mr Buckland: I can only suppose that he was assailed by a
different group, more blind with fury than the men who
attacked me.

The Court: Or else perhaps he attempted some resistance?

Mr Buckland: I know nothing about that.

The Court: What time elapsed between the first noises you heard
and the entry of prisoners into your cabin?

Mr Buckland: A few minutes. I should explain that tumult
among the prisoners—and especially among the half-caste
women—had not been unusual. I should expect it to be dealt
with by the watch on deck.

The Court: Would you not expect to be called, as acting-captain,
at the least sign of danger to your ship?

Mr Buckland: Yes, sir.

The Court: But you took no action?

Mr Buckland: I was confident that I should be called if the
situation required it.

The Court: Thank you, Mr Buckland. Remain, please, while we
hear the next witness. Call Mr Bush.

The impression left with the Court was that Buckland was a

competent first lieutenant but that he had never really assumed command of the ship. A born leader in his position, with only two watch-keeping officers available, with a crew actually outnumbered by their prisoners, would rarely have left the deck. A shot fired would have brought him, armed, to the quarterdeck in a matter of seconds. But Buckland's motto remained 'Let them look out as have the watch!' A good lieutenant he was and a good lieutenant he would always remain. Bush and Hornblower gave their evidence and were both complimented, the one on having fought until overwhelmed, the other on great presence of mind. Mr Clive gave evidence next, proving that Captain Sawyer's illness had made him unfit to command. Other witnesses shed some light on the circumstances in which the prisoners' uprising began, but the story remained obscure in that those immediately concerned were dead. After only a brief recess the Court's conclusion was announced by Captain Armitage:

'It is the opinion of this court that strict inquiry should be made among the Spanish prisoners to determine who it was that murdered Captain Sawyer, and that the murderer, if still alive, should be brought to justice. And as the result of our examination of the surviving officers of H.M. Ship *Renown* it is our opinion that no further action is necessary.

This meant that there would be no court-martial, unless Buckland were to ask for one, and no further investigation. Nothing, of course, was learnt from the prisoners about Sawyer's death but there was another sequel to the inquiry and it came immediately. The *Gaditana*, now H.M. Sloop *Retribution* (18), was to proceed to England, and Hornblower was appointed to her with the rank of Commander. This promotion was almost inevitable—as we can see now—although it came as a complete surprise to Hornblower himself. The capture and destruction of the privateer base in Samaná Bay, with three prizes condemned and a ship taken into the service, was a small but definite victory. It would ordinarily be marked by the promotion of the *Renown*'s first lieutenant, which would be taken as a compliment to the captain. In this instance the captain was dead, the first lieutenant unfit for promotion and the next in seniority was in hospital and might be invalided out of the service. Hornblower stood next in line and he had obviously been the genius of the whole operation. In his report to Buckland, Bush had made it clear that the attack on the fort at Samaná Bay owed its inception as well as its success to Hornblower's initiative. In his report to the Admiral, Buckland had given Hornblower full credit for the recapture of the *Renown*. How could he have done otherwise? As for the crisis which made the counter-attack necessary, Hornblower was, of all concerned, the most completely blameless. He had not been on board the *Renown* but he had reacted at once to the first shot fired. As for giving the command of the *Retribution* to some other officer (say, the flag lieutenant) that would have been manifestly unfair to the captors. Sir Richard Lambert made the right decision, one which Bush at once accepted and which even Buckland had eventually to see as at least logical. Buckland was allowed the captain's share in the three prizes—some slight consolation—and he had to admit that Hornblower was a brilliant young officer.

From this period in Hornblower's career we have two documents worth quoting in full. The first is part of a letter written by Captain Armitage to Sir Edward Pellew and since preserved among the Exmouth Papers. The relevant paragraph reads as follows:

September 12th, 1800

The *Renown* recently came into Kingston after a successful attack on Samaná Bay in Haiti, where three prizes were taken and a privateer schooner destroyed. You will not be surprised to learn that your old acquaintance, David Sawyer, was already confined to his cabin as a lunatic (which *entre nous* was what I had always taken him to be) and that the landing was directed by the First Lieutenant, Mr Buckland. They came away with a shipload of Spanish captives who presently rose against the *Renown*'s crew and overpowered most of them. Hearing the shots which were fired, the young officer who was in charge of the prizes collected the prize crews and laid the largest vessel alongside the *Renown*, boarded her and fairly routed the enemy in a hand-to-hand conflict but not before Sawyer and many others had been killed or wounded. The fire-eater who performed this feat is called Hornblower, aged about twenty-four, a lanky and ungainly figure some six foot high with a hollow-cheeked sad expression, dark hair and brown eyes. When he came before the Court of Inquiry I thought him melancholy, absent-minded and poorly dressed. It was only when he spoke of the fighting that his manner changed directly, his chin thrust out, his eyes flashing and his whole expression one of eager concentration. Sir Richard has made him Commander unto the *Retribution* and I fancy we shall hear of him again, provided that is that war continues for a few more years.

You will want I know to have news of your protegé recommended to you by the Duke of Northumberland. He is midshipman in the *Buckler* but I mean to take him into the flagship when a vacancy offers. Cogshill (you remember him in the *Druid?*) says that he should have a great career before him provided only that he entirely reverses the principles upon which he has begun. . .'

Captain Armitage was unaware that Hornblower was already known to Pellew, who remembered the young man perfectly well and who filed this letter away as proof of his own good judgement.

The other document is the earliest known letter in Hornblower's handwriting, the first anyone bothered to keep. It was sent from the *Retribution* to Mr Bush, still under treatment at the hospital.

September 17th, 1800

My dear Friend,

It is good to hear from Dr Sankey that you are like to recover before the date we were given at first. The negro boatman who delivers this should bring you also some mangoes and a pineapple together with a letter from England that was misdirected. We are hard at work making this ship fit for service and I could only wish that we were to sail in her together. I am hard put to it to find a crew, especially petty officers, and may not sail, whether for England or on convoy duty between the islands, until late October. By then you will be convalescent in England, although I know you would rather be battling the watch on this station with its chances of promotion. I had all the luck this time but I know that everyone gives you full credit for having fought so well. With all your wounds you are I suppose fortunate to be alive. Hoping that the chances of war may again make us shipmates.

Believe me truly yours
—H.H.

What is significant about this is that Hornblower had found a friend, almost certainly his first. Nor would this friendship have been possible had Bush remained the senior. The situation which existed at Samaná, with Hornblower prodding Buckland into giving orders and advising Bush as to how he should carry them out was essentially unstable. Hornblower's impatience was matched by his seniors' irritation and the effect of the Admiral's action had been to place a born leader in his right position. The pyramid which had been balanced on its apex was now resting on its base. Nor was there a trace of jealousy in Bush. He could not and did not pretend to have a tithe of Hornblower's initiative and ingenuity. When they served together again he fell into his natural position as a loyal second-in-command. The turning point in Hornblower's career was the recapture of the *Renown*, or so it seemed to all his contemporaries. Or would it be truer to say that his future was made by the death of Captain Sawyer?

CHAPTER FOUR

Master and Commander

What had been unusual about the *Renown*'s mission was the fact that the raid on Samana Bay took place (for reasons of security) before the ship had joined Sir Richard Lambert's flag. Buckland had known practically nothing about the situation in Hispaniola, his orders (inherited from Sawyer) being limited to a single and restricted operation. Those orders had never been shown to Hornblower, who was to that extent more ignorant still of the complexities with which the Admiral had to cope. He made up for this by a careful study of books and newspapers while the *Retribution* was refitting. Originally a Spanish colony, Hispaniola had been divided between Spain and France. Haiti was the area ceded to France in 1697 and developed as a country of sugar plantations cultivated by negro slave labour. The French Revolution was the signal for negro revolt, followed by a struggle for power among the native leaders themselves. General Toussaint L'Ouverture was the successful candidate and was accepted as such from about 1799. The British attitude towards him was inevitably ambiguous. On the one hand, the expulsion of the Republican French from Haiti was regarded with approval. It gave rise to the possibility of a British annexation, part of the island being actually occupied by British troops from 1793 to 1798. As from then the British were more concerned about the possibility of the negro revolt spreading to Jamaica. At one moment Toussaint was being supplied with arms and gunpowder, at another his emissaries were being arrested and his vessels detained. The French attitude was no more consistent, the earlier talk about Equality (which might or might *not* apply to negroes) giving place to Bonaparte's talk about Empire. The situation was nothing if not complex and the Admiral had little guidance from Lord Spencer, whose policy was undefined and whose information was liable to be out-of-date.

It was November 8th, 1800, when Hornblower was able to

report the *Retribution* ready for service, repaired, altered, re-rigged, provisioned and supplied. She was inevitably ill-manned but so were many of the other ships on the station. Hornblower expected to be sent on convoy duty but the Admiral had other ideas. His own tour of duty was nearly at an end and his successor, Lord Hugh Seymour, had already been appointed. He decided upon one stroke of policy with which to wind up his period of command. If Toussaint L'Ouverture could be deprived of shipping, or of ships anyway which could be used for invading Jamaica, he would feel that something had been accomplished. It was a tricky situation, however, and the officer detailed for the service must be junior enough to discard if things went wrong. Ideal for the purpose was an Acting Commander but one with a knowledge of French and Spanish, one moreover who knew something of Hispaniola. Hornblower was the man and he was given orders which seem to have been destroyed, no copies of which reached the Admiralty. His official report shared the same fate (for reasons which are now apparent) and we have only an outline knowledge of the operation which followed. It seems possible that Hornblower himself kept copies of his correspondence and that these papers may eventually come to light. Lacking these vital documents we can rely only on the *Retribution*'s Log, which gives no more than a laconic account of where she went and when. We are thus certain that *Retribution* sailed for Port-au-Prince on 14th November, 1800, and returned to Kingston on June 27th, 1801. The full story of what happened in the meanwhile remains obscure and may never be told.

At the period of Hornblower's visit to Haiti, Toussaint L'Ouverture had refused a British offer of protection. He could at that moment have established himself as a King within the British Empire. That he rejected what could have been his salvation was due partly to his upbringing as a French-speaking catholic, partly to the fact that British troops had withdrawn as recently as 1798. Toussaint's troops under Dessalines and Christophe had conquered the south of Haiti in 1799, making his power supreme in the island. He was enough of a realist, however, to see that he had to adhere to one side or other in the World War then in progress. What he failed to understand was the character of Napoleon Bonaparte. Who should blame him

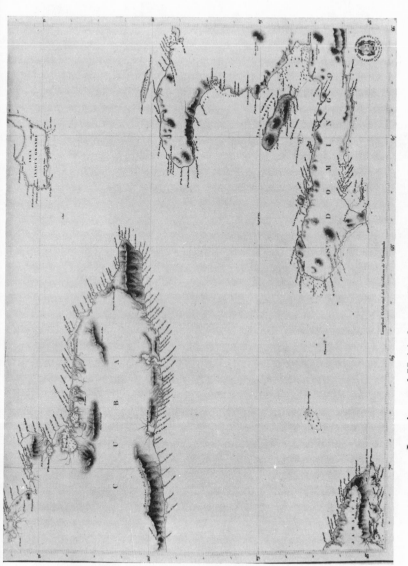

Jamaica and Haiti, from a French map printed in 1801

Swan V, revenue cutter, in action with a smuggler, *circa* 1802, from an oil painting in the author's possession.

for that? Many statesmen were more grossly deceived who had far better opportunities of observing the First Consul. What he failed to anticipate was the Treaty of Amiens, leaving French troops available and French ships free to cross the Atlantic. He could not be blamed for that either for the peace came as a surprise to other rulers of greater experience. His intention was to establish peace and order with himself as General (in the French Army) and President for life. He drew up a remarkably liberal Constitution and sent it to France, asking for the First Consul's approval. He was a man of extraordinary ability and vision and is remembered to this day as the founder of Haiti's independence. Unfortunately there were others in his camp whose greed was more and whose sense of reality was less. Among these was the French Commissioner, Roume, who had come out from France in 1791. It was his ambition to instigate a negro revolt in Jamaica. Ships were collected and armed and spies sent to Kingston who tried to prepare the way there for a rebellion which would not have left a white man alive. This would seem to have been done without Toussaint's knowledge and indeed in his absence, the plan to take effect in March or April of 1801. The historians of Haiti tend to assume that the expedition was abandoned, most probably when Toussaint came to hear of it, but there is evidence that the ships sailed. As they certainly never arrived, it would be natural to suppose that they were lost in a gale or wrecked on some uncharted reef. As against that, Port-au-Prince and Kingston are scarcely three hundred miles apart, while Point Morant and Cape Tiburon (the nearest headlands) are separated by only a hundred miles; a short passage over seas perfectly familiar.

We may never know what happened to the expedition from Haiti or what Hornblower had to do with its failure. What we do know is the sad sequel. General Leclerc, husband of Pauline Bonaparte and so Napoleon's brother-in-law, arrived before the end of 1801 with an army of 21,000 men. Toussaint fought a battle against Leclerc in March, 1802 but afterwards made peace, accepting French rule. He was then treacherously arrested and sent to France where he was imprisoned in the Fortress of St Joux in the French Alps. There he died, a victim to cold or (possibly) poison. Leclerc himself died in 1802 and his army suffered appalling losses from yellow fever and other tropical diseases. What French troops remained were driven out of Haiti and surrendered to the British. Haiti declared its independence on 1st January, 1804, with Dessalines as Emperor. He was killed next year and succeeded by General Henri Christophe, almost as remarkable a man as Toussaint had been. President at first, he became king in 1811 and built first, the Palace of Sans Souci and, later, the astonishing Citadelle, twenty miles from Cape Haitien and three thousand feet above sea level. Hornblower was to be a visitor there in 1822, just after General Jean-Pierre Boyer had made himself President of all Hispaniola. From a chance remark he made on that occasion we might guess that his previous visit had been fairly dramatic. We might even suspect that there had been a romance of some sort, probably his first. Of what actually happened, however, we have no knowledge at all.

When Hornblower reported at Kingston it was not to Sir Richard Lambert but to Lord Hugh Seymour. It at once became clear that policy had changed, that his recent mission (whatever its purpose) was now thought ill-advised, and that the whole affair was best forgotten. In the event of awkward inquiries or questions in the House of Commons it would be desirable to minimise the importance of the affair. It would, for example, be useful to report that Lieutenant Hornblower, in acting command of the *Retribution* (12), had exceeded his instructions; a matter of far less consequence than a display of ill-timed initiative by Captain Hornblower of the *Retribution* (18). While not himself responsible, Lord Hugh Seymour had the good of the service at heart. He reported that the *Retribution* would be returning to England with convoy in July, 1801, and that she had been reduced in establishment. Quite incidental to this manoeuvre was the fact that Hornblower's promotion would not be confirmed. Worse than that, as Hornblower would discover, his pay already drawn as Master and Commander would have been paid in error, making him liable to deduction from his future pay as Lieutenant. As yet unaware of this danger, Hornblower sailed on July 19th, the *Retribution* being part of the escort for a convoy of eighty-seven sail. The voyage was without incident and the convoy reached Plymouth on October 1st. The Preliminary Articles of Peace were signed that very day. For all practical purposes the war was over.

One of the chief difficulties in writing history or biography is

to prevent one's narrative being coloured too much by a knowledge of subsequent events. We know now that the Peace of
Amiens lasted from 25th March, 1802,[1] until the declaration of
war on May 18th, 1803, not fourteen months in all. We are
tempted to add that the ambitions of the First Consul made the
renewal of the conflict clearly inevitable, as everyone at the time
must have foreseen. It was not, however, as obvious as all that.
Most people assumed, on the contrary, that the war was finished
and done with. After all, it had lasted about nine years as compared with the last two wars which had lasted, respectively, for
seven years and eight. Who would have dared predict that there
were a dozen years of conflict still to come? From many prosperous Englishmen the immediate response was a visit to Paris
and one which many of them would have reason to regret. As for
the Royal Navy, it was laid up and disbanded with great alacrity,
to the joy of the lower deck and the despair of the officers.
Promotion was now out of the question and employment most
unlikely. For most of the officers without private means the
choice lay between finding another career and existing on half-
pay until there should be another war.

As compared with most of his contemporaries, Hornblower
was quite peculiarly lost. He had no near relatives and Thomas
Rawson, the uncle who had reluctantly paid him an allowance
as midshipman, had died, as he knew, in 1799. The other uncle
who had helped with the allowance was Jonathan Carter Hornblower, still alive and active, but Horatio had an almost morbid
fear of seeming to ask for help. Any attempt to contact this uncle,
whom he had never met, might have been regarded as a plea for
money or work. He made no such attempt, realising that he was
completely alone in the world. Nor does he seem to have paid any
visit to his birthplace, where he might well be forgotten. When
Retribution was paid off (November 1st, 1801) he went up to
London and applied to the Admiralty for further employment.
He was soon made to realise that the ships in commission would
be a mere handful, officered by men with political interest. He was
also assured that his promotion had never been confirmed and
that his half-pay would be stopped for seven months. After some
frustrating weeks in London he travelled down to Portsmouth,

[1] When the Definitive Treaty was signed. Hostilities had ceased by
Proclamation on October 12th, 1801.

concluding that it would be cheaper to live there. So it was, but the winter was cold and he had little money left. He took a room on the top floor of a house in Highbury Street but had his one daily meal, all he could afford, at an eating house in Broad Street. Mrs Mason was his landlady, the widow of a shipwright (Richard Mason, died 1795) whose daughter, Maria, taught at a Dame School and also helped to make the beds. It was a dull and squalid existence and he was soon in debt for his lodging.

From this wretched way of life Hornblower was temporarily rescued in February, 1802. The Collector of Customs at Cowes, Isle of Wight, had been Mr William Arnold whose death on March 3rd, 1801, had left the office vacant. At the suggestion of Lord Bolton, Governor of the Isle of Wight, the Postmaster-General (Lord Auckland) gave the appointment to Mr Arnold's widow who also became 'Deputy Postmistress of the Isle of Wight'. The actual work of the Customs Office was done by the Deputy Controller, Mr John Ward, whose own promotion had to wait for another dozen years. Mr Ward's duties included the maintenance of a revenue cutter, *Swan V*, built by Mr Gely of Cowes, armed with twelve guns and commanded at this time by Mr William Ferris. It so happened that Mr Ferris was injured in a street accident and kept to his bed for nearly three months in all. It is not clear how Hornblower came to be acquainted with Mrs Arnold or Mr John Ward but the result of Mr Ferris's absence from duty was that Hornblower had the command, as a temporary arrangement, for the whole period of Ferris's absence from duty. The *Swan*'s cruising ground was between Lyme Regis and Beachy Head. At least two smuggling craft were intercepted by the *Swan* while under Hornblower's command and there are indirect references to some other adventures about which no certain facts have so far come to light. There exists an oil painting of the *Swan* in pursuit of a lugger and it might date from this period but the documents, which ought to be at Southampton, are missing. The other fact of interest is that William and Martha Arnold were the parents of Thomas Arnold, later to be the famous Headmaster of Rugby. Thomas spent his childhood at Cowes and did not go to school at Warminster until 1803.[1] It is all but certain that an active seven-year-old like

---

[1] See *At War with the Smugglers* by Rear-Admiral D. Arnold Forster, 1936, p. 247 et seq.

Thomas would have been a visitor to the *Swan* when she was in port and must have met with Hornblower. There is no record of their having met again.

For those three months Hornblower may have made his living, with something extra from the sale of seized contraband. He is thought to have served for another month or two as volunteer in the *Swan* after Mr Ferris's return to duty. By the autumn, however, of 1802 he was back in his Highbury Street attic and receiving his half-pay as lieutenant. If he was miserably poor at this period, as he would seem to have been, it was because he was repaying Mrs Mason for the months of lodging (December 1801–February 1802) when he was without income of any kind. It was now that he became a professional card-player, frequenting the Long Rooms at Portsmouth and accepting a retainer from the proprietor, an emigré called the Marquis de Sainte-Croix. For half a guinea a week he was present in the Room from midday until 2.0 a.m., ready to make a fourth at whist with any other three gentlemen who preferred that game to hazard, vingt-et-un or roulette (games which were played in an inner room). In theory, Hornblower might have lost more than he had to lose but the whist lovers who found it hard to obtain partners were, in practice, the bad players. Their lessons from Hornblower, even at low stakes, were apt, therefore, to be expensive.[1] Hornblower's own play was masterly but he kept ten pounds in reserve against a run of bad luck. The irony of the situation lay in the fact that he hated playing with bad players and could seldom afford to play with good ones. These were hard times for Hornblower but he still had a friend in Bush who lived with his sisters at Chichester but came into Portsmouth each month to draw his half-pay from the Clerk of the Cheque. They sometimes met on these occasions and Bush even stayed the night at Mrs Mason's. He described her afterwards as a short hard-faced woman who trusted nobody and we can take that as being the truth. He was also observant enough to realise that Maria adored Hornblower, who found her affection difficult to resist.

It was manifest by this time that war would break out again in

[1] See *Regency Rakes*, H. R. Warburton, London, 1891. The real gamblers were seldom seen in the Long Room, preferring to frequent the Cockpit, run by 'Captain' Wakefield. See pp. 73–76.

1803. The provisions of the Treaty of Amiens were fully observed, in fact, by neither side, and those which concerned Malta
could not have been carried out by anyone. It was clear, moreover, that the First Consul had not wanted to make peace in the
first instance. He had wanted a pause to recuperate and had used
the opportunity to exercise his fleet at sea; as, for example, in
the expedition to Haiti. By the end of January the early resump-
tion of hostilities was under discussion on either side. On March
8th the King in his Message to the House of Commons spoke
of 'such measures as circumstances may appear to require, for
supporting the honour of his crown and the essential interests of
his people'. The Militia were called out on March 10th and
H.M. Ships began to be commissioned and placed on a war
establishment. War was not actually declared until May 16th but
the intervening weeks were spent in open preparation. Among
many farsighted moves the least important, seemingly, was the
appointment of Horatio Hornblower to command the sloop
Hotspur. He owed this to a chance meeting with Admiral Lord
Parry, with whom he played whist on the night of March 7th.
Parry, one of the Lords Commissioners of the Admiralty, was
impressed with the cool calculations which underlay Hornblower's play at cards. Another player in the same rubber was
Sir Richard Lambert, who evidently took the opportunity to
remind Lord Parry of Hornblower's bad luck over the *Retribution*. The result was his first command, his promotion gazetted on
March 8th, the ship named on the 15th and his commission read
at Portsmouth on the 24th. The *Hotspur* (18) had been built at
Shoreham in 1785 to the design of Mr Edward Hunt. She
measured 410 tons and was peculiar in mounting 9-pounders
where an ordinary sloop was armed with 6-pounders. Her
12-pounder carronades were the normal establishment, six on the
quarterdeck and two on the forecastle. Her officers, under the
Commander, were two lieutenants, the Master and four Master's
Mates. The ship's company numbered 121 all told, good seamen
recruited before the war had even begun. Hornblower was too
junior to expect the command of one of the latest class of sloops
built from 1793 onwards and copied from the French *Amazon*,
but he had a ship unusually well armed and manned. He secured
his old friend Bush as First Lieutenant, with Mr Prouse as
Acting Master. Although originally senior to him, Bush had long

since accepted Hornblower's leadership. Limited as he was in brains and imagination, Bush was a first-rate seaman of unquestionable courage and loyalty. Hornblower was lucky again in having won forty-five pounds at whist, just enough to furnish his cabin with the minimum furniture, silver and stores and rescue his sword from the pawnshop. After ten days of feverish preparation, the *Hotspur* sailed on April 4th for Ushant, coming under the orders of the Hon. Sir William Cornwallis, Commander-in-Chief of the Channel Fleet.

Just before sailing, on April 2nd, Hornblower married Maria Mason at the Church of St Thomas à Becket, Portsmouth. The wedding party was at the George and Cornwallis himself proposed the toast to the newly married couple. There are several mysteries in Hornblower's life but none so baffling as his marriage to Maria Mason.

He was, remember, a man of consuming ambition, without family or interest, a born leader but of merely middle-class origin. He had the beginnings of a reputation but had been unlucky over prize-money. To be confirmed as Master and Commander before he was twenty-seven was quite a rapid promotion for a man without influence. It should have been his cue to marry into a senior officer's family, gaining admission to the charmed circle of the socially acceptable. Failing an Admiral's daughter he might have settled for a Captain's niece or the second cousin, even, of a dockyard official. Instead, he chose to wed—Maria Mason! Or would it be truer to say that the Masons, mother and daughter, had chosen *him*? So far as Maria was concerned it was a love match. She admired and loved him from the beginning. So far as Mrs Mason was concerned it was a matter of calculation as from the moment of his becoming so much more eligible as a husband. So far as Hornblower was concerned, he was a victim to his sense of gratitude and pity. He evidently felt that Maria had stood by him when he was unemployed and penniless. He wanted to rescue her, therefore, from the drab life to which she was otherwise condemned. Apart from that, however, he was particularly vulnerable in never having experienced affection before. When he first went to sea there was literally no one in the world who cared whether he should live or die. After 1799 there was nobody to whom he need so much as address a letter. Leaving Maria two days after the wedding he had, for the first time the feeling that somebody cared for him and would miss him. Saying that, however, one has said all. Maria's physical attractions were merely those of youth, lost for good during her first pregnancy. Her brains and education were negligible and her manners were suited to Highbury Street. All she could offer was devotion, and with that Hornblower had to be content.

Hornblower's orders were to watch the port of Brest, remembering however that Britain and France were still nominally at peace. He found that his opposite number was the French frigate *Loire* (40), clearly detailed to watch *him*. The danger lay in the fact that the French would most probably have news before he did that war had been declared. He ascertained at the outset that there were fourteen ships of the line in the Roads, none ready for sea, with six frigates, of which number only three had their topmasts sent up. So far there was no cause for alarm about enemy preparation. Cornwallis was not yet at sea and the *Hotspur* was merely there to observe and report. The crisis came on May 21st when the *Loire*, a familiar sight in the estuary, showed an inclination to close her distance. Guessing that war had begun, Hornblower cleared for action and kept *Hotspur* four miles to windward of the Frenchman. A gale was blowing at the time and it was soon obvious that the French frigate was both faster and more weatherly. Hornblower kept his advantage for a while by better seamanship but came eventually within range of the enemy. A clever manoeuvre—a minor masterpiece—ended with the *Loire* taken aback, in irons, enabling *Hotspur* to cross her bows and give her a single raking broadside. Nine-pounders could do only limited damage, even at pistol-shot range, but the moral effect was considerable, especially in giving confidence to *Hotspur*'s crew. Rather than be lured beyond Ushant, the *Loire* turned back to Brest with every appearance of defeat, and Hornblower resumed his station off that port and was still cruising there when the Channel Fleet arrived. Within a few days the *Tonnant* (84) appeared, with Sir Edward Pellew as senior officer commanding the Inshore Squadron. Hornblower was once more under the command of Pellew, his old captain in the *Arethusa* and *Indefatigable*, a man for whom he had tremendous respect. His station, almost in a French harbour mouth, just out of range of the shore batteries, was a hazardous one. Beyond him now were

the frigates, beyond them the Inshore Squadron and further seaward again (but invisible) was Admiral Sir William Cornwallis
with his flag in the *Dreadnought* (98) and supported by ten sail of
the line. With this force behind him, Hornblower observed the
movements of the coasters which used inshore channels to slip
into or out of Brest. Armed with that information he proposed to
Pellew his plan for intercepting these coasters, was given the
necessary orders and went in on the night of May 18th, 1803.
He caught the coasters in the dangerous Toulinget Passage and
left about ten of them wrecked or sunk. There was no prize-
money for such a stroke but it served a useful purpose, partly in
depriving the French of needed supplies, partly in discouraging
the use of that route between the rocks and shoals. Information
about this attack and about every other incident at Brest was
flashed to Paris by telegraph—that is, by semaphore signals made
from successive towers, the last being on the north shore of the
Goulet. It was by this device that the *Loire* had been warned of
the outbreak of war.

Hornblower proposed to destroy this last telegraph station as,
also the battery which protected it, and Pellew approved the plan,
reinforcing the *Hotspur* with a strong detachment of Marines.
Hornblower headed the night attack in person, assisted by
Lieutenant Cotard of the *Marlborough*, a Guernseyman picked
for his knowledge of French. The surprise was complete, the
casualties were few and the installation was completely destroyed,
as was also the battery on the Petit Minou. The report on this
affair was the first *Gazette* letter to appear over Hornblower's
signature and it is reproduced in full for that reason. Made
on July 17th, it was the last report made by Hornblower to
Pellew, who was promoted Rear-Admiral at this time and sent to
command the squadron on blockade duty off Rochefort. The
destruction of a telegraph station was unimportant in itself, for
the installation could be and was replaced in a matter of ten days,
but the incident, considered as one of a series, forced the French
to deploy men and guns to defend every possible landing place
and added to their seamen's sense of inferiority. Here were the
British on their doorstep and kicking at the door panels. There
was no question, therefore, as to who held the initiative. The man
who could have been aggrieved over this affair was Bush. Had he
led the landing party he might well have won his promotion.

Unfortunately for him he was junior to Cotard, who was needed to answer the first challenge with a convincing French accent. Cotard could not command because the men would not be from his ship. It was Pellew who decided that Hornblower should lead and that Bush should remain in command of *Hotspur* for the time of his absence. It was the best solution, as Bush had to admit, and he was too good a man to brood over his lost opportunity.

Ships on blockade duty off Brest had no chance, under Cornwallis, of returning to port. Supplies and water were sent to them and the blockade was thus continuous. A series of gales in October, 1803, interrupted the supply system and drove the fleet to its offshore station, seventy miles to seaward. There was no such relief for the watching frigates or for *Hotspur* but they were finally driven into Torbay for lack of provisions; *Hotspur* mainly for lack of water. Maria was seven months pregnant and this unplanned return to England should have given Hornblower the chance to see her. She actually came to Brixham but a number of circumstances—rough weather, other duties and an invitation from the Commander-in-Chief—prevented him going ashore. He was ordered back to his station as soon as his ship was supplied and the wind allowed, having actually seen Maria by telescope as she stood on Brixham Pier. She returned afterwards to the lodgings she had taken in Driver's Alley, Plymouth, where Mrs Mason joined her. There was born there on January 1st, 1804, her first child, a boy who was christened Horatio after his father. At the time of the child's birth Hornblower was actually in battle off Brest. He had been able to report to Rear-Admiral Parker (Pellew's successor) that four of the French ships were armed 'en flute' with yards crossed. Ships with their main armament removed would be used most probably as military transports; perhaps for a small landing in Ireland. Armed with this information, Parker had sent the *Hotspur* up the Goulet, backed by the *Naiad* frigate (38) and the *Doris* frigate (32). A night action was the result, with the capture of an escorting frigate *Clorinde* (40). The task of the *Hotspur* had been to drive the four transports on shore, which was duly performed, but the *Clorinde* had been captured by the *Naiad* in forty minutes and *Hotspur* had no share in the prize-money. Hornblower gained only reputation and the privilege of taking *Hotspur* into Plymouth under jury rig. While the damage was being repaired in dock Hornblower lived with his wife and child, and also (alas) with his mother-in-law. He was glad when completion of the overhaul allowed him to take his ship back to sea.

The *Hotspur* sailed again on February 17th and was soon afterwards detached to cruise with a small squadron to the northward of Ushant. Landing craft were being collected at Boulogne for the invasion of England and efforts were made to intercept them as they crept along the coast. Some rather futile operations were the result and the *Hotspur* went sufficiently close inshore to receive a hit from a howitzer shell. It fell near Hornblower who extinguished the fuse in the nick of time, adding something to his reputation for quick decisions. He had incidentally saved the ship and the life of every man on board. But this moment of danger was enough to give him an idea. The wooden sailing ships of his day were exposed to solid shot, sometimes even to red-hot shot from a shore battery, but they seldom encountered shellfire. This was just as well, for a single direct hit with an explosive projectile would have been enough to destroy any one of them. The resulting fire would have completed what the initial burst began, burning sails being more immediately dangerous than the opening of seams in the ship's hull. There were bomb ketches for use against land targets but no other man-of-war fired that sort of missile. It was rightly thought too dangerous to handle on board ship, partly from fear of the main charge exploding at the same time as the propellant, partly because a high trajectory shell (which was essential) would have to pass through the ship's own rigging. The Bombshells which had long been a feature of siege warfare, were practically unknown at sea. Hornblower wondered whether this need always be so. When the *Hotspur* was back on blockade duty off Brest he submitted to Cornwallis, through Parker, his plan for destroying the French fleet by shellfire. It was dated March 22nd and led to the raid of April 10th, 1804, not an unqualified success but enough to consolidate Hornblower's reputation as a man of initiative and daring.

To understand Hornblower's proposal and Cornwallis's reaction we have to remember that the senior officers of 1793–1815 had all been trained in the War of American Independence; a war fought between gentlemen on either side. Admiral Rodney had been living in France when war began. Howe had thought it enough to defeat the French, if he could; he did not talk of destroying them. Even Pellew had a great friend among his opponents. He and others retained some sense of chivalry. Thus, a ship-of-the-line in battle never fired at an enemy frigate unless she fired first. The game was played according to the rules; rules which might be broken but which were still held to exist. The French Revolution brought about an abrupt change of atmosphere, there being few gentlemen left on the French side. Some idea of fair play lingered even then but Napoleon lowered the tone still more, aiming now at his enemy's destruction. Some senior officers of the Royal Navy became almost as ruthless, Nelson being the chief of these. After them, however, came younger men, and Hornblower among them, who had been trained in this particular war. Theirs was a war against the first of the modern dictators. Of the older and more chivalrous warfare they knew nothing. A world at peace they could scarcely remember, having seen it only from the classroom. Among them, moreover, were some, like Cochrane, who had been influenced by the industrial revolution. There were some inventive minds among these, turning to new and terrible devices. Hornblower belonged to this group, being the grandson of an engineer, the son of a chemist, the nephew of two inventors. With his gift for mathematics and navigation he was receptive to any new idea in technology. The boy who had studied fortification became the man who saw the potential uses of shellfire afloat. He had the germ of a potent idea.

The Hon. Sir William Cornwallis was a man of the older generation, aged sixty and soon to retire. He did not look upon new inventions with the same enthusiasm. He foresaw the difficulties which might arise from entrusting any complicated device to illiterate seamen. He also realised that the invention which could be used today with surprise effect might be used tomorrow by the enemy and could even be of more use to his side than to ours. As the Duke of Wellington was to comment upon a plan to use poison gas: 'Two can play at that game.' The side that is winning has least to gain, in general, from a change in the rules. As against that, he realised the dangers of boredom. Ships on blockade duty had work to do but it was the same work for day after day and month after month. To attempt something against the enemy, even without much effect, was always good for morale. It gave men something to talk about and added to their feeling of confidence. The result was that Rear-Admiral Parker approved Hornblower's plan, as instructed by the Commander-in-Chief, but reduced it in scale. What was conceived as a stunning blow ended as a mere pinprick. While serving the Admiral's purpose, it left the situation much as it was, the morale slightly better on the one side and marginally worse on the other. A hundred well-delivered pinpricks can add up to a sense of superiority over an opponent but no one can tell, even in retrospect, whether any particular pinprick was worth the trouble. It is usually better to do something than nothing, however, if only to test the competence and nerve of the more junior leaders. From this particular test Hornblower was to emerge with considerable credit.

The scheme, as first outlined, was to attack Brest harbour at night with a small squadron of frigates. Each attacking ship would have under tow a hulk or lighter without a mast, mounting a heavy howitzer or mortar and equipped with an anchor and a rowing boat. There would be a noisy cannonade and the frigates would retire as if defeated, leaving the hulks at anchor, unnoticed, within range of the French fleet. About an hour later, when the alarm was over, the mortars would open fire for ten minutes. The men who manned the hulks would then scuttle them and escape by boat on the ebb before the counter-attack could develop. There were several difficulties about this plan, the most obvious being that few seamen had the least idea of how to fire a mortar. Still more difficult, however, was the problem of command. The only captain familiar with the harbour entrance was Hornblower himself, the originator of the plan, years junior to anyone else. The frigates could not be placed under his orders but neither could he serve under a captain who had never been in the Goulet before. The answer was to reduce the operation in scale. Instead of four frigates there would be two sloops, one commanded by an officer junior to Hornblower, and each sloop would have two hulks in tow. Hornblower could then direct from *Hotspur*, with a Master's Mate in each hulk. There was no difficulty in providing the hulks themselves—these were captured coasting craft of about fifty tons—and as little trouble over the howitzers and shells, which were obtained by a raid on the Ile de Rhé. Of the hulks, three mounted a howitzer apiece, bedded below decks amidships on a coil of old rope, and the fourth mounted two mortars and three small cannon to be used at shorter range to cover the withdrawal. April 10th/11th was the night chosen, being moonless with a spring tide making until 2.0 a.m. and ebbing at 2.15 or 2.20. To Bush's disappointment the bomb-vessels (as the hulks were now called) were placed under the command of Lieutenant Marquand, who had once served in the Guernsey Militia. With him went an old Sergeant of Marines from the flagship who had helped to defend Gibraltar in 1782. The other sloop was the *Suffisante* (14) taken from the French in 1795, commanded by Lieutenant Watkin until her new captain came out from England.

The agreed plan involved firing high-angled howitzers from a stationary platform at a stationary target. The range could thus be calculated in advance, assuming that each bomb-vessel were anchored in exactly the right position. As against that, all odds would be against scoring a direct hit in the dark without sight of where the last shell had fallen. And the shell had either to fall on the deck or burst overhead. It would not explode on impact and could achieve nothing if it fell—as it probably would—in the sea. Had the raid been ordered on a bigger scale the chances of hitting would have been much improved. Hornblower could only console himself by remembering that a larger squadron would have been commanded by someone else. He also issued orders to fire deliberately short and then increase the charge fractionally until the splashes—supposing they could be observed —had crept up to the target. No rockets could be fired from the bomb-vessels but the French might well illuminate the scene. This would expose the sloops to fire from batteries and ships but the mastless bomb-vessels might not at first be noticed. First contact was likely to be with guard-boats and with frigates anchored in the harbour entrance. If the effect of this encounter was to hinder the further progress of the sloops and so prevent them towing the bomb-vessels into their correct positions, these would be towed there by the ships' boats; for which purpose each sloop was lent additional seamen from ships not required for the operation. The various problems were solved, one after the other, and the night of April 10th was suitably calm with a westerly wind and a starlit sky. The two sloops glided in under easy sail, covered by a squadron of frigates and supported, more distantly,

by the Inshore Squadron. The *Hotspur* headed the raiding force
and both sloops had, ready to display, the French night recognition signal, the secret of which Hornblower had obtained from
one of the French fishermen he had come to know. Lieutenant
Marquand was on the forecastle ready to reply to any challenge
in French. Bush stood near the leadsman in the main chains, who
gave him the depths in a quiet voice. A boy then ran aft with the
information to Hornblower who thus groped his way into the
harbour. All he could see were distant lights ashore and a faint
glow from where the French fleet was anchored. The approach
was made in silence.

'Silence', in this context, is a relative term, for no sailing ship
could be completely silent. There was, inevitably, a creaking of
cordage, a sound of wind in the rigging, a recognisable slap and
rush of the bow-wave. The first challenge came at 1.10 a.m. and
Hornblower unmasked his recognition signal (two red lanterns
on the fore yardarm). Either he had been given wrong information or—more probably—the signal had been changed, for the
response was a warning musket shot. Marquand answered a hail
from the guard-boat but again there was something wrong, a
missing password or an incorrect wording, for three musket shots
were now fired, evidently as a signal. The guard-boat vanished
astern and did not re-appear, but the mischief had been done.
A minute later a rocket soared into the sky and burst with a white
light, illuminating the harbour for a few seconds. Hornblower
could see the frigate from which the rocket came and noted that
there were two others forming a protective line. Four cannon
shots were fired—two-pause-two—and Hornblower could picture for himself the guards being summoned and the batteries
being manned. He realised that another half mile would involve
him in a close action from which neither sloop could escape. He
ordered Marquand, therefore, to part company and take the
three bomb vessels up the harbour. Each would have a ship's
cutter alongside but there would be no rowing at first—the tide
would take them in. The fourth bomb-vessel was lashed alongside
Hotspur on the port side, hidden from the French as the sloop
turned northward. Hornblower now opened fire at extreme
range, not with the object of damaging the frigates but merely
to distract attention from the bomb-vessels. He was soon under a
heavy but distant fire from both ships and shore batteries. With

rockets used for illumination on both sides, this action was bound to be the focus of interest. Tacking at about 1.35, and swinging the bomb-vessel over to his disengaged side, Hornblower began his withdrawal, firing alternate broadsides as the ship went about. The three frigates followed, firing at long range and gaining slowly on their prey. To the French at this stage the whole operation must have seemed daring but pointless. The *Hotspur* and *Suffisante* suffered only minor damage and their opponents must have been virtually unharmed. Their moment of greatest danger would come later when they were trying to recover the boats.

What, meanwhile, of the bomb-vessels? One of these became detached from the other two, drifted too far southward and ended aground on a sandbank, far out of range of any possible target. The crew did nothing and eventually surrendered to a guard-boat. Two of them reached position unobserved, dropped anchor and, at about 2.15, opened fire on the nearest French ship-of-the-line. Only three of these were within range and only two were engaged. For some minutes the French were not even aware of their danger for the bombs, falling vertically, did not skip over the surface as solid shot would often do. The howitzers made a noise of gunfire but this was lost in the noisier cannonade from seawards; and their muzzle flash was invisible, firing as they did from below deck-level. Eventually, one splash was near enough to be observed and the result was a rocket, bursting white, which did not reveal the bomb vessels but did enable the British to see where their last bomb had gone. It was short for length and far to the right. Mr Marquand realised that there must be more wind at the top of his missiles' trajectory than there was at sea level. He corrected his aim and told the other crew to make the same correction. Fire was resumed and more rockets fired by the enemy. A splash sighted was still short and the range was increased by using cartridge with a bigger propellant charge. At this moment the bomb-vessels must have been sighted, for the nearest ship fired her broadside. There was little for the gun layers to see and few shots came near the target. The howitzers continued their fire but still without effect, and their supply of bombs was nearly exhausted. The French guns were now beginning to make better practice and one shot struck the second bomb-vessel at the moment its howitzer was firing. There was a

Rochfort. L'Adour is pierced for twenty guns, and was commanded by le Capitaine de Frégate, Moudelot, who was totally unacquainted with the war.

I have the honour to be, etc.

CHARLES PAGET.

The Hon. Admiral Cornwallis, &c., &c., &c.
Copy of another letter from the Honourable William Cornwallis, Admiral of the Blue, &c., to Sir Evan Nepean, Bart., dated the 24th instant.

SIR,
I have much satisfaction in acquainting you, for the information of the Lords Commissioners of the Admiralty, of the recent success of Captain Hornblower, in his Majesty's ship Hotspur; and I enclose a copy of his letter addressed to Sir Edward Pellew, commanding the inshore Squadron.

I am, &c.

W. CORNWALLIS.

SIR,   *His Majesty's Ship Hotspur, in the Bay of Brest, July 17, 1803.*
In accordance with your orders I took the ship under my command into the Goulet on the night of July 16, having on board, additional to establishment, Lieutenant Côtard of H.M. Ship Marlborough and a detachment of Marines from H.M. Ship Tonnaut. The ship's boats were lowered and manned off the Petit Minou and I led the landing party ashore at a point near the Telegraph Station and the adjacent battery I had been instructed to destroy. Mr. William Bush, my first Lieutenant, had very handsomely volunteered his services, but I directed him to remain in command of the ship. Lieutenant Charles Côtard, who had volunteered for the expedition, gave invaluable assistance as a result of his knowledge of the French language. I regret very much to have to inform you that he received a wound which necessitated amputation, and his life is still in danger. The Telegraph Station was seized by the party under my personal command without the slightest opposition, and was set on fire and completely destroyed. Captain Jones of the Royal Marines, having gallantly secured the battery, was unfortunately involved in the explosion of the magazine, and I much regret to have to report his death. While several other Royal Marines of his party are dead or missing. Lieutenant Reid of the Royal Marines guarded the flank and covered the retreat with small loss. His conduct under heavy fire calls for my unreserved approbation. It is with much gratification that I can inform you that the battery is completely wrecked. The parapet is thrown down along with the guns and the gun-carriages destroyed, as will be understood because not less than one ton of gunpowder was exploded in the battery. The retreat was effected in good order, Mr. Alexander Cargill, Master's Mate, being allotted by me the duty of superintending the re-embarkation, which he carried out very much to my satisfaction. I append the list of killed, wounded and missing.

I have the honour to be, &c., &c., &c.

HORATIO HORNBLOWER.

Admiral Pellew.
Copy of a letter from Mr. Daniel de Putron, Commander of the Private Ship of War Alarm, to Sir Evan Nepean, Bart., dated Guernsey, July 23, 1803.

SIR,
I beg leave to acquaint you, for their Lordships' information, that on the 28th ult. in lat 42 deg. 45 min. N and long 11 deg. 7 min. W., I fell in with, and, after a chase of fourteen hours, captured the national schooner La Legere, commanded by Mons. Collinet, Lieutenant de Vaisseau, and mounting two brass four-pounders, and 14 brass swivels, with 36 men. She was bound from

The funeral of Vice-Admiral Viscount Nelson, seen from Bankside, Southwark, from a contemporary engraving

bright flash and a loud explosion on board a French ship-of-the-line. Laid inaccurately for range, the howitzer had been corrected by the French cannon ball and had made a direct hit! There were no other hits and Marquand's men took to the boats, leaving both bomb-vessels under fire and sinking. They began their long pull seawards but the ebb tide was with them and they had a good chance of escape.

The time came, at about 3.0 a.m., when Hornblower had to keep his rendezvous with the ships' boats returning from the attack. He hove to and ordered the *Suffisante* to make for safety. Then he ordered the remaining bomb-vessel to cast off, drop anchor, and prepare for action. As the nearest frigate came up to engage *Hotspur* she was surprised by the overhead detonation of a mortar bomb. Others followed, all in the sea, but one went off at surface level. The frigate received neither damage nor casualties but the surprise effect was all that Hornblower could have hoped for. The French attack was never pressed home and the boats' crews were recovered. The two sloops then tacked down the Goulet, firing occasionally, until the inshore frigates came to their rescue. By daybreak they were out at sea and able to survey the damage they had sustained. *Suffisante* had been hardest hit, oddly enough, with seven casualties and a hit on the waterline. *Hotspur* had suffered in her rigging but had only three men wounded. One boat's crew had been lost, numbering a Master's Mate and fourteen seamen from the *Marlborough*. As against that, a French ship-of-the-line, the *Proserpine* (80) had received one direct hit from a howitzer shell. It was some days later before Hornblower was able to report 'from information received' that the shell had gone down the after-hatch and burst between decks. The resulting fire was extinguished with difficulty but not in time to save the mizzen mast. By morning the pumps could barely keep her afloat. She was immediately taken into dock for extensive repair but doubts were expressed about her ever being seaworthy again.[1] The raid had been a success but Hornblower had to admit when reporting verbally, that his technical experiment had been a failure. The fact was that the idea was perfectly sound but that much of the essential equipment

[1] In fact she never did sail again. She was used for a time as a receiving ship and later as a sheer hulk. For active service she was beyond repair, being broken up in 1813.

had still to be invented. Cornwallis did not worry about that. It was enough for him that the French had been given a fright and put still more on the defensive. Another gazette letter went to prove that the Channel Fleet was in good heart and ready to fight the world.

Hornblower's only immediate reward was a chance to make prize-money. In expectation of war with Spain, not yet declared, Cornwallis sent a squadron to intercept the Spanish flota or treasure fleet. Four frigates went on this mission, parting from the Channel Fleet on July 23rd, 1804, and the *Hotspur* was ordered to Cadiz to gather information about the flota from the British Consul, thereafter to rendezvous with Captain Moore, senior officer of the squadron. A French frigate, the *Félicité* (44) was in Cadiz when the *Hotspur* arrived and was on her way, as Hornblower learnt, to warn the flota of the impending danger. Having joined Moore's squadron at the expected point of interception, Hornblower was assigned to the most northerly post in a line stretched over sixty miles. In this position he sighted the *Félicité* on September 19th and managed to cripple her in the course of an action lasting for many hours. When Hornblower rejoined the fleet off Ushant he learnt that the flota had been intercepted in his absence, laden with six million dollars: a fortune for all concerned but one in which he would not share. After a further spell of blockade duty, Cornwallis sent him back to Plymouth for a needed refit (in December, 1804) and there he heard that Moore and his men would receive no prize-money after all. The capture had taken place before war was declared at Madrid on December 12th and the prizes belonged, therefore, to the Crown as 'Droit of Admiralty'. More fortunate in two other respects, Hornblower found that Maria was pregnant again and that Mrs Mason had gone back to Southsea. When Hornblower returned to the Channel Fleet, on March 14th, 1805, he knew that his noble gesture had actually cost him nothing. It was appreciated, however, by one man in the service and that was Cornwallis. Sending for Hornblower, the Admiral told him that he was about to haul down his flag, that he was allowed to make certain promotions on the eve of retirement and that Hornblower was his choice for promotion to post-captain. He was to quit *Hotspur* and proceed to England, where he would expect to be gazetted in three weeks' time. Fortune he seemed destined to miss but promotion he had achieved and that the most important step of all. If he continued to serve and avoided death in action, mere seniority would bring him his flag in the end.

CHAPTER FIVE

Secret Agent

On 17th May, 1805, Hornblower was relieved as Commander of the *Hotspur* by Captain James Percival Meadows, who came out from Plymouth in the water hoy *Princess*. Hornblower took passage home in the same vessel, leaving Bush still as first lieutenant. But a contrary wind kept the hoy in the fleet's vicinity and Hornblower was summoned back to the flagship on the 20th. Meadows had lost the *Hotspur* by stranding on the night of the 18th and Hornblower was needed as a witness at the Court-Martial. All he could say in evidence was that there were navigational risks round the Black Rock. So, indeed, there were and are. His comments on them were nullified, however, by the fact that he had himself been off the Goulet without mishap for the best part of two years. The Court-Martial acquitted Bush and Prouse and let Meadows off with a reprimand. Whether he would be employed again was another matter. In the meanwhile, he and his officers were given a passage to Plymouth in the *Princess*. To have in the one small and overcrowded vessel a captain going home on promotion and his successor, senior to him, who had lost the ship and been reprimanded, was decidedly awkward. To make matters worse, the headwinds continued and the hoy made little progress towards her destination. While still battling northwards the *Princess* sighted a French privateer brig. There was now every likelihood of the hoy being captured before nightfall. It was in fact evening before the privateer had overhauled his prey. The *Princess* hove to and the privateer sent her boat to take possession. This would have been easily accomplished in normal circumstances but the hoy carried thirty men above her usual complement of six. The boat's crew were silently overpowered and the boat headed back for the privateer with different men but the same arms. A second boat followed with reinforcements and the brig's deck was cleared by a surprise attack in the course of which Meadows was killed. The French had been driven below rather than subdued, however, and the boarding party could not retain their prize. All they could do was wreck the vessel, so cutting up the rigging that no sail could be hoisted for hours. The British returned to the *Princess* and made with a fair wind for Plymouth. Among the privateer's papers, which Hornblower had removed, was a document of obvious importance wrapped (for sinking) in a sheet of lead.

When Hornblower presented the captured papers to the Port Admiral, that officer decided to send Hornblower with them to the Admiralty. The post chaise was ordered immediately and all Hornblower saw of Maria and Young Horatio was a glimpse at the dockyard gate before his journey began. When examined by experts the dispatch proved to be a letter of encouragement addressed by Napoleon—who had recently assumed the title of Emperor—to the Governor of Martinique. The content of the letter was mildly interesting, showing that Napoleon intended no more than a small reinforcement of his West Indian Colonies, but the style of the communication was new and the thing had been found intact as addressed and officially sealed, the first specimen of its kind to fall into British hands. Mr Marsden, the Secretary to their Lordships of the Admiralty had in his hands the means of forging a Napoleonic letter of instructions, the seals reproduced and the signature copied. In the ordinary way this might not have been important but Britain was faced at this moment by the very crisis of the war at sea. A forged letter might never be delivered, might never be accepted as genuine, might not even be obeyed. It was too small a card to take a trick in any normal rubber. A time might come, however, when every card would have to be played. Background to this situation was the treaty between France and Spain signed at Paris on January 4th, 1805. The treaty defined the forces which were to be committed to the invasion of Britain. Napoleon's armies comprised 30,000 men at the Texel, 120,000 deployed between Ostend and Le Havre, 25,000 at Brest, 4,000 men at Rochefort and 9,000 men at Toulon; making a total of 188,000 with means of transporting them all. From Spain were to come another 24,000, bringing the grand total to 212,000. To clear the way for the flotilla and transports, France and Spain had over seventy sail of the line between them, distributed between Brest, Rochefort, Toulon, Ferrol, Carthagena and Cadiz. The British had eighty sail of the line but deployed, of necessity, between the East and West Indies, between Newfoundland and the Baltic. If the Channel Fleet could be lured off its station, if the North Sea Fleet could be defeated off the Dutch Coast and the allies given the command of the Channel—even for a week, perhaps even for forty-eight hours—England would be invaded and conquered. The danger was very real and seemed the greater when Lord Nelson did in fact pursue Villeneuve to the West Indies. The French Admiral reached Martinique on May 16th and heard of Nelson's pursuit soon afterwards. Hornblower reported to the Admiralty on May 29th at a moment when the First Lord had every reason to be worried. In Hornblower's interview with Mr Marsden—when the captured despatch was on the table—it transpired in conversation that Hornblower had some knowledge of both French and Spanish; a fact which Mr Marsden remembered.

While Hornblower was well received at the Admiralty as the bearer of a captured document, there was no immediate command for him. Vacancies existed but in ships for which he would be too junior. He was gazetted, nevertheless, as Captain in the Sea Fencibles which at least gave him seniority from June 1st, 1805. The Sea Fencibles were a sort of coastal 'Home Guard' organisation, ready to repel the French invasion whenever it should materialise. Naval officers regarded it with mixed feelings. It admittedly provided employment on full pay for men whose seagoing days were over. As against that, it saved from impressment a number of fishermen and boatmen whose services were desperately needed at sea. In Hornblower's case his posting was temporary, as he must have been assured, and so much so that he left Maria at Plymouth. His Fencible command extended from Rochester to the North Foreland and he was assisted by three elderly lieutenants, one with a special responsibility for the Isle of Sheppey. Their work, such as it was, involved a weekly and mainly convivial meeting at the Ship Inn in the Market Place at Faversham. Remembering no doubt that a Post-Captain must be aloof from his officers, Hornblower fixed upon Maidstone for his own centre of operations, travelling from there on his visits of inspection to Sheerness or Whitstable. In so far as the French were threatening Kent, it cannot be said that Hornblower did much to deter them. What he did do was to discover Maidstone as his family's place of origin. So far as we know, this was his first visit to the place.

Hornblower's connection with Maidstone was not a mere matter of remote ancestry for his father had been apprentice there in his great-uncle's business. There would be people still around who would remember James Hornblower, the apothecary; a few even who might have seen Jeremiah, the corn merchant, Horatio's great-grandfather. That the family came from this neighbourhood, Horatio must have learnt from his father. This knowledge was confirmed at this time by inspection of tombstones and a glimpse of the parish register. It was near here, he decided, that he must eventually live. It is a common belief that a sailor should want to live within sight of the sea. The sailor's preference is often, rather, for a place in the depths of the country. Hornblower's choice was more of a compromise but influenced by family connections. A place near Maidstone might also be within ten miles of the dockyard at Chatham. It would be situated perhaps on an actual tributary of the Medway. It would be a very proper place for the retirement of a Captain, R.N. Hornblower began to look around the countryside with a new interest. While he expected to see further service at sea, he was secure now of a dignified retirement. It might be no more than a cottage he would eventually own but he could expect a certain position in society. He would be a Justice of the Peace, very likely, and might even keep a carriage. It was while thinking on these lines that he came, by accident, on Smallbridge Manor.

Smallbridge lies five miles south-westward of Maidstone but too far from the main road to be discovered by a traveller on the way to London. Hornblower's Sea Fencible business took him, however, to places quite remote, with the natural result that he often lost his way among the blind and wandering Kentish lanes. It was on an evening in July that he thus went astray on the way back to Maidstone from Tunbridge. He was riding a hired horse and attended by a friend's servant, also mounted, who was supposed to be acting as a guide. When it became clear that they were lost, but with a lodge gate in sight, Hornblower stopped, meaning to ask for directions at the lodge. It was untenanted and he rode up the drive, resolved to ask his way at the house. What followed is best told in his own words dated 4th November, 1805:

. . . I gained admittance only with difficulty and it was only after a long delay that the old maidservant who opened the door could be finally prevailed upon to announce me. The Squire, who sat in the Library, was a strange old gentleman dressed in the fashion of an earlier age and evidently much of a recluse, rambling excessively in his speech and hearing little and understanding less of what was said to him. The house, I learnt from the maidservant, for he seemed to have no other attendance, is called Smallbridge Manor and was built perhaps fifty years ago by the Squire himself, whose name is Tom Barnett and who was then betrothed to a young lady who died from a fall while hunting on the eve of the day fixed for the wedding. It would seem that Mr Barnett has scarcely left the house since the day of this tragedy and the park and garden show evident signs of an almost total neglect which extends even to the parish church and the adjacent village. I ascertained that the estate, which Mr Barnett inherited, will pass to a distant cousin who is in possession of a much more extensive property in Shropshire. I incline, therefore, to suppose that this estate may well be sold when Mr Barnett dies, he being a man of seventy-five years of age or thereabouts. I should be obliged if you would take note of what happens and be ready to act on my behalf should this estate come on the market. Such has been the neglect that possible buyers may be somewhat discouraged, bringing the asking price down to what I can afford when I finally come ashore.

Trusting to your good offices, my dear sir,

I remain,

Your ob't servant,

Horatio Hornblower

This is almost the earliest example to have survived of Hornblower's private correspondence. It was written after he had left the Maidstone district and was addressed to an attorney, Mr Hodge, in whose possession it remained as the oldest item in a deed box marked 'Smallbridge Manor'. It is doubtful whether Hornblower can have thought very seriously about Smallbridge in 1805–6. For one thing, he had no money. For another, he could not have regarded Maria as a possible wife of a future Squire. Restoring Smallbridge to its classic elegance would cost a small fortune and the result would have terrified Maria out of her wits. It was a dream, nevertheless, of the sort of estate which

Hornblower would have liked to inherit or acquire. Some recollection of it remained for years at the back of his mind.

While Hornblower was in Kent the world crisis was becoming more urgent. This was the result of the battle fought by Vice-Admiral Sir Robert Calder on July 22-23, an indecisive action taking the place of a needed victory. News of this event reached the Admiralty early in August and the French claim to have won a victory was published soon afterwards in the British press. It led to a public outcry, a demand for Calder's court-martial and indeed for his imprisonment. With inferior numbers Calder had engaged Villeneuve on his return from the West Indies and captured two of his ships. If this was so culpable, a French author asked, what did Villeneuve deserve whose fleet had been superior in numbers and who had *lost* two ships? In the meanwhile the situation remained extremely tense, with Villeneuve's fleet still more or less intact. He put into Vigo on July 28th, landing his wounded there, and reached Ferrol on August 1st. When he sailed again on the 9th it was still open to him to make a junction with other forces and steer, as ordered, for the Channel. There was a clause, however, in his orders which allowed him, in certain circumstances, to sail for Cadiz. On the 15th he decided to do this and by the 20th he was there. News of this was received at the Admiralty on September 1st and Lord Barham, the First Lord, was in trouble. Cabinet Ministers wanted to know what Lord Nelson was doing, Members of Parliament were concerned about the danger to trade and the newspapers were demanding Sir Robert Calder's court-martial. If only Villeneuve would put to sea! The destruction of his fleet was the only solution to the main problem by which Lord Barham was faced. It was at this moment that Mr Marsden remembered Hornblower and the possibility of sending Villeneuve his orders over a forged signature. There were fifty other things to do but this was one idea and its failure, if it failed, would cost practically nothing. A special messenger rode down to Maidstone on the evening of September 1st and Hornblower reported to the Admiralty on September 2nd. While still drawing pay as Captain in the Sea Fencibles, he was seconded to the Secret Service, and sent on a secret mission into enemy territory. Were he to be captured he would certainly be shot as a spy.

The difficulty about recording this episode in Hornblower's

career is due to the fact that what was secret then is mostly secret still. For his strictly naval career we have official reports, gazette letters, printed despatches and even ships' logs. For his brief career as a spy we have no documentary evidence at all. He himself referred to this episode very guardedly and the Admiralty kept no written record of what was done or said. What we do know, in retrospect, is the object of the exercise—to drive Villeneuve into battle. We can easily guess why Hornblower was the chosen agent: he was fluent in Spanish and French and it was from him, most likely, that the suggestion had come. As for the actual operation we may never know what, if anything, was achieved. Unless some new material should come to light, we must rely upon guesswork. One thing we know for certain is that speed was of the essence. If Villeneuve were not ordered to sea by a fake order within a matter of weeks he might receive genuine orders directing him to lay up his ships for the winter. For that matter, he might be superseded by another Admiral to whom Napoleon had given verbal orders to avoid battle at all costs. Whereas so complex an operation should have been carefully prepared and rehearsed, this mission left England on September 6th, four days after the orders were issued. The vessel used was a French coasting vessel of a type familiar in the Bay of Biscay. She was commanded by a Cornish smuggler, reprieved on certain conditions and watched by his nominal mate, Mr Dinford of the Revenue Service. The landing party was led by Hornblower and comprised a Spaniard called José Miranda, a French emigré physician called Guichard, an agent from Jersey called Legros and an agent from London called Wicks. All these names were, of course, assumed and Hornblower himself took the name of Martin Lopez (Miranda's servant from Corunna). Hornblower carried the forged letter, addressed to Villeneuve from Napoleon, with a covering letter from Decrès, the French Minister of Marine. It was undoubtedly a work of art, written by a French emigré, signed by Dr Claudius (a clergyman in Newgate Prison who had been condemned to death for forgery but who thus earned his reprieve) and sealed by a reproduction of the Imperial seal made by an expert in Cheapside. In it Villeneuve was told to sail for Toulon even at the risk of fighting a battle, provided only that he had five more ships than the opposing fleet.

The road from Paris to Madrid, and so to Cadiz, is almost

entirely inland. From the French Ministry of Marine the courier must ride to Orleans, Tours and Bordeaux. He does not reach the sea until he approaches the Spanish frontier at Bayonne. From there to San Sebastian on the Spanish side his route is parallel with the coast. Then he must go inland again to Vittoria and Burgos, seeing nothing more of the sea until he reaches Cadiz itself. The place to intercept the Imperial messenger would be in the neighbourhood of Bayonne or at some point on the road between there and San Sebastian. The problem would then be to substitute one order for another or else replace the courier by a spy who would deliver the letter in person. Guichard was an expert in opiates, Legros in forgery and Wicks in the picking of locks. There was, moreover, at least one agent resident in Bayonne, the man with local knowledge who had been fore-warned of the landing that was to be made. Provided the sub-stitution was possible this was clearly the team to undertake it, well chosen if not perhaps sufficiently trained. If all went accord-ing to plan, Hornblower would be at Bayonne on about Septem-ber 16th, Villeneuve would receive his orders on about the 25th and the allied fleet would sail in October, to be destroyed by Lord Nelson within a matter of days. Nelson actually joined the blockading fleet on September 25th as from which day the scene was set for a decisive battle, one which would establish British naval predominance for a generation to come.

What success did Hornblower have? We have no means of knowing. What we do know is that his forged letter was paralleled by a genuine letter which had almost the same purpose. Napoleon abandoned his plan for the invasion of Britain on September 2nd, the day after he learnt that Villeneuve had reached Cadiz. He issued new orders on September 14th, instructing Villeneuve to sail for Naples. Decrès added his covering letter on the 16th and sent the courier on his way. On the 18th Napoleon decided to replace Villeneuve, appointing Vice-Admiral Rosily as his successor. Rosily himself was entrusted with Villeneuve's letter of recall and he left for Madrid on September 24th. Napoleon's orders of the 16th were delivered to Villeneuve on September 27th and it was in obedience to these—and not to any substitute orders—that he sailed on October 19th. So much is clear but there is a mystery about how Villeneuve came to know—as he seems to have done—that Rosily was to supersede him. Was that

Hornblower's achievement? Was this the spur which drove Villeneuve into battle? There is a further mystery about the relative speed of the courier and the Admiral. If it took eleven days for the courier to reach Cadiz, why did it take three weeks for Rosily to reach Madrid? He complained of delays over horses and escort. Could these delays have been brought about by British agents? Whoever gained time for Villeneuve to sail before he could be replaced had at least some share in winning the Battle of Trafalgar. We do not know, perhaps we shall never know, what share of the credit should go to Hornblower.

Whatever the result (if any) of the mission to Bayonne, Hornblower would seem to have been back in England before the end of October. After reporting to the Admiralty, he was sent on leave and took the opportunity to join Maria at Plymouth. It was there, on November 4th that he heard the news of the Battle of Trafalgar and the death of Lord Nelson, news brought by the *Nautilus* (26). While there in November he also received his letter of appointment to command the sloop *Atropos* (22), a 6th Rate and just large enough to support the dignity of a Post-Captain. She had been built at Chatham in 1781, measured 481 tons and was established for a crew of 155. She had originally mounted twenty-two 9-pounders but eighteen of these had been since replaced by 12-pounder carronades. Her captain, Caldecott, had resigned his command for reasons of health. Being neither the latest nor the best she was very suitable for the most junior officer but one on the list. At much the same time he would appear to have heard from his uncle, Jonathan Carter Hornblower, who was currently working at Birmingham. It was this uncle, remember, who had contributed something to Horatio's allowance as a midshipman. When Jonathan suggested a meeting, therefore, Horatio felt obliged to agree. As he must travel to Deptford, where *Atropos* was coming out of dock, he named Gloucester as the rendezvous. It was not on the shortest route from Plymouth to London but it was a reasonable compromise as between Plymouth and Birmingham. The journey, via Bristol, was done by coach but Hornblower was increasingly worried about Maria, now expecting their second child but insistent, nevertheless, that she and little Horatio should come with him to London on what would be a first visit for both of them. On December 10th, at the Fleece in Westgate Street,

Gloucester, the Hornblowers came together, Jonathan and Horatio, Martha and Maria. It then transpired that Jonathan had a favour to ask. He wanted Horatio to find a berth in the *Atropos* for a grandson, another Jonathan, the son of Jeremiah. This boy was born early in 1795 and was now aged nearly eleven. Horatio agreed to take the young Jonathan on his quarterdeck but not until he was somewhat older. Horatio, who entered himself at seventeen, was no believer in the theory that a boy should know the ropes from the earliest possible age. His emphasis was always on the need for previous education, especially in mathematics and French. He advised his uncle accordingly and promised to accept young Jonathan as soon as he reached the age of fifteen. This promise was faithfully kept and the young man afterwards did credit to the family.

It was probably Uncle Jonathan who persuaded Horatio to continue his journey by canal rather than by road. The birth of Maria's child was almost due and there seemed every likelihood that the rattling of the coach would bring about a premature labour, perhaps in some remote part of the Cotswolds. Although himself a mechanical rather than a civil engineer, Uncle Jonathan was enthusiastic about canals. A canal boat, he pointed out, made a smooth passage. There would be no rattling or swaying and no risk of being overturned in a ditch. The Thames and Severn Canal, completed as recently as 1789, offered the best possible means of reaching London from Gloucester. With his concern for Maria and his interest in technology, Horatio instantly accepted the idea and took passage in a canal boat called the *Queen Charlotte*. His uncle came down to see him off on the evening of December 11th and the voyage began. For Hornblower it was memorable because one of the boatmen was injured in an accident, allowing him to become a volunteer helmsman. This was his first experience on an inland waterway and he was to talk about it in after-years. The canal boat had to cover over two hundred miles and did well to reach Brentford on the 13th. From there Hornblower hired a wherry to take him and his family down the Thames to Deptford. There they went ashore and found accommodation at the George on Deptford Hard; the place where Maria's second child was destined to be born. Higher up the river but below the Pool of London lay, at anchor, the sloop *Atropos*.

Hornblower took command of his ship on the 14th and Mr John Jones, the First Lieutenant, presented him at once with a letter from the Admiralty in which he was appointed to organise Lord Nelson's funeral procession. The *Victory*, with the Admiral's body on board, had reached the Solent ten days before but had been ordered round to Chatham. In a week's time the body would be at Greenwich Hospital, whence it was to go by river to Whitehall and from there along the Strand to St Paul's for burial. Hornblower was to co-operate with the College of Arms so as to ensure that the proper ceremonial was observed in so far as consistent with seamanship and safety. The funeral was to be on January 9th, 1806 and the river procession would take place on the previous day. Hornblower had just over three weeks in which to plan and execute a combined (if peaceful) operation of unbelievable complexity. The officers and men of the *Atropos* were all unknown to him and he had no other staff he could use whether in writing letters or delivering them. The people whose movements had to be timed and co-ordinated included the most senior Admirals, the Lord Mayor and Sheriffs, the Heralds and the Mourners. His only consolation was that his chief responsibilities ended at Whitehall Stairs where the coffin was to be landed. After that he had merely to disperse the thirty-eight barges and boats which would take part. All went well on the day and Maria gave birth almost simultaneously to a small daughter, who was named after her mother. Hornblower's only reward was to be presented to George III at a Levée and to have posted to his ship, as midshipman, His Serene Highness the Prince of Seitz-Bunau; a princeling whose territories were occupied by Napoleon but who retained as his chief asset a kinship to George III. He was a great-nephew, acceptable as such at court and destined for the Navy. Sole survivor of his original retinue was a certain Dr Eissenbeiss, a medical man who had been ennobled and promoted High Chamberlain and Secretary of State. The policy decided upon was to appoint Eissenbeiss as surgeon to the *Atropos* and so procure his continued attendance on the Prince. It was not, of necessity, a happy arrangement but Maria was delighted to think that her husband had this contact with the royal family.

The *Atropos* was under orders for the Mediterranean and there was no special point in Maria returning to Plymouth. With the baby as well as young Horatio (aged one) to look after, Maria did better to lodge with her mother at Southsea. By the time she did so the *Atropos* was at anchor, fogbound, in the Downs. One odd circumstance was that Hornblower was there almost opposite the village of Worth, the scene of his birth and upbringing. The other odd circumstance was the penetration of the anchorage by a French privateer from Dunkirk disguised as a Ramsgate trawler. The only clues to the plot were a single pistol shot and a floating oar. Following these up in the fog, Hornblower found a West Indian packet, the *Amelia Jane*, with a prize crew on board. She was easily retaken and the privateersmen were persuaded to indicate where their privateer was. Captured by boarding in the fog, the *Vengeance* was a useful capture and brought Hornblower a sum in prize-money which was to help him on his return to England. In the meanwhile, he sent the *Vengeance* and his report into Chatham, the prisoners being put ashore at Deal. As soon as the fog cleared, the *Atropos* sailed with convoy for Gibraltar on January 23rd and dropped anchor there on February 11th. Orders awaiting him there from Lord Collingwood directed him to join the Fleet and, in the meanwhile, take on board Mr William McCullum of the Honourable East India Company's Service, together with his native assistants. Mr McCullum turned out to be a wreck-master and salvage director of the Coromandel Coast, his assistants being pearl divers from Ceylon. With no idea what the object might be of this strange reinforcement, Hornblower sailed up the Mediterranean and joined the Admiral's flag off Cape Perro in Sardinia. He reported to the Admiral and was given orders to proceed to Marmorice Bay in the Levant. It was there that the fleet and transports had collected in 1801 before the landing in Egypt. While the expedition had been there, the *Speedwell* transport had capsized and sunk, taking with her a quarter of a million sterling, gold and silver for paying the troops. The *Atropos* was to proceed to Malta, where Mr George Turner would join the ship as sailing master; he having been present (and taking bearings) when *Speedwell* sank. Hornblower's orders were to recover the money, using Turner to locate the spot and McCullum to do the salvage. No European diver could dive to sixteen and a half fathoms, the depth in which *Speedwell* had gone to the bottom; hence the Sinhalese brought all the way from India for the purpose. One added complication was the need to conceal the purpose of the visit from the Turks, in whose harbour the treasure lay. No offence was to be offered but they might conceivably prove difficult and might even be unreasonable enough to want the treasure for themselves.

The *Atropos* came into Valletta harbour on February 24th and Hornblower made his demands on the dockyard, which included (at McCullum's request) a mile of half-inch line, a quarter mile of slow match and five hundred feet of leather 'fuse-hose' (whatever that was). He was inevitably invited to dine with the Governor—Rear-Admiral Sir Alexander Ball, who had taken the island in 1798–1800—and he as inevitably took with him the Prince of Seitz-Bunau. It was at this dinner party that he heard for the first time of a problem which was later to be his special concern—the plight of Maltese prisoners in the Barbary States. He took little interest in this matter at the time, however, all his attention being given to his immediate mission. On his return to his ship he was told that a duel had been fought between Dr Eisenbeiss and Mr McCullum with the result that McCullum had been shot through the lungs. On inquiry of the surgeon at the hospital, Hornblower was told that the pistol bullet had entered the chest cavity at the level of the fifth rib (near the heart, in other words) and that death might be expected within a few days. Furious that this duel should have happened, furious with himself for not knowing of the bad relationship which had led to it, Hornblower decided to bring McCullum aboard, sail for Marmorice Bay at dawn and hope to arrive there while the patient still lived. Without McCullum the work of salvage would be impossible. He was their only expert and the only man who could instruct the divers or understand what they had to report. The task of keeping him alive must be assigned to Dr Eisenbeiss, whose pistol had fired the bullet. Hornblower assured the doctor that his own life was also at stake, that he could be hanged for murder. This may not have been strictly true but the threat gave McCullum his best chance of survival. As the voyage progressed, however, there seemed little chance of his living for long. He was still alive, nevertheless, when Rhodes was sighted on March 8th. By then Eisenbeiss had come to the conclusion that the bullet was not in the chest but in the muscles of the back. There was a chance of extracting it by an operation if the ship were at anchor

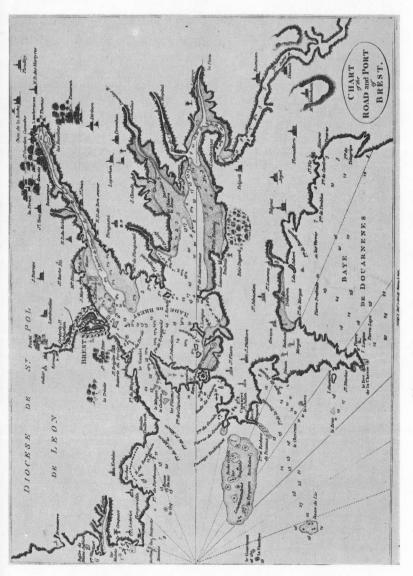

Chart of the Harbour at Brest in 1801

Lady Barbara Leighton, from an engraving by Thomas Wright after the portrait by Sir Thomas Lawrence, R.A., painted in 1810

in sheltered waters. On the evening of the 8th the right conditions existed. The *Atropos* was at anchor in Marmorice Bay.

The operation succeeded to the extent that the bullet was
extracted, together with the shreds of clothing which had entered
with it. Whether the patient would survive was still in doubt but
Hornblower's hope was that McCullum might be well enough to
advise. He ordered his boats to locate the wreck by dragging.
From the local Mudir (the Turkish district officer and harbour
master) he obtained leave to fill water casks and buy fresh provisions; a useful excuse to remain in the harbour while vege-
tables were brought in from the surrounding countryside. The
wreck was found without difficulty, being exactly where it had
sunk, and the three divers, instructed by McCullum from his
sickbed, were able to buoy the exact spot. The wreck was capsized, keel-upwards, and was possible to enter at the break of the
poop. The treasure had been in the lazarette abaft the mizzen
mast and was probably still there. To gain access to it would
mean blowing a hole in the ship's hull with explosive—splitting
it open without breaking it up. To sink a keg of gunpowder and
place it in the correct position would be relatively easy. The
difficulty was over the fuse. This could be applied in one of two
ways; by letting the fuse burn its way along a leather hose-pipe
or by flying-fuse—the lighted match being enclosed with the
explosive itself. The first and less dangerous way failed, probably
because the hose-pipe leaked under water pressure at the lower
end. The alternative method was risky but now inevitable. A
double-ended keg was made and the fuse (to burn for an hour)
was coiled and stapled to the inner head. The whole keg was
covered with a canvas jacket, the final opening in which had to
be stitched and painted with pitch after the fuse had been lit and
the keg stoppered. Then the divers, working one at a time, had to
work the keg into position on board the sunken vessel. Finally,
the boat had to withdraw to a safe distance before the explosion
took place. To work too slowly would mean death and disaster.
To work too hurriedly, as one would be tempted to do, would
mean a leak in the powder keg and the necessity of beginning
again with another keg. In McCullum's absence, still in sickbed,
Hornblower supervised the work in person—realising, as the
others did not, that the slow match would burn faster in the heat
which it would make in that confined space. The explosion

actually took place before the launch had reached the ship. Then the divers went down again and located the silver. By the time the salvage operation could begin, the expert McCullum was sufficiently recovered to supervise the work in person.

It was too much to hope that all this could happen without the Turks taking notice. The Mudir had actually pressed him to stay as a protection against pirates but this was merely a ruse to gain time and lull him into a false security. Observing the salvage operations and drawing his own conclusions, the Mudir had reported the matter to higher authority. The result was the appearance of the Turkish flag on the fort which crowned the Ada peninsula and thus covered the harbour mouth. Another flag waved above the fort on Passage Island, indicating that the batteries there were also manned. Hardly had these preparations been observed than an archaic-looking two-decked ship entered the harbour under Turkish colours and dropped anchor within a quarter of a mile of the *Atropos*. The trap had closed with a vengeance, and the Mudir came to propose terms. After explaining that the Vali (or Governor) had appeared with an army and that the man-of-war was the *Mejidieh* (56) with a crew of a thousand men, he conveyed an offer from the Vali. If Hornblower would hand over all the treasure so far recovered, he would be welcome to what else he could find. As two-thirds of the gold and nearly all the silver was on board the *Atropos*, and as the remainder was nearly impossible to retrieve, this offer was unattractive. The only alternative, however, seemed to be a battle against heavy odds and an official rebuke (whatever the result) for causing an international incident. Hornblower and the *Atropos* were in the worst position imaginable. It was the 15th of the month, incidentally; the Ides of March.

What suggested a possible way out of the dilemma was the night breeze, springing up after midnight, the pale light of the rising moon and a careful study of the chart. If the *Atropos* suddenly made sail and sheered for the passage between Sari Point and the Kaia Rock she had a chance of escape. She would be under fire from the shore batteries but the manoeuvre attempted would come as a surprise, the channel being ordinarily thought too narrow and intricate for a ship of any size. Hornblower gave his orders in a low voice and they were repeated in a whisper, men went quietly to their stations, the waisters to the capstan and the topmen to the yards. At a given signal the cable was cut and sail was made, all in a matter of seconds. *Atropos* was gathering speed before the alarm was given on board the *Mejidieh*. She was out of range before the Turkish ship was ready to fire. There remained the shore batteries, however, and a gun fired from the *Mejidieh* was enough to put them on the alert. To increase the range from Passage Island, Hornblower took the *Atropos* right under Sari Point. This was a feat of seamanship in itself, more than most navigators would have attempted in daylight. To do it at night and under fire seemed mere suicide but the thing was done and the surprised Turkish gunners failed to secure a single hit. The treasure (£200,000 in gold and silver) was duly landed at Gibraltar on April 8th, 1806, from there to be shipped to England. The *Atropos* came under the orders of the Port Admiral, who now required her for a special service.

During the French Wars, with Spain usually on the side of France, the British Mediterranean Fleet was often dependant for its supplies on the Barbary States, the pirate kingdoms in North Africa centring respectively on Morocco, Algiers, Tunis and Tripoli. The Arab corsairs ranged the Mediterranean in a state of perpetual warfare against the smaller countries of Christendom, capturing the vessels and raiding the coasts of Genoa, Sardinia, Naples, Sicily and the Ionian Islands. All prisoners taken were retained or sold as slaves and the philanthropists of Europe, hearing of Britain's proposal to abolish the African slave trade, were apt to ask why the British were not as concerned about *white* slavery? The fact was that the pirates never attacked British shipping. This gave British merchantmen a distinct advantage over other freighters. They could offer greater security at lower insurance and cost. As for the fortress of Gibraltar and the fleet anchorage there, it would have been useless without a supply of provisions from places like Oran and Tetuan. Hornblower himself had been sent to Oran for cattle back in 1796, and knew all about that traffic with the Barbary Coast. In dealing with these Arab States the British used a mixture of threats and bribery, trying always to avoid any actual conflict. What had altered the situation to some extent was the British occupation of Malta, for the Maltese, some of whom had been enslaved, were now to be regarded as British subjects. The coast of Malta, dotted with forts and with fort-like farmhouses, had been raided often enough in the past but never since the British flag was hoisted there. This did not help the Maltese slaves already in Algiers or Tunis, whose relatives had brought pressure to bear on the Governor of Malta. Unable to take any action himself, he had written in turn to the Governor of Gibraltar. It was now the Port Admiral who gave Hornblower his orders but the Governor who explained to him what the problem was.

The Maltese in Arab hands were mostly from captured fishing boats but a few, more prosperous, had been taken in a brig on passage between Valletta and Palermo. This prize had fallen to a Tunisian corsair in 1796 when the Maltese islands were still under the rule of the Knights of St John. The power and activity of the Knights had declined to a point at which they could do little to protect their subjects or even provide a ransom for them. The occupation of their island by the French, followed by its occupation by the British, had given the Maltese other things to think about. It was only in about 1805 that they began to regard British rule as (possibly) permanent. It was only in 1806 that they came to realise that Maltese captives in Barbary could now be regarded, possibly, as British citizens. Until the final peace treaty the legal point was actually open to dispute. The argument was tenable, nevertheless, and Rear-Admiral Ball wanted to do all he could for the Maltese; for people he had come to know and like. A number of them had been enslaved for ten years but news had come that they were still alive, some in Tunis itself. It might have been possible to pay ransom for them but Ball was opposed to this as a bad precedent. He thought that negotiations might succeed if backed by some show of force and the offer, perhaps, of a merely token payment. Agreeing with this suggestion, the Port Admiral chose Hornblower to do the actual work. His removal of the treasure from the Bay of Marmorice had been a clever feat of seamanship as everyone had to admit. If these slaves were to be freed, he was just the man to do it.

There was by now an obvious danger that Hornblower might be regarded as more of a secret agent than a fighting seaman. He had some reputation as a linguist and for his cloak-and-dagger exploits, both real and imagined, and this could have side-tracked him from the path to higher command. He must have seen the drawback in the role for which he was now to be cast, but orders are orders. With less than a year's seniority as captain, he could not expect to have his wishes considered or his preferences discussed. His orders, dated April 21st, were as clear as they were unwelcome. He was to proceed to Malta and collect information there about the people he was to rescue, taking on board a sum of money which might be used in negotiation. He was then to visit Tunis and secure the release of the persons listed, bringing them back to Malta. That mission accomplished, he was to join the Commander-in-Chief's flag at one or other of the rendezvous as laid down in general orders. He was always to remember that the Bey of Tunis was at peace with Britain and that no action of his was to imperil the good relationship which existed between the Bey and King George III. The *Atropos* sailed from Gibraltar on April 22nd and entered Valletta again on June 4th. Reporting to the Governor, he was soon provided with a list of eighty-four captives, eleven of them having been children at the time of capture and three of them too old, perhaps, to have survived. Of the eighty-one he might expect to rescue, nine would be women and four would be young girls, grown up in captivity. The cost of recovering all of these by ransom would come to about 74,500 Spanish dollars at the current rate. Ball would provide no more than 10,000 dollars and Hornblower agreed that this was the limit of what he should offer. Some of the relatives were interviewed, one family called Bezzina being of local importance and greatly concerned over a daughter who would by this time be aged seventeen. The Redemptionist Fathers were able to report where they thought the captives would be. There were a number of meetings and Hornblower ended with a very real sense of what this enslavement meant to the relatives if not to the victims themselves. He gathered all the information he could about Tunis and evidently came to the conclusion that threats would be useless and that persuasion would be a mere waste of time. He had to find some other way and it is clear from the sequel that he found it.

What is maddening is the fact that his plan of campaign is almost as secret now as it was when he sailed from Malta on June 11th. Almost all we know for certain is that *Atropos* re-entered the harbour at Valletta on July 30th and that Hornblower then reported as follows to the Governor.

His Majesty's Ship Atropos
Valletta, July 30, 1806.

Sir,

I have the satisfaction to acquaint your Excellency that I have on board and am about to land seventy-seven inhabitants of Malta who were until recently enslaved in or near the city of Tunis. Several of these Maltese prisoners died in captivity so that I have reason to believe that, of those still living, all are returned with the exception of two young women who elected to remain in Tunis. The names of those that have died are listed in the attached enclosure I, the names of those released in enclosure II, the names of those who remain in Tunis in enclosure III. Not listed are the names of the several children born in captivity and still awaiting baptism. These numbered seven at the time of embarkation and one more was born during the passage hither from Tunis. I have further to report that the Bey of Tunis was persuaded to release these unfortunate people without ransom as a gesture of friendship towards His Majesty, under whose protection the Maltese islands are now happily placed. The money apportioned for ransom will be returned therefore to the public Treasury.

I also have the honour to report that on June 19th the *Atropos*, under my command, was fired upon by a Tunisian frigate, the *Ibrahim* of 28 guns. An action followed in the course of which the *Ibrahim* was dismasted and driven aground on the island of Lampedusa off the African coast. It then transpired that the attack had been made in error, the captain of the *Ibrahim* mistaking the *Atropos* for a merchant ship belonging to a country with which the Bey of Tunis is at war. When the error was explained, I rendered assistance to the *Ibrahim* and have the satisfaction to report that she was refloated and was able to reach Tunis under jury-rig. The casualties on board the *Atropos* were fortunately light, comprising only three seamen slightly wounded. The *Ibrahim* suffered more heavily and I was given to understand that nine of her crew were killed and sixteen wounded, eight seriously, and that the ship herself will require docking. The Bey of Tunis is fully cognisant of the circumstances in which this encounter took place and is satisfied that no error is attributable to me. He wishes to maintain a friendly relationship with

His Majesty and also with your Excellency and asks me to convey the assurance that no Maltese vessel will be molested in future by any ship under the Tunisian flag. I have written a more detailed report addressed to the Port Admiral at Gibraltar, under whose orders I sailed, for transmission, if he sees fit, to the Commander-in-Chief.

I have the honour to be, etc.
Horatio Hornblower.

This report is clearly a masterpiece of reticence and while his other and more official report is more detailed, naming the men wounded, listing the damage and doing justice to the loyalty and courage of Mr James, First Lieutenant, Mr Stile, Second Lieutenant, Mr Turner the Master, Midshipman Smiley and Midshipman His Serene Highness the Prince of Seitz-Bunau, it tells us nothing about the circumstances in which the captives came to be released. Two facts stated are more significant, however, than they might seem. In the first place, the whole operation lasted over seven weeks. Since Malta and Tunis are little over two hundred and fifty miles apart, and Lampedusa about half that distance from Malta in a different direction, the process (whatever it was) took time. In the second place, the Tunisians' failure to recognise the *Atropos* was presumably the result of her sailing under false colours. There can be no doubt that Hornblower's real report was made and approved verbally and that nothing more was meant to be on record. Whatever the full story may be, the success he achieved was enough to make him extremely popular in Malta. We know nothing of what immediate celebrations he attended ashore, but his return to Malta in 1829 was made notable by a deputation of the Maltese who, but for him, might have died in captivity. One would like to know more about the two girls who preferred slavery! It seems doubtful, however, whether the full story will ever be known.

The *Atropos* duly reported to the Commander-in-Chief, Lord Collingwood, off the north point of Sardinia at Cape Perro. On August 9th he was given fresh orders to reconnoitre the Mediterranean coast of Spain and report what efforts were being made to reconstitute the Spanish fleet after the Battle of Trafalgar. Hornblower duly looked into Malaga, Motril and Almeria without seeing a single man-of-war. There remained Carthagena, the naval base, and *Atropos* appeared off that port on August 23rd. From the masthead four sail of the line and a frigate could be seen in the inner harbour, none with yards crossed, and one frigate in the outer bay apparently ready to sail. She was identified as the *Castilla* (44) and she came out of harbour to chase *Atropos* off. Hornblower set a course eastward and found that he could just hold his own. Twice the wind moderated and reefs were shaken out. On the second occasion Mr Midshipman Prince (as the King's great-nephew was known for short) attempted a stupid feat on the yardarm, lost his hold and fell overboard. Had he not bounced off the shrouds he might have been killed. As it was Hornblower had either to risk the ship or abandon George III's relative. Making an instant decision he threw the emergency life-buoy overboard, ordered the mizzen topsail aback and had the quarter boat dropped into the sea. While the boat went to the rescue he hoisted signals as if to another British ship to leeward. The ruse worked and the *Castilla* hauled her wind, fearing that she might be cut off from her base. The royal youngster was rescued and instantly caned for his folly. Hornblower decided, meanwhile, to keep the *Castilla* under observation. He did so during the night and kept to windward of her next day as the Spaniard headed (apparently) for Minorca. The situation then altered abruptly with the sighting of other sail further to leeward and beyond the *Castilla*. These turned out to be a small convoy escorted by a small frigate, the *Nightingale* (28), commanded by Captain Ford. The Spanish Captain decided to give battle, closing with the *Nightingale* before the *Atropos*, to windward, could intervene. Hornblower realised, to his horror, that Ford was closing with the enemy before any help could be expected from *Atropos*. In a short time the *Nightingale* was a ruin, her main-topmast gone, her foremast over the side. There was only one thing to do—board the *Castilla* and hope that Ford would do the same. These tactics worked and the Spanish were over-whelmed by two waves of attackers, one from either side. With great difficulty the *Nightingale* and prize were brought into Palermo on September 10th, shortly before the flagship arrived with Lord Collingwood aboard. Hornblower then set his men to work on a repair and refit which included repainting the entire ship. As the sequel showed he might have done better to leave her as she was. As things were, she was seen by King Ferdinand, of Naples and Sicily, on his way out to visit the flagship. Naples had been lost to this unattractive monarch and Sicily remained to him as the result of British protection. He pointed out, nevertheless, to the British Ambassador, Lord William Bentinck, that an island king should not be without a Navy of his own. He asked for the *Atropos* to be transferred to his flag. Needing his alliance at a time when Britain had few other allies, fearing moreover that he might come to a separate peace with Napoleon, Lord William Bentinck advised Lord Collingwood to hand the ship over. He agreed with reluctance, sent for Hornblower and told him what the decision had been. If he cared to transfer to the Sicilian Navy he would have the rank of Commodore. This he promptly refused but the mediocre Mr John Jones (the Ninth) agreed to remain as Captain—having no other chance of promotion—and took twenty volunteers with him. These were, of course, the bad characters, the remainder being distributed among the other ships of the squadron present. The Prince of Seitz-Bunau was given a berth on board the flagship, saying goodbye to Hornblower and the *Atropos* with tears in his eyes. Hornblower himself was given a passage to England in the *Aquila* transport. He came ashore at Portsmouth on December 13th after a rough passage with contrary winds.

There can be no doubt that Hornblower was in a bitter mood at this stage of his career. He had made an efficient ship out of the indifferently officered *Atropos*. He had made a success of two important missions, neither of which could be given publicity. He had finally played the crucial part in the capture of a Spanish frigate. Unluckily for him, however, he had been the junior captain (he was still junior to almost everyone) and Ford, taking most of the credit for himself, had written a report on the action in which the reference to the *Atropos* had been—well—ambiguous. It was this letter which would appear in the *Gazette* and it had read as follows:

While the action continued with the *Nightingale* and her opponent locked together I made the signal to the *Atropos* to engage the enemy more closely. This signal was obeyed by Captain Hornblower who did not take in his royals and courses until he was nearly within range. After enduring the enemy's fire for upwards of half an hour, sustaining great damage and suffering heavy casualties we were relieved to see the *Atropos* on the further side of our opponent. Until shortly before this time our anchor had been hooked in the Spanish ship's fore-chains but it was cut free by a party of axemen ably led by Mr John Huggins, Master's Mate. The alteration in the two ships' relative positions enabled us to board the enemy and I therefore called for boarders and led them over our bowsprit and across the enemy's forecastle. The enemy made a determined resistance which would have been still more prolonged had not Captain Hornblower now attacked the enemy ship on its undefended side. The enemy struck soon afterwards and turned out to be the *Castilla*, a heavy frigate of forty-four guns. I am indebted to Captain Hornblower for his timely assistance in making this capture, much of the credit for which must go to Mr Richard Lucas, First Lieutenant of the *Nightingale*, but for whose intrepid conduct . . . etc., etc.

Without being precisely inaccurate, Ford, whose tactics had been inept, conveyed the general idea of a co-operation which might have been useful if it had not been so belated. The fact was that he had failed to identify his opponent and had manoeuvred so as to make a quick capture before the *Atropos* could fire a gun. Given a measure of common sense he should have played for time and kept away from *Castilla* until the *Nightingale* and *Atropos* could act together, forcing the *Castilla* to distribute her fire between them. The losses suffered by the *Nightingale* had been mostly unnecessary, so many lives merely thrown away. How many readers of the *Gazette* could see all that between the lines? Not the Lords of the Admiralty, who promoted Mr Lucas to the rank of Commander. Not the directors of the Patriotic Fund, who would in due course vote Ford a gold-hilted sword to the value of a hundred guineas and one for Hornblower worth just half that sum. If any man understood it was Lord Collingwood, whose representation would govern their Lordships in deciding upon the ship to which Hornblower would be appointed. Unaware of what their decision would be and still sore over the fate of the *Atropos* Hornblower landed at the Sally Port and found a barrow to take his luggage round to Highbury Street. It was Maria who answered the door and who told him at once that the children were sick. The apothecary had been sent for but had not come and it was Hornblower himself who made the diagnosis. They both had smallpox. . .

The two children, Horatio and Maria, died within a day of each other and were buried in the churchyard of the church in which their parents had been married. The double funeral took place on December 18th, the bells tolling from the belfry of St Thomas à Becket. It was a sad Christmas that year and there was all too little that Hornblower could say or do. Maria herself was prostrate and ill and weeks passed before he could persuade her to celebrate what success had come his way; the *Gazette* letters, the comment in the newspapers, the paragraph in the *Naval Chronicle*, the presentation of the gold-hilted sword. For Horatio himself the only news that mattered was that received on February 5th, 1807; news of his appointment to the frigate *Lydia* (36), now fitting out at Chatham. It was with something like relief that he announced his intention of going there immediately. This would not mean a final goodbye before returning to sea. He would almost certainly have the chance to bring the *Lydia* round to Portsmouth before she went further afield. For the moment what mattered was to escape from the stuffy and sordid atmosphere of Highbury Street. For Maria he felt sympathy in plenty. What he did not feel for her, and had never felt for her, was love.

CHAPTER SIX

Frigate Captain

From Portsmouth Hornblower travelled by coach to London and called at the Admiralty with a view to securing Bush as his First Lieutenant. This application succeeded, Bush being available (as Hornblower knew) and there was some little discussion about the other appointments, Mr Gerard as Second and Mr Crystal as Master. His main points gained, Hornblower continued his journey to Maidstone where he called on Mr Hodge, the attorney, and was told that Mr Barnett was still alive and that Smallbridge Manor was more neglected than ever. Repeating that he was interested in the property, Hornblower went on to Chatham and ended his journey there at the Golden Cockerell. Calling at the dockyard on February 16th, he learnt that the *Lydia* was completing a refit and would be in dock for copper sheathing between the 23rd and the end of the month. The *Lydia* was a middle-sized Fifth Rate built at Woolwich in 1796 to the design of Sir William Rule. She measured 951 tons and 143 ft long, mounted twenty-six 18-pounders on the gun-deck, eight 9-pounders on the quarterdeck and two 12-pounders on the forecastle. She was established for a crew of 274 men and had cost £19,070 to build. Having been aground in the Shannon Estuary, her captain had been dismissed for negligence and the ship herself brought in for repair. Her new commission would begin, it was agreed, on March 12th, 1807.

The *Lydia* finally sailed from Chatham on March 22nd and came into Portsmouth on the 24th. Maria came aboard there to view the frigate and Hornblower took the opportunity of entertaining his officers ashore. For him at least this was a moment of relative affluence for he had shared in the prize money from the *Castilla*: not a fortune, to be sure, but a useful sum, the two captains sharing an eighth of the value between them. He was better dressed now with some silver for his cabin table, and Maria's simple needs were more than provided for. His orders, when he received them, were to sail for Malta, taking with him

Captain Owen Griffith, R.N. and Mr John Withinshaw. He was told, in strict confidence, that Alexandria was to be occupied by British troops. Captain Griffith was an expert in combined operations, sent to command the actual landing. Mr Withinshaw was a civil engineer, sent to report on the possibility of making a canal at Suez to connect the Mediterranean with the Red Sea. The *Lydia* was to join the expedition at Malta, remain at Alexandria for as long as Mr Withinshaw required co-operation in his work and then bring him (but not Captain Griffith) back to Portsmouth. Their Lordships stated their expectation that the *Lydia* should be home again by the end of August. She would then be required for a special service. After his two passengers had joined the ship, Hornblower said goodbye again to Maria and sailed from Portsmouth on March 28th, 1807.

Whoever drafted Hornblower's order would seem to have made a mistake for the expedition to Alexandria had long since sailed—had sailed indeed while the *Lydia* was at Chatham—so that there was no fleet at Malta which Hornblower could join. When the *Lydia* reached Alexandria, moreover, on June 11th, it was to find that historic seaport at least temporarily in British hands. There was nothing for Captain Griffith to do. Mr Withinshaw, by contrast, had an interesting task ahead of him and one with which Hornblower could assist. By the end of July Hornblower knew something about Egypt and something about civil engineering, while Mr Withinshaw had learnt something about navigation and even more about ancient history. The content of his report is not to our present purpose but it reveals, indirectly, why the *Lydia* was sent on this unusual mission. The Suez Canal of classical times was being studied, not merely with a view to its revival but as the example, technically, of what might be done at Panama. Someone in government and perhaps even in the Cabinet, was interested in the idea of developing a route there across the Isthmus or perhaps, and more hopefully, via Lakes Managua and Nicaragua.[1] Horatio Nelson had been sent to investigate the possibilities of this route in 1780. His expedition

[1] The statesman concerned was almost certainly George Canning, Treasurer of the Navy from 1804 to 1806, whose subsequent policy towards the Spanish colonies was to be of great importance. He went out of office before Hornblower was given his orders but the scheme was probably his, drawn up and approved in 1806.

tried to reach Nicaragua Lake via the San Juan River, with a view no doubt to capturing the city of Granada. The attempt had failed but the idea remained alive and especially the idea of attempting the same thing from the Pacific side. Some such plan seemed the more feasible in 1807 in that there were reports of a rising against Spain centred upon the Gulf of Fonseca. Were the conquest made, with local help, the next problem could be to decide upon the exact route to be followed and the best means of transport. On the map there would seem to be no great difficulty about joining the existing waterways with a relatively short length of canal. The concept under discussion was the same as would underlie the eventual construction of the Panama Canal; a sensible solution to a tiresome problem.

If some statesmen were intrigued with the possibilities of Nicaragua, others were *not*, and among them, most probably, were the naval members of the Board of Admiralty. They could not see what Nicaragua had to do with the defeat of Napoleon. The effect of their intervention was threefold. In the first place, they reduced the expedition in size, sending one ship instead of the four originally planned. In the second place, they briefed a civil engineer with experience on the Aire and Calder Canal. In the third place, and finally, they decided (as we have seen) that the engineer should look at Egypt first. There had been a canal there in ancient times, linking the West with the East, and an expert might learn something from the way in which the problem had once been solved. For reasons of security neither Hornblower nor Mr Withinshaw was told, initially, about the Nicaragua scheme. They would be briefed about that on their return to Britain. This programme was observed, *Lydia* being at Portsmouth by August 25th. While she was repaired, refitted and supplied for a long voyage, Mr Withinshaw was in London and being told about Nicaragua under an oath of secrecy. The result was that he flatly refused to go. He may have known more about Central America than his employers at the Admiralty. He may even have talked with somebody who had survived the expedition of 1780. Whatever his source of information, he knew enough about Nicaragua to decide against it. Their Lordships could find someone else, so far as he was concerned, and all good luck to the man chosen—he would need it. Muttering to himself about official stupidity, Mr Withinshaw returned to his native Lancashire. Without seeking a substitute, their Lordships promptly decided that Hornblower should go by himself. He was known to be a good navigator, fluent in Spanish, and a capable sort of man. No doubt he would know what to do when he saw the place. For the sake of security they told him little but made him sail under sealed orders, to be opened only after leaving Madeira.

The gist of the orders, when he came to open them on November 19th, amounted to this: he was to make contact with a Landowner called Don Julian Alvorado whose property lay along the western shore of the Gulf of Fonseca. Don Julian intended to rise in rebellion against Spain and Hornblower was to deliver to him five hundred muskets and bayonets, five hundred pouch-belts and a million rounds of ball ammunition. He was to assist the rebellion in every way, not excluding financial support,[1] and recognise Don Julian's rule over any territory he might conquer. Coming to the heart of the matter, Hornblower was told that an arm of the Bay of Fonseca, called (it was believed) the Estero Real, approached the inland Lake of Managua, which was known to communicate with the Lake of Nicaragua and so with the river San Juan, which flows into the Caribbean. Hornblower was to open up this route across the Isthmus, with Don Julian's help, and report on the best means of improving this line of communication, whether by canal or otherwise. Only when all this had been accomplished was Hornblower free to attack treasure ships in the Pacific, and even then he must avoid giving offence to inhabitants who might otherwise favour the revolt. He was informed, finally that the Spaniards patrolled the Gulf of Fonseca, retaining there for the purpose a two-decked ship, the *Natividad* (50), which the *Lydia* (36) was encouraged to capture, sink, burn or otherwise destroy. To attack a ship of nearly double the *Lydia*'s size was thus incidental to a programme which began with founding a new kingdom and ended by cutting a canal through the Isthmus. The final paragraph ended with a warning against letting the Spaniards know of his approach. He was thus to avoid sight of land between Cape Horn and the Gulf of Fonseca, displaying a standard of navigation which perhaps one captain in a hundred might claim to possess. The programme as outlined was nothing if not ambitious. The first step, however,

---

[1] Hornblower brought with him fifty thousand guineas in gold coin, a source of anxiety throughout the voyage.

was the simplest, at least in concept: he was to deliver a load of arms and ammunition to a named individual without previously allowing his presence to be known.

The secrecy of the outward voyage was easily preserved as long as the *Lydia* remained in the Atlantic. She was at the Cape de Verde Islands on November 28th, crossed the Line on Christmas Day and reached Rio de Janeiro on January 12th. Whereas Portugal itself was under French control, Brazil remained to the King of Portugal, with whom Britain was in alliance. Hornblower had no difficulty, therefore, in obtaining supplies and water at Rio. He told the Portuguese authorities that he was under orders to cruise off the River Plate. They told him, in reply, that they knew all about it; that another attack on Montevideo was being planned and that they fully understood the British reluctance to give up the attempt. Hornblower knew, of course, about the failure of Popham's expedition in 1806, as also about the further failure in July, 1807. That another effort should be made was not improbable, although Hornblower knew for a fact that none was intended. His story was accepted, however (and, indeed, improved), and there was no danger of his officers or men indulging in careless talk, for to none of them had he divulged anything. This was the period of his life when his reputation was established as a taciturn and cold-blooded disciplinarian, giving clear orders but saying nothing about any future plan. He sailed from Rio de Janeiro on February 4th, watered at the Falkland Islands, which he knew to be uninhabited, on March 10th, and set off from there to round the Horn. He had his first sight of the Horn on April 17th, was driven back into the Atlantic and then sighted it again, and for the last time, on the 30th. He saw no more of South America after that, sailing into the Gulf of Fonseca on June 18th, 1808.

In performing this considerable feat of navigation Hornblower had been lucky, as he fully realised. Few British navigators rounded the Horn and those who had done so came back, many of them, with reports of appalling weather. Captain Cook had been fortunate in this respect on his first voyage, being off the Cape in January—midsummer in that latitude—and Hornblower was almost as lucky in April. The voyage from there northwards was far from easy without sight of land (say, at Quito) but Hornblower's skill in making lunar observations brought *Lydia* to the

MARRIAGES.

Lately, the *gallant* Robert Hope, Esq. Purser of his Majesty's ship Puissant, aged fourscore, to the lovely and amiable Miss Fanny Paul, of Portsmouth, aged 13!

EPIGRAM ON THE ABOVE.
Said an ancient Apostle,
   Of Faith, Hope, and Love,
The latter by far
   Must all ages approve.
But one Angel (Miss *Paul*)
   Acted quite the reverse;
For *old Hope* above all
   She preferr'd—with his *purse!*

Captain Anderson, to Miss Eggleston of Kilham.

At Greenwich, Lieutenant Alexander Robert Kerr to Miss Raison.

At St. John's Church, Westminster, by the Rev. Dr. Vincent, Subalmoner to his Majesty, Lieutenant John Hotchkis, to Miss Pearce, daughter of the late Richard Pearce, Esq. of Westminster.

James Lucas, Esq. Lieutenant of his Majesty's ship Ardent, to Miss S. Langham, youngest daughter of Mr. Langham, of Cockfield, Suffolk.

The 1st instant, at Doncaster, by the Rev John Eyre, Captain George Eyre, to Miss Georgiana Cooke, daughter of Sir George Cooke, Bart. of Wheatly, in the county of York.

The 15th ult. at Minorca, Lieutenant Francis Hastings, to Leonora St. Croix, only daughter and heiress of Don Emanuel St. Croix, of that island.

On the 17th instant at Stockbridge in Hampshire, Rear-Admiral Sir Percy Wetherall Leighton, Knight of the Bath, to Lady Barbara Wellesley, youngest daughter of the 1st Earl of Mornington. As soon as the ceremony was performed the bridal party was met by Sir Percy's numerous and respectable tenantry; who, after offering their heartfelt congratulations on the joyful event, preceded them in procession, accompanied by a band of music, to Woodland Hall, where a reception was held. Afterwards the happy couple set off for Markby House, lent to them for the occasion by Lord Hambledon of Petersfield.

Lately, Captain Anderson, of the Navy, to Miss Eggleston, of Kilham.

The 5th instant, at Stoke Damerell, Devonshire, William M'Donald, Esq. Surgeon in the Royal Navy, to Miss Knight, daughter of Captain Knight, of his Majesty's ship Montague.

The 9th inst. at St. James's Church, Captain Temple Hardy, of the Navy, only surviving son of the late Sir Charles Hardy, to Miss Warre, of Belmont Lodge, Herts.

Lately, Sir Thomas Williams, Captain of the Endymion, at Salisbury, to Miss Whapshare, eldest daughter of the late Charles Whapshare, Esq.

15. By special licence, G. Nelson, Esq. of the Temple, London, brother to the Secretary of the Navy, and a relative of Lord Nelson, to Miss Browne, of Stoke Newington.

The 23rd inst. Admiral Sir Hyde Parker, to Miss Onslow, daughter of his brother Admiral. The difference of their ages is exactly forty-three years. Lady Parker has a settlement of 2000l. *per annum.*

24. At Kingston, by the Rev. W. Bussell, Lieutenant A. Wilson, of the Navy, to Miss E. B. M'Kay, of Gibraltar.

The 25th, at St. Martin's in the Fields, Captain Dundas, of the Navy, to Miss Charlotte Wood.

At Truro, James Obrien, Esq. Captain in the Navy, and nephew to the Earl of Inchiquin, to Miss Bridgman Williams, daughter of James Williams, Esq. of the same place.

Notice of the marriage of Rear-Admiral Sir Percy Leighton to Lady Barbara Wellesley, reproduced from the NAVAL CHRONICLE of 1810

H.M. Cutter *Witch of Endor*, from the coloured aquatint by J. Cartwright, published by T. McLean in 1818, by which period the vessel had reverted to the revenue service for which she had been originally designed

Smallbridge Manor, from the aquatint made by T. Baker after the oil painting by A. Stewart of 1823

Gulf of Fonseca without even making the approach along the right parallel—the time-honoured way to make certain of a landfall. Shortly before making his final approach, on June 1st, Hornblower reached three years of seniority on the captains' list. This enabled him to sport two epaulettes instead of one. On that day he invited his wardroom officers to dine on the anniversary of the Battle of the Glorious First of June (1794). Bush gave a toast to the new 'senior captain' and all thought the occasion might be marked by Hornblower telling them the object of the voyage. While politely grateful for his officers' good wishes, Hornblower told them precisely nothing. When the *Lydia* made that astoundingly accurate—or lucky—landfall on June 18th, only the captain knew why she was there. All he said, moreover, was 'Clear for action', and then, 'Load and run out the guns'. Ready thus to meet any emergency the *Lydia* ran up the bay with the tide making and dropped anchor in seven fathoms. The first phase of the operation was over.

The second phase, as he soon grasped, was going to be a great deal more difficult. Don Julian Alvorado was still alive and in rebellion. He was even in effective control of the area south of La Libertad. The trouble was that power had driven him mad, leading him to proclaim his divinity as 'El Supremo'. Alliance with this lunatic was vital, nevertheless, for the *Lydia* needed a minimum of eight months' provisions to reach England again. Luckily he had arms and ammunition with which to trade and 'El Supremo's' men produced (besides water) a fair equivalent in cattle, pigs, bread, sugar, tobacco, coffee, potatoes and rum. He was still landing arms and shipping supplies when a messenger came with warning that the *Natividad* had been sighted by a lookout posted in the mountains. He calculated that she could not enter the bay until about midnight. Instead of putting to sea, as many captains would have done, Hornblower shifted *Lydia* into a new berth, an ambush position behind Meanguera Island. When the *Natividad* came in by moonlight the *Lydia* suddenly appeared from nowhere, shot alongside the Spaniard and fired a single broadside. The grapeshot was followed by a wave of boarders who cleared the upper deck in a matter of minutes while the lower deck was cleared by men from the frigate's boats which attacked from the other side. As a Spanish officer was later to point out to him in conversation, the *Natividad*, in twenty years

of service along the Pacific coast, had never been less than four
thousand miles, by sea, from any possible opponent. She was
captured in fact, with surprising ease. The sad sequel was that
'El Supremo' promptly demanded her as the nucleus of the fleet
he was to lead against La Libertad. Hornblower could only agree
and assist in an operation which began at least with complete
success and was the prelude to 'El Supremo's' further attack on
San Salvador.

Leaving 'El Supremo' to his own devices, Hornblower sailed
his frigate down to the Gulf of Panama, partly as a diversion in
'El Supremo's' favour, partly to intercept the Spanish trade in
that area. Before she had intercepted anything, *Lydia* was herself
intercepted by a Spanish lugger under a flag of truce. The officer
on board informed Hornblower that Britain and Spain were now
at peace. More than that, they were allies! Napoleon had deposed
King Ferdinand, replacing him by his own brother, Joseph.
What remained of the real Spanish government had formed an
alliance with George III as a result of which all the ports in
Spanish America were open to the *Lydia*. Hornblower hoped
wildly that the news might be untrue but the lugger also bore
despatches; one from the British Admiral on the Leeward Island
station, sent overland from Porto Bello, and one from the Viceroy
of Peru. These documents, unquestionably genuine, made the
situation all too clear. It was apparent, incidentally, that the
Viceroy had not yet heard about the *Natividad*, nor about 'El
Supremo's' campaign in the Captaincy General of Gautemala.
Here was a dreadful situation! By a strict obedience to his orders
Hornblower had created a situation of the most difficult kind,
encouraging a local revolt against one of Britain's allies. He could
not be court-martialled for obeying his orders but he might well
be left unemployed as a gesture to placate the Viceroy. His was a
black situation and not at all improved by a third communication which accompanied the other two. This read as follows:

> The Citadel
> Panama
> July 20th, 1808
>
> Lady Barbara Wellesley presents her compliments to the
> Captain of the English frigate. She requests that he will be so
> good as to convey her and her maid to Europe, because Lady

Barbara finds that owing to an outbreak of Yellow Fever on the Spanish Main she cannot return home the way she would desire.

The name 'Wellesley' had a momentary effect but Hornblower's other problems were too pressing for him to feel more than a passing annoyance about this arrogant and obviously impossible request. The Spanish officer expressed his relief that he had been able to convey the news before the *Lydia* fell in with the *Natividad*. To this Hornblower's best reply was to bring the prisoners up from the cable tier—providing an embarrassing scene for all concerned. Even then he did not know the worst of it, for—as he now learnt—the Manila galleon was due at Acapulco the following month and the rebel *Natividad* would be awaiting her. The capture of her cargo, worth a million or more would cripple the government and give heart to the rebels, to oppose whom Spain would have neither ships nor men. By the time the *Lydia* dropped anchor at Panama, Hornblower realised that he would have to fight the *Natividad* for the second time and without the advantage of surprise. It was while still digesting that fact that he found himself confronted by Lady Barbara Wellesley, who came on board—with her coloured maid and baggage— calmly assuming that her request for a passage would not and could not be refused. Hornblower had good reason to send her ashore but found that there were three objections to that idea. In the first place, she was in Panama by the accident of war. She had been visiting the West Indies and the packet in which she sailed had been captured by a Spanish privateer and brought into Porto Bello. She was there as a prisoner when a yellow fever epidemic began and she went to Panama to escape it. In the second place the epidemic was almost certain to reach Panama. In the third place she was a Wellesley and seemingly used to having her own way. For a Post-Captain without influence to make enemies of the Wellesley family would amount to professional suicide. Hornblower had to welcome her aboard, although one suspects that he did so with a bad grace. There were many inconveniences in having a lady on board ship, the surrender of the captain's cabin being merely one of them. Apart from that, moreover, there was an action to be fought and a voyage round the Horn to be faced, the one perhaps as dangerous as the other. What if the *Lydia* were captured and what if Lady Barbara Wellesley were to fall into the hands of the lunatic 'El Supremo'? She was beset by perils on either hand but might be forgiven for thinking yellow fever the worst of all.

We may doubt whether Hornblower had at this time even heard of Lady Barbara and he certainly had no work of reference to which he could turn for information about her. The fact is, however, that she was not the least remarkable member of a very remarkable family. Garrett Wellesley, 1st Earl of Mornington (1735–1781) having married Anne Hill, had by her a series of children, beginning with Richard in 1760 and continuing with Arthur (who died), William, Francis (who died), Anne, Arthur, Gerald, Henry, Mary Elizabeth and (finally) Barbara, in 1781. Richard, the 2nd Earl and 1st Marquess, was destined for a brilliant career in politics, Henry played a respectable role in diplomacy and became 1st Baron Cowley, and the second Arthur (b. 1769) was to be the greatest soldier of his day. Barbara was very much of an afterthought, born just before her father died and at a period when the rather impoverished family had moved from Ireland, their proper home, to Knightsbridge. There was no fortune for Barbara to inherit but when the brilliant Richard went to India, as Governor-General, in 1797, he took his youngest sister with him. She was aged eighteen, attractive and gay, and well placed to marry the best man India had to offer. She returned from India unmarried, however, in 1799–1800, accompanying her brother Henry, who had been Richard's private secretary. She had been left an encumbered estate in Ireland, the bequest of a cousin, and she went there at this time, meaning to develop its possibilities. She was in Ireland for several years, staying mostly with relatives in Dublin, and then received (in 1806) another bequest, this time of a small plantation in Jamaica. A keen traveller, she resolved to go there in person. The capture of the ship in which she made the voyage marked the end of this attempt and her present resolve was to go home again. It was at this point that she went on board the *Lydia* and demanded a passage.

We have no description of Barbara Wellesley at this exact moment of her life. It so happens, however, that she is mentioned in a letter of Lady Bessborough to Lord Granville written the year before.

Brocket House
Saturday, 18th June, 1807.

... The greatest news I can tell you, and what most occupies
all our Society at present, is that Palermo, the Don's[1] horse,
won at Ascot against all odds. Lord Jersey has bought him and
we all wait, in fearful apprehension, the *details* which for the
next two months we shall probably hear. I came here to-day in
the hope that change of society would take off a little from the
depression of Spirits I labour under. The fine weather has done
something to soothe me but I cannot say the same about the
visit here of Lady Barbara W. who was to have married the
eldest son of Lord Brandon. Unluckily, Lord Brandon wrote
to her eldest brother in such a style, setting forth the honor
he was doing them, that he offended the whole family and led
to the proposal being refused outright. I had not met B.W.
before and must confess to being a little out of sympathy with
her at first although not a little astonished that she is not
already married. She is over the middle height with dark hair,
fair skin and grey-blue eyes, her face a little too long and her
nose a little too imperious for everyone's taste. She went to
India with her brothers and it was assumed that she would
return a married woman. No such thing happened, although
offers cannot have been wanting, the story goes that she is too
arrogant and not pretty enough. I inclined at first to think this
true but found, on making her better acquaintance, that she
can be quite beautiful when she becomes animated and that
she is more diffident than she seems. Her family was poor, I
fancy, throughout her younger days and found it difficult to
live up to the titles they had inherited. They are also numerous
and she, the youngest, has missed some opportunities for want
of fortune. All of us came to like her in the end and hoped that
she would make a suitable match before she becomes too much
of the old maid (she being over 25, I believe). I din'd yesterday
at Sally's—her Husband, Ld Erskine, Ld Yarmouth, the
Prince, Ld Lauderdale and some others. The Prince of Wales
was so out of Spirits he could not speak three words and ate
nothing. The rest of us had no earthly thing to talk of but
duels and the Yorkshire Election. . .[2]

[1] 'The Don' was Lord Boringdon.
[2] *Letters of Lord Granville*, 1781–1821, Vol. II, p. 253.

There are one or two other references to Barbara in the books which have been written about her two more famous brothers, but they shed little light on her character and the 'B.W.' of the *Creevey Papers* may well be someone else—Beatrice Willoughby, for instance. There can be no doubt that Hornblower misunderstood Barbara at first, thinking her arrogant and wilful. His mental picture was of a woman bred in the midst of fashionable society whose every whim had been satisfied since childhood. He could not know that her father had been more or less bankrupt when he died and that the Anglo-Irish Wellesleys had all lived by their wits since she was born. Her rather overbearing manner did not come from boundless wealth but from a titled poverty, of which her single coloured maid was the proof. A lady of real consequence would have had a dozen servants at least and would never have been satisfied with the cabin which Hornblower had (reluctantly) to offer her. He could not refuse, of course, thinking her more influential than she was, but he gave way with a bad grace, warning her that the ship might be in action and that the passage round the Horn might be rough. She stayed on board, nevertheless, and was present when the *Lydia* met the *Natividad* for the second time.

Hornblower sailed from Panama on July 24th, leaving the Viceroy to plan his reconquest of Nicaragua,[1] and headed north for the point at which the *Natividad* might hope to intercept the Manila galleon. With some of the Spanish prisoners to navigate, with a crew of 'El Supremo's' ruffians and with 'Vice-Admiral Don Cristobal de Crespo' to threaten them with death, the *Natividad* would be no easy victim in the action that was to be expected. Hornblower looked vainly for the rebel ship in the Gulf of Fonseca, tried again at La Libertad and Champerico and finally sighted her in the Gulf of Tehuantepec on July 20th, 1808. It was blowing a gale, as it often does in those waters, and Hornblower saw this as an advantage, hoping that *Natividad* would not be able to open her lower gun-ports. In the early manoeuvres the handier British ship had the advantage, but the result of exchanging broadsides was to bring down the *Lydia*'s mizzen mast. Twice the frigate's stern was raked but Hornblower's men, making frantic efforts, managed to cut the

[1] In which he was successful, defeating 'El Supremo' at San Salvador and hanging that lunatic afterwards at Panama.

wreckage away and bring the ship under control. In the next exchange the *Natividad* lost her foremast. The two ships drifted apart and out of range and victory would go to the first one ready for action. There was all hell let loose on board the *Lydia* with the gale still blowing, the ship leaking where she had been hit below the waterline, a gun broken adrift on the main deck, fifty men wounded or dying in the cockpit and everything to be done first before anything else could be tackled. Somehow the problems were solved, a sail stretched over the ship's bottom to check the leaks, the guns secured, the rigging repaired, the fourteen dead buried overside and finally (by a supreme effort) a jury-mizzen mast fished to the stump that was left. By nightfall the *Lydia* was ready to renew the action but the weather prevented it. Hornblower remained hove-to and slept in a chair on deck, knowing that the *Natividad* would probably be out of sight by daybreak. Sail was made that night when the wind moderated and everything depended now upon Hornblower's guess as to what Crespo would do. He guessed right and first light on July 21st revealed his opponent ten miles away and under a poorly contrived jury-rig. Unfortunately, the wind died away soon afterwards and Hornblower's only means of closing the range was to have *Lydia* towed by ner boats. It was a laborious process and had the disadvantage that the *Lydia* came under fire from the *Natividad*'s 18-pounder stern chasers for an hour or so before her own 9-pounders could reply. It was late afternoon before this gruelling pursuit was over. Then, at long last, Hornblower gave the order to open fire. The range was then about four hundred yards and the firing was continuous for the next hour and a half.

A light wind sprang up towards evening and the smoke was blown aside to reveal the *Natividad* as a battered wreck with only her mizzen-mast standing. As the light began to fail, Hornblower placed the *Lydia* in a position across the *Natividad*'s bows, raking his opponent with every shot and at a lessening range. After sunset there was a moment when the two ships touched but they drifted apart again. By now the rebel guns were silent and Hornblower, seeing that his opponent was on fire, called on Crespo to surrender. 'Never!' was the reply and the *Natividad* actually sank before the fire could destroy her. There were only eight survivors in all and the *Lydia* was alone on the ocean, a ship with spliced rigging and torn canvas, barely kept afloat by the working of the pumps. There were another twenty-four men for burial, making twenty-eight in all, with four men drowned and seventy-five wounded. When Hornblower went to visit the orlop, he found that the person in effective command there was Lady Barbara. The surgeon having died earlier in the voyage, the purser's steward had been made acting surgeon. The task was, not surprisingly, beyond him and he coped badly with the problems of first aid. With no more knowledge, Lady Barbara had seen what needed to be done and was doing it. That did not, however, save many of the wounded from death by gangrene—Mr Galbraith among them—and there were many more burials over the next ten days. When the *Lydia* reached Panama on August 19th, there was a certain friendship established between Hornblower and Lady Barbara. There was none, by contrast, between Hornblower and the Viceroy of Peru. With the *Natividad* sunk, the Spaniards on the Pacific coast had no further use for the British alliance. They were merely resentful that the *Lydia* was in their waters and that their only man-of-war had been lost rather than recaptured. Spanish jealousy reasserted itself and the *Lydia* was denied entrance to any port in Spanish America. There was no question of Hornblower rounding the Horn in a leaking and damaged ship, even granted that his supplies would last out. Hornblower decided, therefore, to refit the *Lydia* at the uninhabited island of Coiba. There his toiling crew emptied the ship and then beached her in a sheltered cove, covered by her own guns mounted on either headland. The shot holes in the hull were plugged, the copper replaced, the main yard made to replace the mizzen mast, the ship re-rigged and made ready for sea. This tremendous task was finished in sixteen days. By September 14th *Lydia* was ready to begin the homeward voyage.

Hornblower was not under orders to sail for England but he had long since decided that his original orders were no longer in force. He had been sent to assist in a rebellion against Spain, with a further view to developing a route across Nicaragua. The Spaniards were now allies; to whom, however, his presence was unwelcome. His logical course was to return home, and the more logical in that he had expended most of his ammunition. The distances, however, were considerable and his supply position gave cause for anxiety. He was 4,500 miles from Cape Horn and another 3,000 miles from St Helena, his next source of supply. The voyage to Britain would be one of 12,500 miles all told, taking perhaps six months in all, with due allowance for storm and calm. With a quarter of his crew dead his supplies would last the longer but he decided nevertheless to make a final call—against the Viceroy's injunction—at some point on the coast of Spanish America; perhaps at Conception or Valdivia, somewhere beyond the Viceroy's reach. This would have the further advantage of bringing him to Cape Horn at about the local midsummer. To make such a call was admittedly risky, for he would certainly be blamed for any friction with Spain which might result. As against that, he had to be certain of food for his men. There might have been enough had not the ship leaked so badly after the second encounter with the *Natividad* but there had been over five feet of water in the hold at one time and much of his bread had been spoilt.

Hornblower's report to the Admiralty is reticent on the subject of his visit to Conception, referring only to a call at Sta. Maria for wood and water, and at San Pedro for beef and bread. So common are these place names that either might be almost anywhere along the coast of Chile, and while the supplies were obtained there is no mention of payment for them. He was on that coast in October, sailed south again in November and finally rounded the Cape just before Christmas, reaching St Helena on February 2nd, 1809. It had been cold and windy while the frigate was in the Roaring Forties but the sun was shining again by the time the *Lydia* dropped anchor off Jamestown. Her arrival there coincided with that of a homeward-bound East India convoy under the escort of Rear-Admiral Sir James Saumarez. The passengers included the Earl and Countess of Manningtree, on their way back from India, and Lady Manningtree immediately insisted that Lady Barbara should transfer to the *Hanbury Castle*. Her offer was accepted and Hornblower said goodbye to a lady for whom he had a great admiration. Sir James took the *Lydia* under his command and she returned to England as part of the convoy's escort, reaching Portsmouth after a swift passage on March 4th. The frigate was immediately taken into dock for replacement of her mizzen mast but the crew were not paid off. Frigates were all too few for the work that had to be done and *Lydia* was soon afloat again and under orders to join Lord

Gambier's fleet off the Basque Roads. Hornblower reported to Lord Gambier on March 26th, being the bearer of despatches from the Board of Admiralty.

Any account of the action which followed in the Basque Roads and of all the events which took place there between the 17th March and the 29th of April must inevitably end as another inquiry into that unhappy affair, written either to exonerate Lord Gambier or add still more to the case which Lord Cochrane brought against him. Such an inquiry has no place in a biography of Horatio Hornblower, whose part in the affair was creditable but not prominent. The *Lydia* was one of eight frigates present and came off without material damage. We know from his comments made in later life that Hornblower had a poor opinion of Lord Gambier but he never joined in the outcry against him nor would agree that Cochrane was blameless. On his return to port Lord Gambier was tried by court-martial at his own request. The trial took place at Portsmouth on July 26th and Hornblower was one of the witnesses. His testimony was extremely circumspect, probably from his foreknowledge that Gambier would certainly be acquitted. He made no enemies and added a little to his reputation. Of more immediate importance was the fact that the *Lydia*'s service in the Basque Roads rather overshadowed her doings in the Pacific. Copies of the gazette letter from Panama had been brought home by Hornblower himself, the originals being sent to the flag officer on the Leeward Islands station. So long was it before the originals were received and so long before they were forwarded, that their publication almost coincided with those sent by Lord Gambier. The public might otherwise have been rather mystified by the *Natividad* affair in which the same ship was captured and later engaged again and sunk. Many a captain had been knighted for a smaller achievement but Hornblower's feat was so distant, so complex and so belatedly reported that he was grateful for oblivion. The chief sufferer was Mr Bush, who had certainly earned promotion, but he was now willing to be regarded as Hornblower's follower, destined to follow him into a larger ship. Hornblower's last service with the *Lydia* took place in the autumn and winter of 1809, taking the form of a last cruise off the Basque Roads and a short visit to the Channel Islands. He was at Portsmouth in December and knew by January that he was to be posted to a ship of the line.

This chapter of Hornblower's life cannot close without some reference to the woman he had married and the other woman he certainly loved. He evidently lived with Maria, now childless, in 1809–10, and treated her with every kindness and consideration. It is at least as clear that he found her a dull companion as compared with Lady Barbara. Had he and his guest been lovers on board the *Lydia*? So far as one can tell from the scanty evidence available they had been something short of that. Hornblower could not afford a scandal nor could he dare to offend the Welles-leys, who were rapidly gaining importance. It would appear from the sequel that Lady Barbara would have been more reckless and that it was Hornblower's caution which prevented the friendship from becoming a romance. It was apparently this circumstance which ended the friendship. They parted coldly it would seem and Lady Barbara showed her disdain by marrying Rear-Admiral Sir Percy Leighton, K.B., in March, 1810, after a three weeks' courtship. It was not a particularly brilliant match, despite the Leighton wealth, and there are grounds for supposing that Lady Barbara soon regretted the impulse which led her into it. In the meanwhile, it was undoubtedly through her influence that Horn-blower's new ship was added to the squadron which Leighton was to command. It might have amused her for a day or two to think that Hornblower should be under her husband's orders but the mood passed and she realised soon enough that Leighton was only a second-best, a man without imagination or humour or brain. The deed had been done, nevertheless, and Hornblower saw the record in cold print:

NAVAL CHRONICLE
Marriages

On the 17th instant at Stockbridge in Hampshire Rear-Admiral Sir Percy Wetherall Leighton, Knight of the Bath, to Lady Barbara Wellesley, youngest daughter of the 1st Earl of Mornington. As soon as the ceremony was performed the bridal party was met by Sir Percy's numerous and respectable tenantry; who, after offering their heartfelt congratulations on the joyful event, preceded them in procession, accompanied by a band of music, to Woodland Hall, where a reception was held. Afterwards the happy couple set off for Markby House, lent to them for the occasion by Lord Hambledon of Petersfield.

This was the end, seemingly, of whatever there had been between Hornblower and Lady Barbara. He was a married man and bound to take care of Maria, who was soon to be with child again. Even had he been free to marry, he would have been a poor match for even the last of the Wellesley daughters. Leighton, the son of a wealthy London Alderman, was only just acceptable, a man to whom Lady Barbara's brothers would be no more than civil. But Hornblower was nothing, by comparison, an officer without family or influence and one who had been consistently unlucky over prize-money. He was now sufficiently far up the list to command a ship of the line, a promotion which would in itself lessen his chances of making anything more than his captain's pay. He had the beginnings of a reputation in the service but he was not one of the dashing frigate captains whose names had become known to the press. Years would pass before he would achieve his flag, even supposing that he remained in employment, and the coming of peace would probably place him again on half-pay. He could still dream of acquiring an estate but he could never see Maria as the squire's wife. She might do her best but she would always be shapeless, unfashionable, awkward and common. After even the shortest stay in Portsmouth Hornblower longed to be at sea. He had not yet despaired of higher command, of recognition, of seniority and fame.

CHAPTER SEVEN

Senior Captain

Hornblower's new ship was the *Sutherland* (74), originally built by the Dutch as the *Eendracht* and captured off the Texel in 1797. Because of the shoal water on the Dutch coast, the ships of the Dutch Navy were all on the small side, the *Sutherland* measuring no more than 1,562 tons with a length of 167 feet on the gun deck. She thus compared ill with the more recent 74's built in the British dockyards. The *Bulwark*, for example, of 1807 measured 1,925 tons, with a gun-deck 182 feet long; a far roomier ship to mount the same number of guns and accommodate 590 men. With twenty-eight 32-pounders, thirty 18-pounders, eight 9-pounders on the quarterdeck and six on the forecastle,[1] she was top heavy and yet floated too high in the water; an unweatherly and ugly ship, newly coppered and painted but drab in appearance and squat in outline.

With Bush as First Lieutenant, Gerard as Second, Rayner as Third, Crystal as Master and some good Master's Mates, the *Sutherland* was well officered; with Hornblower's cousin Jonathan aged sixteen as midshipman afloat for the first time. She was commissioned at Plymouth, where Maria was temporarily lodged, on May 2nd, 1810. As from the day he assumed command Hornblower received 13s. 6d. a day with certain additional allowances, a big improvement on the 6s. a day he was paid while commanding *Hotspur*. He was at least properly uniformed now, with real gold lace on his coat and genuine silk for his cravat. He was better off indeed than he had ever been but lacked what was needed for his initial outlay on silver for his table, extra stores for his steward, smart outfits for his boat's crew and gold leaf for his ship's figurehead. His main anxiety, however, was in finding a crew, in which he might have failed had he not managed to transfer two hundred men from the *Lydia*. With marines and boys and convicts sent from the Assizes at Exeter and Bodmin, he

[1] The 9-pounders were replaced by 12-pounder carronades at Hornblower's request.

had just enough men to sail the ship, four hundred and forty in all, leaving him short of establishment by a hundred and fifty. Seamen were impossible to enlist by 1810 and the pressgang roved the streets of Plymouth without result. He was desperately short-handed even when he finally put to sea.

On May 4th, Hornblower received an invitation from Rear-Admiral Sir Percy and Lady Barbara Leighton. Would he and Mrs Hornblower dine at the Angel Inn that afternoon? We know little about this meeting between Hornblower and Lady Barbara, the first after her marriage, nor do we know what she thought of Maria or what Hornblower thought, at this stage, of Leighton. All our information comes, instead, from Mrs Elliott, wife of the Flag Captain, whose letter of next day was addressed to her sister, Lady Fanshaw and came to be published in Lord Fanshaw's *Life and Letters*.[1]

Plymouth
May 5th, 1810

My dear Harriet,

Many thanks for your very kind note which finds me going on most prosperously both as to health and to knowledge of matters nautical. The weather here has been fine and we have seen something of Devonshire as well as of this town which is full of the dullest people imaginable, saving only Susan and your cousin by marriage, Colonel Graham, who is as entertaining as ever. Yesterday we dined at the Angel with Admiral Leighton and his bride, Lady Barbara Wellesley, the youngest sister of our Fabian General in Portugal. The dinner was dismally dull at first and I felt sorry for Lady B. who did her best but is newly married to a heavy sort of man who has little but money to commend him. This match was arranged somewhat in haste after her recent escapade, a voyage to the West Indies which ended in her returning from the South Seas as sole passenger in a frigate commanded by a Captain Hornblower, who was actually present with his wife at this very dinner! She had been originally accompanied by her cousin (or is she an aunt?), Miss Bunbury, who parted company

___

[1] *Life and Letters of Augustus, Lord Fanshaw, Ambassador in the Netherlands and Spain.* Edited by the Rev. Stephen Fanshaw, London, 1861.

with her after a quarrel between them at Antigua or some such place. Following this imprudent and headstrong adventure she was unlikely to marry anyone of consequence and owed it to her brother's influence that Sir Percy would have her, she having little fortune of her own. I never met her before but was more than a little curious, having heard the gossip, to meet the lady in person. She must be well over thirty[1] with dark hair, bright eyes and a well proportioned figure in the style of Juno with white shoulders and a full bosom which her muslin gown did little to conceal. It was all the men could do to avoid staring but my Harry was discretion itself as befits a Flag Captain. I could not resist the impression that she was playing off her two men against each other but must confess that she acted hostess also to the ladies. As for Captain Hornblower, he looked utterly confused at first, a rather handsome man but melancholy, middle-aged and weatherbeaten, awkward in company and little used to fashionable society even such as is to be met with in Plymouth. He is married to a plain and ill-bred little woman with very low connections, as I have heard, of whom he tries hard not to be too obviously ashamed. She confided to me the information that her two children had died of smallpox but that she was happily pregnant again. Her husband said little at first and Mrs Bolton, another Captain's wife, said nothing at all but ate her way through the evening as if she had starved for the whole of the week preceding. It was her husband who finally asked Captain Hornblower to tell us of his action with a Spanish ship called the *Natividad*. On this subject he became quite eloquent, his manner showing the man of action and courage, determined, energetic and alert, much as he must have appeared in the battle itself. What was most remarkable in this affair—as I learnt afterwards from Captain Bolton, who had known Captain Hornblower when they were midshipmen together—was that a mere frigate had not merely defeated but had sunk outright a two-decked man of war, a feat almost without parallel, it would seem. I caught a look of admiration on Lady B's face which I should not have liked had I been in Mrs H's shoes, or Sir Percy's either, but she was too stupid, I thought, and he too complacent, to take anything amiss. It was only Captain H's narrative and Lady B's hero-worship,

[1] She was actually twenty-nine but might have looked a little older following her Pacific voyage.

that was memorable about the evening, which was otherwise as insipid as can be imagined.

I hear delightful accounts of your nephew and my godchild, George, who is returned from Staffordshire and who is said *entre nous* to be interested in the pretty Miss S.G. . . . etc., etc.

This letter is interesting in itself and doubly so in containing almost the earliest known reference to Hornblower in contemporary gossip. No early letters of his exist, with two exceptions (see pp. 77 and 103) and he was quite unknown to the fashionable world even in 1810. Judith Elliott had heard the scandal about Lady Barbara but knew nothing previously about Hornblower, whose Pacific exploit was reported too long after the event to attract much notice. She is mildly critical of Lady Barbara but impressed also despite herself, as she had reason to be. The earliest surviving portrait of Barbara was painted just after this time by Thomas Lawrence, R.A., afterwards knighted but even then sufficiently established as court painter to George III.[1] To judge from this she must have been at her loveliest at this period, more attractive than she had been as a girl and less arrogant in appearance than when Hornblower first saw her. This is guesswork, admittedly, for there is no earlier picture of her, not even a miniature or family group, but there is reason to think that she looked too imperious and insecure while young and that she was most beautiful in maturity. That the dinner party at the Angel was agony for Hornblower is certain. That it was exciting for Barbara is at least highly probable, for she had her mischievous side. For at least some of the others it must have been very embarrassing indeed.

Leighton's squadron was under orders for the Mediterranean and comprised the *Pluto*, *Caligula* and *Sutherland*, the first of 98 and the others of 74 guns. The first duty of this force was to escort an outward-bound East India convoy out of the Channel and as far south as latitude 35°. Leighton entrusted this task to Hornblower and sent the *Caligula* with two storeships to Port Mahon, he himself escorting some transports to Lisbon before proceeding to Palamos Point, where the other two ships would

[1] Another portrait was painted at the time of her engagement but this was taken to sea by Leighton and so came to be destroyed at the Battle of Rosas.

The Château of Graçay, near Nevers on the River Loire, from the engraving by Petit of 1838

of the pan, is to be covered, and this part of the priming is to be bruised with the round part of the horn. The apron is to be laid over, and the horn hung up out of danger from the flash of the priming.

7th. POINT YOUR GUNS.----At this command the gun is, in the first place, to be elevated to the height of the object, by means of the side-fights; and then the person pointing is to direct his fire by the upper-fight, having a crow on one side, and a handspec on the other, to heave the gun by his direction till he catches the object.

The men who heave the gun for pointing are to stand between the ship's side and their crows or handspecs, to escape the injury they might otherwise receive from their being struck against them, or splintered by a shot; and the man who attends the captain with a match is to bring it at the word, "POINT YOUR GUNS," and, kneeling upon one knee opposite the train-truck of the carriage, and at such a distance as to be able to touch the priming, is to turn his head from the gun, and keep blowing gently upon the lighted match to keep it clear from ashes. And, as the missing of an enemy in action, by neglect or want of coolness, is most inexcusable, it is particularly recommended to have the people thoroughly instructed in pointing well, and taught to know the ill consequences of not taking proper means to hit their mark; wherefore they should be made to elevate their guns to the utmost nicety, and then to point with the same exactness; and, having caught the object through the upper-fight, at the word,

8th. FIRE.----The match is instantly to be put to the bruised part of the priming; and, when the gun is discharged, the vent is to be closed, in order to smother any spark of fire that may remain in the chamber of the gun; and the man who spunges is immediately to place himself by the muzzle of the gun in readiness.

9th. SPUNGE YOUR GUNS.----The spunge is to be rammed down to the bottom of the chamber, and then twisted round, to extinguish effectually any remains of fire; and, when drawn out, to be struck against the outside of the muzzle, to shake off any sparks or scraps of the cartridge that may have come out with it; and next, its end is to be shifted ready for loading; and, while this is doing, the man appointed to provide a cartridge

tridge is to go to the box, and by the time the spunge is out of the gun, he is to have it ready.

10th. LOAD WITH CARTRIDGE.----The cartridge (with the bottom end first, seam downwards, and a wad after it) is to be put into the gun, and thrust a little way within the mouth, when the rammer is to be entered; the cartridge is then to be forcibly rammed down, and the captain at the same time is to keep his priming-wire in the vent, and, feeling the cartridge, is to give the word *home*, when the rammer is to be drawn, and not before. While this is doing, the man appointed to provide a shot is to provide one (or two, according to the order at that time) ready at the muzzle, with a wad likewise, and when the rammer is drawn, at the word,

11th. SHOT YOUR GUNS.----The shot and wad upon it are to be put into the gun, and thrust a little way down, when the rammer is to be entered as before. The shot and wad are to be rammed down to the cartridge, and there have a couple of forcible strokes, when the rammer is to be drawn, and laid out of the way of the guns and tackles, if the exercise or action is continued; but if it is over, the spunge is to be secured in the place it is at all times kept in.

12th. PUT IN YOUR TOMPIONS.----The tompions to be put into the muzzle of the cannon.

13th. HOUSE YOUR GUNS.----The seizing is to be put on again upon the clinched end of the breeching, leaving it no slacker than to admit of the guns being housed with ease. The quoin is to be taken from under the breech of the gun, and the bed, still resting upon the bolt, within the carriage, thrust under, till the foot of it falls off the axle-tree, leaving it to rest upon the end which projects out from the foot. The metal is to be let down upon this. The gun is to be placed exactly square, and the muzzle is to be close to the wood, in its proper place for passing the muzzle lashings.

14th. SECURE YOUR GUNS.----The muzzle lashings must first be made secure, and then with one tackle (having all its parts equally tight with the breeching) the gun is to be lashed. The other tackle is to be bowsed tight, and by itself made fast, that it may be ready to cast off for lashing a second breeching.

Care must be taken to hook the first tackle to the upper bolt of the carriage, that it may not otherwise obstruct the reeving of

the

Page from Hornblower's copy of the GUNNERY MANUAL

rejoin his flag. As from then Leighton was to operate on the Spanish coast as commander of the Inshore Squadron, his role to harass the French forces in Spain. The squadron sailed from Plymouth on May 16th and the *Sutherland* soon parted from the flagship, keeping her convoy in fairly strict formation, made Ushant and set a course for Finisterre. Hornblower's main anxiety centred upon his shortage of men. He had enough to work the ship and enough to man the guns but not enough to do both. And, as luck would have it, he was in action before he had a chance to find more men or even train those he had. The six East Indiamen were attacked by two French privateer luggers and it took all Hornblower's seamanship to beat them off, leaving one of them dismasted. After thus earning the gratitude of the Company's officers and of Lord Eastlake, bound for the governorship of Bombay, Hornblower went on to press twenty seamen from each of the Company's ships. This high-handed proceeding was contrary to Admiralty instructions but he answered the protests of the Company's senior captain by an assurance that all who did not volunteer would be returned. He ended the incident by signalling that all *had* volunteered which, in a sense, was true. He parted company from the Indiamen as ordered, feeling confident that months would pass before the Admiralty would receive a protest from East India House. He also recalled that Nelson had once impressed men from an East Indiaman in London River itself, firing a broadside to suppress the resistance that had been offered. His own offence was nothing by comparison and far more remote from public notice. He had an even chance of escaping reprimand and there is no record, in fact, of any reproof ever reaching him. In the meanwhile, he had a ship properly manned and ready, or soon to be ready, for battle.

Caligula and *Sutherland* were the first at the rendezvous, the latter ship on June 12th, and it seemed unlikely that Leighton would appear for another week. So Bolton, the senior, authorised Hornblower to begin the harassing operation and return to the rendezvous in three days. When the *Amelie*, a French merchant brig, fell to him, too late in her attempt to escape, Hornblower realised that the *Sutherland*, with her round bow and Dutch lines, was not typical of the Royal Navy and could easily pass as French. He promptly hoisted the tricolour and came close in with the enemy coast. He stormed the battery at Point Llansa, sending the boats in at the moment his true colours were hoisted. The cannon were tipped over the cliff, some coasting vessels captured, and the *Sutherland* moved on to Port Vendres. Appearing off that harbour on the 14th, the *Sutherland* stood out to sea after what might have seemed a casual reconnaissance. Closing again with the port after dark, Hornblower himself led the cutting-out raid at moonrise, an affair which led to the capture of a valuable merchantman. He followed this by a quick descent on the Lagoon de Vic, near Cette in the Gulf of Lions. Burning a laden coaster there, he headed back for Palamos Point as ordered, missed the *Caligula* there and gained information of a column marching by the coast road near Malgret, just north of Barcelona. The column comprised two Italian divisions under French orders and Hornblower found deep water from which to command the road. He broke up the march with fairly heavy casualties and then headed back for the rendezvous, where Rear-Admiral Leighton received him rather coldly. He had acted too independently and he should have been at the rendezvous sooner.

The sequel to this unfriendly meeting was the freak hurricane of June 17th, which caught Leighton's squadron at a point almost due west of Cape Creux. The *Pluto* lost all three of her masts and even her bowsprit, very nearly capsizing but just righting herself in time. She was drifting down on a lee shore, however, and it was Hornblower who came to the rescue. He managed to take the *Pluto* in tow and bring her out of danger, a considerable feat of seamanship and one to which Leighton owed his life. Both ships were actually under distant fire from Cape Creux at the moment when they came nearest to disaster. The immediate result was that the *Pluto* was sent to refit at Port Mahon while the Rear-Admiral shifted his flag into the *Caligula*. With his force thus reduced, Leighton decided against any major operation and detached the *Sutherland* to cruise between Barcelona and Cape San Sebastian while he himself would do the same from Palamos northward to Cette. There was a rendezvous appointed on July 20th, at Port Mahon, by which date the *Pluto* might be expected to rejoin. This was an arrangement which suited Hornblower very well and he resolved to make the best of it. From the master of the *Amelie*, an incautious conversationalist, he had learnt of the presence, at Barcelona, of the *Artemis*. To be exact, he had known about the *Artemis* before but he had since learnt, from this probably reliable source, that she was under repair and would soon be ready for sea. The *Artemis* had once been a British sloop but had come down in the world with age, being relegated to the role of storeship. She had thus patiently served the British squadron off Toulon, plodding back and forth between Cape Sicie and Port Mahon, with occasional visits to Gibraltar. On one of her less inspired passages in the autumn of 1809 she had been snapped up by two French privateers and taken into Barcelona, the port from which they were operating. Rumour had it that the commanding lieutenant had been drunk, taking her absurdly close to an enemy base, and that he had still been incapable when she was carried by boarding. Certain it was that she had been taken, undamaged, into Barcelona, where her cargo of naval stores must have been more than welcome. If she was being fitted for sea, it would be as a privateer; a role, however, for which most people would have thought her too slow. It was a question, incidentally, whether she might not have been damaged in that hurricane of June 17th. Hornblower did not know whether Barcelona had been affected by it—he rather supposed not. Anyway, the *Artemis* was a possible prey but secure, of course, under the batteries of Barcelona. Any direct attack on that sea-port was, also, of course, out of the question. It remained in doubt, however, whether something might not be achieved; a minor success but a useful capture in terms of prize-money.

In a not very hopeful situation Hornblower had two main assets. In the first place, Napoleon had over-reached himself in making his brother King of Spain. The Spanish had been too stunned to react immediately (that is in 1808) but Joseph Bonaparte's position was now becoming daily more insecure. He was supported by a French army but the bulk of this was deployed against Wellington in Portugal. The Spanish were now more than restive, seeing that Wellington was undefeated, and the French lines of communications, stretching from the Portuguese frontier to the Pyrenees, were extended and vulnerable. The Spanish officials and garrisons were nominally under King Joseph's orders but other people, lower in rank or displaced from office, were ripe for treason, stratagems and spoils. Hornblower had already made contact with some Spanish insurgents and he knew that the Catalans, the folk round Barcelona, were traditionally hostile to France in that they lived so close to it. He had little faith in the Spanish as allies, knowing that they were too apt to quarrel with each other. He had every use for them as informants, however, and could only wish that Catalan, rather than Castilian, had been the language he had learnt. His other asset lay in the ambiguous appearance of the *Sutherland*. He had known from the outset that she was easy to mistake for a Frenchman. It seemed to him now that she might pass as readily for a merchantman or, better still, as a storeship. He had used the quite usual ruse of hoisting French colours at the attack on Point Llansa but that had only a limited object: it made a battery commander hesitate and lose time. For a real deception plan it was essential to make the disguise complete. More than that, the appearance assumed must be that of a particular ship, identifiable and familiar. A privateer captain, operating for profit rather than glory, wanted to know beforehand the strength and the value of his intended prey. Balancing the risk against the incentive, he could then decide whether to intercept the vessel or whether to leave her severely alone. His dream was always one of riches easily acquired. His nightmare was of a ship defended to the last man and the last round, wrecked by the process of capture and then found to have been sailing in ballast. The commander of the *Artemis* would not be lured to sea by anything short of precise information and that was exactly what Hornblower planned to give him.

For purposes of the immediate campaign Hornblower invented the storeship *Pembroke*, a former 64-gun ship, originally taken from the Dutch and now used to supply the squadron off Toulon. She was to do much the same work as the *Artemis* had done and her practice would be to visit Gibraltar on every other voyage, bringing back not only provisions but specie to pay some British troops which were serving as marines. Her captain was an elderly Lieutenant called Francis Sweeney, passed over for promotion and all but cashiered for the loss of the *Antelope* in 1806. The *Pembroke* mounted ten carronades (12-pounders) and had a crew of forty, half of them Italian or Portuguese. The *Sutherland* had plenty of paint and spare canvas, taken from the *Amelie*, and the disguise was completed in calm weather and well away from the coast. With agony Bush watched his ship assume the appearance of a battered and shabby merchantman, her gun ports painted out, her canvas patched and stained, her rigging made to look slovenly and careless and a number of her guns dismounted and struck below. Thus disguised, the *Pembroke* made her way southward along the Spanish coast. At a point north of Malgret Hornblower made contact, after dark, with some Spanish insurgents. He persuaded and bribed them to send some of their number into Barcelona, conveying the news which their friends there would circulate as common gossip. He thus ensured that privateersmen there would know about the *Pembroke* within two days at the outside. Coasting southward again, he looked out for fishing craft and presently fell in with one, beyond Arens de Mar, and brought some of the crew on board. So important was this part of the plan that all the seamen visible were disguised. There had been three previous rehearsals, moreover, the chief parts being allotted to men who had been prominent in theatricals. Hornblower was not himself among the actors, Lieutenant Rayner taking command during the play's one and only performance. The most dramatic incident was provided by the hoisting out of a water cask. The rope broke and the cask burst on the deck amid a scene of confusion and blasphemy. Led carefully near the ship's boats, all clearly marked with the name 'Pembroke' the fishermen took away with them a story they were bound to repeat, one in which the drunken captain would be the principal character, his men an example of indiscipline and slackness. Once his audience had gone, Hornblower took his ship past Barcelona, almost but not quite unseen from the shore, and then, further south again, staged a last performance. On this occasion a dummy figure fell overboard, causing the ship to heave to and lower a boat. Every mistake of seamanship was made and the rescue was accompanied by a deplorable exhibition of boat-pulling. All this took place within view of Cabellas and Sitges. After this final display of ineptitude the *Pembroke* went out of sight to the southward, clearly on her way to Gibraltar, when she would return with specie on board.

Allowing time for a voyage to Gibraltar and back, Hornblower then came back over the same route, confident that the *Pembroke* was now a laughing-stock and easy to identify. He appeared off Tarragona towards sunset on the 6th July and was lucky to have only a light breeze during the night. He might thus expect to be intercepted next day and most probably at daybreak. He turned in with the feeling that his trap would almost certainly succeed.

It was with annoyance, therefore, that he learnt of light signals being made from the shore. Coming on deck he saw the lights for himself but had to agree that they were apparently meaningless. It was Mr Crystal who thought that they most nearly resembled the Mediterranean Fleet's night recognition signal of about 1808. It was Mr Midshipman Hornblower who now suggested the possibility that the signal might be made by British prisoners of war, by men whose captivity had begun in 1808. Could they, in fact, be the crew of the *Artemis*, taken in 1809? It seemed a faint possibility but Hornblower was annoyed, at this point, to think that the possibility even existed. He was in the midst of setting a trap and these prisoners (if they *were* prisoners) were at best a distraction; at worst a trap which was being set for *him*. He took bearings, nevertheless, and studied the map. So far as he could make out, there was some sort of monastery on the headland from which the signals had come; disused, it was the sort of place in which prisoners might well be kept. Santa Barbara was equally the sort of place in which the same prisoners might be used as bait. Resolving to ignore the problem, Hornblower turned in again. He was called before dawn and there, silhouetted against the lightening sky, was the *Artemis*, just where she should be to windward, placed so as to prevent her victim's escape (and unable, therefore, to escape herself). Last move in the game was the *Pembroke*'s clumsy and belated effort to avoid battle. She was already cleared for action, but with ports closed, and the *Artemis* swooped on her prey without any sign of hesitation. After firing warning shots the privateer ranged alongside at half pistol shot. It was only then that the colours were hoisted and ports crashed open, revealing the '*Pembroke*' as a two-decked man-of-war. The *Artemis* surrendered (July 7th) without firing another shot, her captain well knowing that resistance would be suicide. He struck his colours and came aboard, handing over his sword with what grace he could and failing to destroy his secret documents. In its way this was a classical example of deception, memorable above all for thorough preparation. But Hornblower was thinking ahead and was ready to make the next move, still under false colours but now possessed of the current French signal book.

The *Artemis* retaken, Hornblower's first order was to re-hoist the tricolour in the privateer and hoist the tricolour over the blue ensign in the *Sutherland*. He could now approach the Spanish coast with impunity, the *Artemis* and her prize being the very ships the French would be expecting to see. Off Barcelona he did no more, however, than hoist the recognition signal before turning southward again. The procedure might seem unusual but not exactly suspicious. To land his prisoners at Santa Barbara before the prize had been condemned would be irregular but it was the sort of senseless thing a privateer captain might just possibly do. Eyebrows would be raised but no guns would actually open fire. The *Artemis* and prize appeared off Santa Barbara on July 12th and signalled that she had prisoners to land. There was some consternation ashore, the Commandant having had no warning that more prisoners were to be expected. He was handicapped, however, by a shortage of signal flags and unable to argue at long range. When he saw boats lowered he came down to the landing place, ready to explain that he had no room for more prisoners and no authority to receive them. The guns of his three-gun battery were silent, for the boats were filled, as everyone could see, with British prisoners guarded by armed privateersmen. No sooner had the landing taken place, however, than the prisoners turned out to be armed. The guard at the landing place was over-powered, the battery taken from the rear and the monastery gate captured without difficulty. The inmates of the prison camp were mostly deserters from the Spanish army, probably awaiting trial, but there were British sailors as well, one hundred and thirty-four of them, mostly but not all from the *Artemis*. It was a group of petty officers who had devised the recognition signal, lowering it from a window on the seaward side of what had been the monastery chapel. They had eventually been caught in the act and were in the punishment cells when rescued; subdued but still defiant. Hornblower brought off the Commandant and his men as prisoners of war, releasing the Spanish captives and leaving the prison empty. He then steered north again and appeared once more off Barcelona. He had learnt, meanwhile, from his French prisoners—some of whom were indiscreet—that the port contained a second privateer, *L'Alceste* which had often worked with the *Artemis*, being owned, in fact, by the same syndicate. Offered his freedom as incentive, a quartermaster of the latter vessel, a Portuguese, devised a signal which would bring *L'Alceste* out of port. It had to be a rather elaborate message, telling of an enemy prey to the southward, too fast for the *Artemis* to capture but likely to strike her flag to *L'Alceste*. The inference from this was that the expected prize was to be caught in a triangle against the coast—quite a normal manoeuvre. What remained a mystery ashore was why the '*Pembroke*' was not sent in for condemnation by the prize court. There was a further exchange of signals, some from the *Artemis* being probably incorrect, and it was not until the late afternoon that the second privateer put to sea. Her puzzled captain made a cautious approach and Hornblower was forced in the end to open fire. *L'Alceste* lost her foremast before she surrendered (July 15th) but was otherwise little damaged. There could be no further deception after that and Hornblower laid a course for Port Mahon, where Leighton would be found as from July 20th. The capture of two valuable prizes did something to improve the atmosphere at his next meeting with the Rear-Admiral. In the matter of prize-money, Hornblower's luck was beginning to turn.

The regulation concerning prize money laid down that a vessel condemned as a lawful prize should either be sold by auction or else bought, at a valuation, and taken into the service. For a privateer or warship the better price would be paid by the Royal Navy, partly because she might be poorly designed for trade, partly because a private purchase might lead to her returning (through intermediaries) to her original owners and so to her interrupted career of destruction. A merchant vessel like the brig *Amelie* was relatively more valuable because of being laden, the cargo being often worth more than the ship. The sum raised by the sale of the prize, whether by auction or otherwise, was divided (less the agents' commission) into eight parts of which one went to the Flag-Officer on the Station, three to the Captain, one to the officers, one to the petty officers and two to the remainder of the crew. Were a hostile ship destroyed there could be no prize-money but the Commissioners of the Navy paid an estimated five pounds a head for 'every opponent who was living at the beginning of the engagement' the sum total to be divided in the same way as if the enemy ship had been taken and sold. The system was heavily biased in the Captain's favour but he was also answerable for damages if the prize were not condemned. The lower deck men seldom received more than a guinea or two apiece, a sum more likely to be wasted than saved. Unlucky up to this point, Hornblower made a considerable sum from his prizes in 1810, the *Artemis* being taken back into the service and the *Alceste* bought into it. He would seem to have collected about £6,000, enough to buy himself a small country estate. As from this time the acquisition of Smallbridge Manor became actually possible, provided at least that it came on the market.

At Port Mahon on July 24th Rear-Admiral Leighton's flag was hoisted once more in the *Pluto*, his squadron ready again for a more ambitious stroke than he had so far attempted. This was to be no less than the capture of Rosas, a Catalonian seaport second only in importance to Barcelona itself. The success of the operation hinged upon the help to be expected from the Spanish insurgents, led by General Rovira. He was said to have seven thousand men in the vicinity of Olot. The French garrison of Rosas was supposed to number about two thousand men. Between Olot and Rosas is a distance of thirty miles with Gerona in between, also garrisoned by the French. If Rovira circled Gerona, using mountain paths, he would be in a position to attack Rosas but would lack any siege artillery. The guns would therefore be landed by Leighton at Selva de Mar with a covering force of six hundred seamen and marines. Landing four days after Rovira was due to march, but with only six miles to go, the British contingent should reach Rosas at almost the same time as the Spanish. As the French Seventh Corps was stationed south of Barcelona, the allies would have a clear week in which to capture Rosas. Once taken it could probably be held, forming a bridge-head through which other Spanish forces could be landed, thus creating a serious threat to the French communications. The plan was to that extent attractive but its success depended upon Spanish promises, Spanish information and (in the last resort) on Spanish troops. Leighton's guns might make the breach but Rovira's regiments would have to storm it. That Rovira and his men hated the French might be true but they were amateurs at war, vague in their intelligence, optimistic in their calculations and as inexperienced as they would be ill-equipped. Hornblower, who was to command the landing party, was quite unable to share Leighton's confidence in their Spanish allies. The whole operation was more complex than the Rear-Admiral seemed able to understand but Hornblower, once the orders had been given, kept his misgivings to himself.

The landing took place as planned on the night of July 29th and Hornblower was met on the beach by Colonel Juan Claros, who had a thousand men and enough horses and mules to drag the guns to Rosas. Ten 24-pounders were landed and were clear of the beach by daybreak, with a hundred rounds per gun and a day's rations for six hundred men. Then began the back-breaking task of covering the six hilly and rock-strewn miles which lay between Selva de Mar and Rosas. Riding ahead on a borrowed horse, Hornblower came within sight of Rosas but there was no sign of any activity before its walls. General Rovira had not appeared. Halting his column, Hornblower made the Spaniards send a messenger to find Rovira while a midshipman carried a report back to Leighton. He dared advance no further with a siege train uncovered by infantry. When Leighton's reply came it was to ask whether the fortress could not be attacked with the force he had? Before any such operation could begin the French garrison marched out to meet the allies, revealing a strength far in excess of the number supposed to be in the town.[1] Hornblower ordered a general withdrawal, posted the marines as a rearguard under Major Laird, and informed Leighton that all the squadron's boats would be needed. The Spanish irregulars vanished at this point but failed to remove, as they would like to have done, the horses and mules. The withdrawal, which took the rest of the day, the 30th, was a nightmare of effort and danger but the men and the guns were saved and even the horses and mules —to be returned to the insurgents—and Hornblower, the last to re-embark, came back exhausted to the *Sutherland* with a bullet through his hat.

A week later (August 8th) the *Sutherland* was detached on a cruise to the northward with orders to reconnoitre the coast as far as Toulon. The flagship was returning to Port Mahon and with her went the mail addressed to England. One letter among the rest was written by Mr Midshipman Hornblower, of whose previous career we know very little. It is the earliest letter from which we can learn anything about Horatio Hornblower's reputation among his actual shipmates. Jonathan Hornblower was

---

[1] We know now that the garrison had been recently reinforced and that it comprised about 3,500 effectives. See *The Peninsular War* by R. Whitehead, p. 379 et seq.

aged sixteen at this time and his letter was addressed to his father, Jeremiah, at Birmingham.

Sutherland at Sea
August 8th, 1810

My dear Sir,

I hope you are all well at home as I am. I write this to you from our rendezvous off Cape Creux and am sure of it reaching you because it goes with the Admiral to Minorca. I have had no letter from you nor from Mother since June but have written several times to give you the news. We are just escaped from a perilous situation ashore in Spain, where we landed to help the insurgents capture the port of Rosas. Our captain, your cousin, was in command ashore but was completely let down by the Spanish whose army never appeared. There we were with our cannon making to assault a place where the French vastly out-numbered us! We were lucky to find ourselves on board again with no greater loss than the round shot we had landed and could not recover. That we came so near to disaster was the fault, we all agree, of the Admiral we call Old-late-on-divisions. Things go very differently when Horny, as he is known on the lower-deck, is left to himself. We recently took two privateers by the neatest trick you ever saw, the *Sutherland* made to look like a clumsy old transport or storeship, so well disguised that the Frenchmen came out to attack us from under the batteries of Barcelona where they would have been safe for ever. You can't imagine their rage and fright when they found themselves opposite our lower-deck guns, the port lids suddenly open and not a chance of escape! There is a good sum of prize-money due to all of us and we owe this good fortune to our Captain's cleverness. We are also much better manned than is usual and for this I can claim some of the credit myself. Some light signals were made from a headland which the Master thought were like the Fleet Recognition Signal of two years back and it was I who suggested that they might have been made by prisoners of war. So it turned out and we eventually rescued them, bringing our crew up to strength with more besides for the other ships of the squadron. So we now feel ready for anything, fit to do battle with a three-decker, and this con-fidence we owe to our Captain than whom there is no better officer in the service. We have hands aboard who talk of Nelson and Collingwood and one even who served under Rodney in the last war but the younger men all say that Captain Hornblower is just as good and will be an Admiral some day himself. It is his way to be stern and unsmiling, a man of few words and a tyger for discipline, but we know that he is more kindhearted than he seems, doing everything to care for his men especially those who are sick, not malingerers though. He will pace the quarterdeck for an hour together, saying nothing to anybody and look thoughtful or even meloncholy but let there be but the prospect of action and he looks a different man his eyes as bright as his sword ready to dare anything and fool his opponent into the bargain. I could not be in a better ship than this nor learn seamanship under a better chief. He asks us midshipmen to dine with him in turn and shows himself a kind host. What we rather dread, though, is being invited to play whist with him, he being a very good player and a stern critick of his partner's play. After each game he is apt to discuss the mistakes made at rather tedious length. Luckily there are lieutenants enough who play and we midshipmen are seldom called upon. We are about to proceed on detached service and may make some more money from prizes before the cruise is over. Do not worry about the danger for we care nothing about the French who mostly skulk in harbor or keep out of our way. Remember me to John, Sarah and Penelope and please give Rover a pat on my behalf. We shall have to refit some time next year which may give us the chance for leave. Until then, when I shall have much to tell you, you may believe that both Hornblowers in this ship are well, the Captain much respected and liked by all hands, the midshipman on his way, he hopes, to becoming a good practical seaman and navigator. Give my love to Grandfather[1] and to Uncle Jabez[2] as also to my Friends at Walsall. My love to Mother and sisters.

I remain Dear Father

Your affectionate son

Jo. Hornblower

It was not given to everybody to succeed as Captain of a ship-of-the-line. Some men who had been successful in frigates were

[1] This would be Jonathan Carter Hornblower, the engineer (1753–1815), associated with James Watt.

[2] Jabez Carter Hornblower (1744–1814), engineer.

failures when given a larger ship and a larger crew. Hornblower turned *Sutherland* into a most efficient ship, well-manned, well exercised and well disciplined with morale much raised by the '*Pembroke*' pantomime and prize-money. It is clear, nevertheless, that morale had suffered with the setback ashore at Selva de Mar. That Hornblower had done well to bring the landing party away with only a very few casualties was admitted by everyone in the squadron. But a successful withdrawal is not the same thing as a victory. Beneath their apparent self-confidence the officers and senior ratings all knew that a tangible success was needed. Leighton, whose fault it was that disaster had been so imminent, was the more aware of the situation in that morale was lowest in the *Pluto* because of her narrow escape off Cape Creux. He had to do *something*, and soon, if the squadron was to remain an effective force. It is thus that one mistake leads to another, the attempt to save the situation being more disastrous than the error which brought it about.

The *Sutherland* cruised without incident as far as the Gulf of Lions and there, on August 18th, fell in with the frigate *Cassandra* (32), commanded by Captain Frederick Cooke. The wind was north-east and the *Cassandra*, to windward, signalled that four hostile ships-of-the-line were to windward of her again. It was evident that *Cassandra* had been the inshore lookout off Toulon, that the French squadron had escaped, heading south-west, and that the frigate had run before them so as to keep them under observation. Hornblower reached the correct conclusion that the French had been sent to deal with Leighton's squadron, the presence and strength of which would be known (by this time) in Paris. As the French force was plainly insufficient for the purpose it became his object to lure them within range of *Pluto* and *Caligula*. Ordering the *Cassandra* to make all sail and search for the Rear-Admiral, he followed at a more leisurely speed, keeping the enemy just in sight. He lost sight of them during the night of August 18th but saw them again next day. By then he was heading westwards towards Cape Creux with the wind backing south-easterly and the French ships now to leeward and bound, seemingly, for Barcelona. At this time (August 19th) the *Cassandra* reappeared, evidently in contact by signal with Leighton, who was out of sight to the northward. The French must have glimpsed the *Pluto* at the same moment for they tacked and steered directly for shelter in Rosas Bay. The *Sutherland* lay directly between the French Admiral and his chosen refuge, her opportunity being so to cripple the French that Leighton could come up with them. The French squadron comprised, as we now know, the *Ville de Bordeaux* (98) flagship, the *Méduse* (74), the *Turenne* (74) and the *Didon* (80), the whole commanded by Vice-Admiral Bouvet de Neufchateau, with Rear-Admiral Gallois's flag in the *Méduse*. At this juncture it was open to Hornblower to avoid battle, assuming that the French Admiral would remain on course for Rosas Bay, distant about six miles. That he would have fought in any case is virtually certain but the decision was made for him by a signal from *Pluto*, repeated by *Cassandra*, No. 21 'Engage the enemy'. Leighton afterwards denied having made the signal, which could have been due to a mistake on board *Cassandra*, but Hornblower took it as an order and one reasonable in the circumstances. It would have made more sense, in fact, if Leighton, twenty miles away, could have come up in time. The odds were against this and the question about the Rear-Admiral's signal is really immaterial, for it was Leighton's decision in any case. It was, after all, open to him to have made the signal of recall and he certainly never did. In the game of war *Sutherland* was merely a pawn and due now to be sacrificed.

Hornblower steered the *Sutherland* to meet the French and managed so to outmanoeuvre the *Didon*, their leading ship, that he was able to cross her stern and rake her with a tremendous broadside. Unable to finish that opponent off, Hornblower next engaged the *Méduse* at close range and had the satisfaction of seeing her main topmast go over the side. He might have broken off the action at this point but he decided that to cripple the other two ships would be worth while, even if it meant the loss of the *Sutherland*. He now steered to meet the three-decked *Ville de Bordeaux*, broadside to broadside, and was soon locked in a desperately unequal duel. After the *Sutherland* had lost mainmast and foremast she was engaged on the other side by the fourth French ship, the *Turenne*. It was this last attack and the firing of two gunboats which finally compelled Hornblower to surrender. By the time he struck his colours 117 of his men had been killed and 145 wounded, of which number 44 subsequently died. The *Sutherland* herself was a mere wreck, beached by her captors to prevent her sinking. As the smoke cleared, however, Hornblower

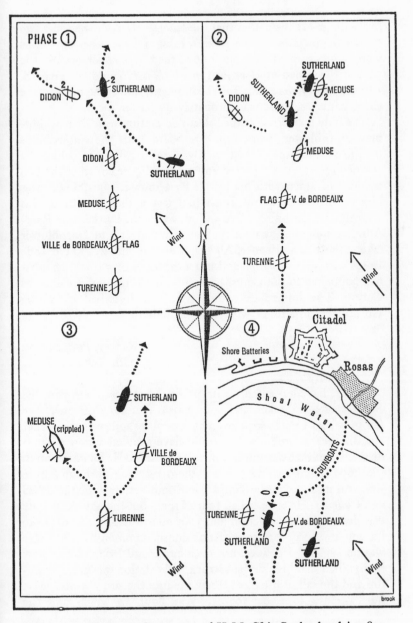

Diagram to illustrate the capture of H.M. Ship Sutherland *in 1810*

saw with grim satisfaction that the *Ville de Bordeaux* had lost two topmasts, the *Turenne* her mizzen mast and the other two ships were more crippled still. Not one of them was fit for sea and the port of Rosas had no dockyard in which they could be repaired. Although they were safe, for the moment, under the guns of the shore batteries, there was ultimately no escape for them.

The only man who escaped death or capture was Mr Midshipman Hornblower, who went overboard with the *Sutherland*'s mainmast and was picked up by a rowing boat in which he reached the *Pluto*, a dejected and solitary figure covering the two Spanish oarsmen with his pistol. By a miracle Hornblower was himself unwounded but Bush had lost a foot and there was scarcely another officer alive and unwounded. By the time Rear-Admiral Leighton arrived the battle was over and Hornblower taken ashore as a prisoner. All Leighton could do was to blockade Rosas with his two ships and use a captured brig to report what had happened to the Commander-in-Chief, Admiral Sir Charles Cotton. The immediate sequel was well described by young Hornblower in a letter written to his father.

Rodney, Port Mahon
28th August, 1810

My dear Sir,

Things have gone badly with us since last I wrote to you, the *Sutherland* being taken and your cousin Horatio a prisoner. We fell in with a French Squadron of four ships, one a three-decker and another of 80 guns. We could have avoided action without discredit but that was never our captain's style. He fought them in the hope that he could prevent them reaching harbour before Rear-Admiral Leighton could come into action with the *Pluto* and *Caligula*. He crippled all four of them but the old *Sutherland* was destroyed in the action and your cousin had finally to strike his colours. I say that as an expression in common use but there was no flag left, I believe, nor mast either and I don't know how he signified that his ship had struck.[1] My station was in the maintop and the fall of the mast threw me into the sea, not otherwise hurt, I clung to a spar for nearly an hour, by which time the

---

[1] We know from other sources that he hung over the ship's side the tricolour flag he had used for purposes of deception. See *The Naval Miscellany*, Vol. IV, Navy Records Society, 1932, pages 421, 435.

battle was over and the firing had ceased. Boats were picking up survivors and I was lucky to be rescued by two Spanish fishermen. While they were attempting to save another seaman, who turned out to be dead, I managed to re-load and prime my pistols with powder I had kept in a waterproof pouch. I then made them row seawards until we reached the *Pluto* but persuaded the First Lieutenant to let them go rather than make sailors out of them. The flagship had taken as prize a small vessel called *San Gennaro* and I was sent in her to carry despatches to the Commander-in-Chief off Toulon. I was more frightened on board the flagship than I was in the action but the Admiral spoke very kindly of our Captain and I was able to assure him that he was unhurt, to the best of my knowledge, when the *Sutherland* struck. Having told him all I knew about the situation at Rosas the Admiral said that I should be posted to the 74-gun ship *Rodney* bearing the flag of Rear-Admiral Martin and commanded by Captain Hollis. I soon realised that the *Rodney*, *Repulse* and *Achilles* were destined to finish the work at Rosas which your cousin had begun and that I was to go in case my knowledge of the place might prove of value. Rear-Admiral Martin is senior to Rear-Admiral Leighton, who will thus be made merely second-in-command. In conversation with other mids I gained the impression that Rear-Admiral Leighton is thought to have bungled things. More than that I overheard the Flag-Lieutenant refer to 'Late-on-the-scene' with almost a suggestion that he had been lacking in courage. This I do not believe because nobody in the *Pluto* thought that he could have come any sooner to the *Sutherland*'s help, the wind being light and variable. Whether he had been right to disperse his squadron is another question and a better tactician would perhaps have recalled the *Sutherland* at the outset. My own idea is that the Rear-Admiral was smarting over his defeat ashore and thought of Rosas with an almost personal hatred. He could have had no better revenge on the place than the destruction of a French squadron in the harbour mouth. His desire to see this happen so distorted his calculations that he judged falsely of what was possible, confusing what he wanted with what was likely. He is nothing of a seaman and unpopular because of this very cholerick disposition which clouds his judgement. That, I suspect, is why Sir Charles Cotton has appointed Rear-Admiral Martin to command while allowing Leighton to regain something of his reputation for courage at least. You see the result of my being on board the flagship—I busy myself with the politicks of the fleet rather than with frustrating the enemy! We are here at Port Mahon making some last preparations before returning to finish our business at Rosas. My love to Mother and tell her not to worry about what the French may do to us. It is little we care about them and little they can do to save themselves!

I remain, Dear Father,

Your Affectionate Son

Jo. Hornblower.

The preparations to which young Hornblower refers included the equipment of four fireships and the squadron which reached the rendezvous off Cape Creux on September 8th comprised three sail of the line, the frigate *Apollo*, the fireships and the *San Gennaro* brig. It was the last named vessel which carried Martin's orders to Leighton, taking him under command and ordering him to join the rest of the squadron. The plan which Martin now issued was masterly. Having withdrawn *Pluto* and *Caligula*, allowing the French to assume that the blockade was over, he ordered a night attack for 2.0 a.m. on the morning of September 12th. The five sail of the line, headed by *Pluto* and *Caligula*, in that order, would enter the bay in line ahead and engage the shore batteries. The *Apollo* would lead the fireships in from a different direction and launch them against the French ships at their anchorage. The *San Gennaro* would operate independently with the special task of burning the *Sutherland*. The *Rodney* would be third in the line of battle but Martin's flag would be in the *Apollo* from which signals would be made, including the signal to break off the action.

This plan was carried out to the letter and with negligible loss. The ships-of-the-line drove away the guard-boats and drew the fire of the ships and shore batteries. Under cover of the noise and confusion the real attack was launched, one fireship destroying the *Turenne* (the prime target as the ship least damaged) while the others so threatened the other ships that their cables were cut and they went ashore. The *Sutherland* was boarded and set on fire, subsequently burning to the waterline, and the signal of recall was made at 3.30 a.m., the withdrawal being completed

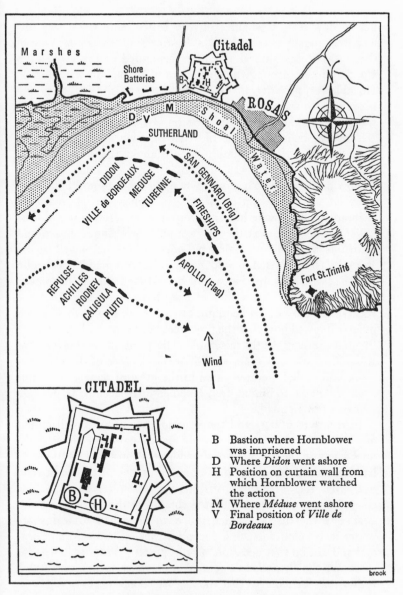

B   Bastion where Hornblower
    was imprisoned
D   Where *Didon* went ashore
H   Position on curtain wall from
    which Hornblower watched
    the action
M   Where *Méduse* went ashore
V   Final position of *Ville de
    Bordeaux*

brook

Diagram to illustrate the Battle of Rosas in 1810

before daybreak. Casualties on the British side were very few and were mostly confined to the leading ship, the *Pluto*. One of them was Rear-Admiral Leighton, wounded in the groin by a wood splinter. Among the spectators of the action was Horatio Hornblower, prisoner, in the citadel, who was allowed, on giving his parole, to watch from the curtain wall on the seaward side. It was a bad moment for him when he saw the destruction of the *Sutherland*, believing as he did that his own career had ended with her. He heard something more about the action from a solitary prisoner who was brought ashore, a seaman from the *Pluto* who had gone overboard when her main topmast was shot away. It was from him he heard of Leighton being wounded, without knowing whether the wound were serious or not. His belief at this time was that he would be exchanged and would return to England on half-pay, never to be employed again. Who, he asked himself, would give another command to a captain who had lost his ship? He would have done better to have been killed in action. That would at least have saved him from the court-martial by which he might be cashiered. From what he said in later life we know that the first weeks of his second captivity in Spain were completely miserable. His position, moreover, was worse than he even realised. For while his fear of disgrace was quite unfounded, he now stood in the greatest danger of execution. Unknown to him at first, Napoleon had decided to put him before a firing squad.

In trying to understand the situation, we have to realise, first of all, that Hornblower had already made a name for himself. His operations on the Spanish coast had been a constant irritation and had reached a climax with his bombardment of the coast road near Malgret. From the various reports received Napoleon singled out one which attributed the fall of the battery at Point Llansa to the ruse by which the *Sutherland* had come inshore under false colours. Such a deception was, of course, quite normal and not on that occasion very important. What mattered far more was the *Sutherland*'s general appearance, which was Dutch rather than British. All that the flag had done was to save Hornblower a few casualties—the battery would have fallen in any case. Fastening on this minor incident, however, Napoleon chose to regard it as a violation of the rules of war: an act, as it were, of espionage, punishable by death. As soon, in fact, as the news of

Hornblower's capture reached Paris, the order was given to bring him there under escort with a view to his trial by a military court. The same order applied, incidentally, to Bush who was treated as his accomplice.

On November 17th, 1810, Hornblower and the crippled Bush were put in a carriage under the eagle eye of Colonel Jean-Baptiste Caillard, an Imperial Aide-de-Camp, the carriage guarded by fifty mounted gendarmes. By nightfall the coach and escort had crossed the frontier into France and halted for the night at Port Vendres. Until that point had been reached it had been still possible for Hornblower to be rescued by the Spanish irregulars. General Rovira and Colonel Claros were still in the field and there were a score of partisan groups acting independently. Any one of them might have ambushed the coach, supposing that it contained treasure. No attempt was made, however, and Hornblower had to realise that his position was almost hopeless, his fate decided. Caillard was an unpleasant man but no fool and his gendarmes knew what would happen to them if their prisoners escaped. Their vigilance was therefore exemplary. Apart from that, moreover, Hornblower was handicapped by the presence of Bush. His coxswain, Brown, who had come with them as servant, was a strong man, unwounded. Hornblower himself was a man of brains and daring. How could he escape, however (even given the chance) and leave his old friend, Bush, to be tried and executed? As things were, Bush had a chance of acquittal on Hornblower's evidence. He could say, and with perfect truth, that the tricolour was hoisted on his orders and that Bush had nothing to do with it. More, he could deny that Bush was even present—and who was there to prove that he was? It was likely enough that Hornblower's evidence would go for nothing and that both of them would die as proof of British perfidy. It was a possible policy, nevertheless and there was just a chance that it might succeed. As for three prisoners escaping when one of them could not even walk, the thing was manifestly impossible. It was the realisation of this appalling handicap that brought Hornblower nearer to despair than he had ever been before. Realising this, Bush begged him to escape if given the opportunity—to which Hornblower could only reply that escape seemed out of the question. Each day they travelled northward brought them nearer to the prison where they would die. They came to Perpignan on November 26th and the only cheerful aspect of the situation was the removal of the ligature from Bush's leg, the first step towards recovery. The coach lumbered on through Clermont-Ferrand and was approaching Nevers on December 19th. On that day, to complete their misery, it began to snow.

CHAPTER EIGHT

Commodore

In later life Hornblower would say that his luck changed on a day in December 1810, the day on which the snow fell over central France. On that day, the 19th, the coach journey began to go wrong. One of the four horses went lame, to begin with, and progress became slow. Then the snow began to fall, becoming heavier after nightfall, and the coach had to stop at intervals so that the hardened snow could be scraped out of the horses' hooves. Finally the coachman lost his way in the darkness and nearly drove the coach into a river. It was all but upset and so bogged down that it could not be moved. Caillard sent the sergeant ahead to ask for help at Nevers, with another man to post at the turning where they had gone wrong. Other men were told to dig the snow away from the coach, which had been lightened by the removal of Hornblower and Brown, and others again were holding the horses. It was pitch dark but the coach lamps had revealed one thing of tremendous interest; a small rowing boat, moored to a post. Choosing their moment, Hornblower and Brown suddenly overpowered Caillard and bundled him, stunned, gagged and tied-up, into the coach. They then lifted Bush, on his stretcher, into the boat, followed themselves and pushed off into the darkness. Nobody saw them go or gave the alarm. Taking a scull each, they began the most perilous voyage of their lives. The river was in spate after heavy rain and was impeded by rapids and shallows, through which they managed to press, passing Nevers and finally wrecked the boat in a waterfall. Still in darkness, they staggered towards a distant light, prepared to surrender. Instead they found themselves the guests of the Comte de Graçay, hidden in his Château until the hue-and-cry was over. Finding fragments of their boat and of the blanket in which Bush had been wrapped, the gendarmes were soon convinced that they had been drowned. Their report was accepted in Paris and published in the *Moniteur*, so reaching

England where it was believed for a time by Maria, Lady Barbara and the relatives of Bush and Brown.

The Château where they were hidden lies, or rather lay,[1] on the upper reaches of the River Loire between Nevers and Briare. The Count had fled to England during the Revolution but returned to France, accepting the amnesty when Bonaparte became First Consul. Three of his sons served in Napoleon's armies and all were killed: the eldest, Marcel, having first married a peasant girl called Marie. There was no other family and the Count was the last of his line, with only his daughter-in-law Marie, the Vicomtesse, to keep him company. His few servants were utterly loyal to him and his English guests were in no danger as long as they kept out of sight. Their only chance of escape was by river and at earliest in April after the floods were over. The plan agreed was that Bush and Brown should build the boat they would need and that the women of the house should make for them uniforms of the Imperial Customs Service, for use when they reached Nantes. Apart from the need for a boat and a disguise, they had first of all to provide Bush with a wooden leg and he had then to learn how to walk with it. It cannot be said that they were idle during the four months of their concealment but they had leisure enough for romance. It is known that Hornblower gained the love of Marie while Brown— who learnt French as Bush never succeeded in doing—was as successful with one of the maids; a girl he was afterwards to marry.

The voyage down the Loire began on April 17th, 1811, with the three voyagers intended to pass as men out fishing. The weather was good and the navigation easy and no one wanted to know who they were. They drifted past Sully and Jargeau, Orléans and Blois and so came finally to Nantes on the evening of May 3rd. It was there that they put on their uniforms as officials of the customs service, continuing their voyage unquestioned and looking about them for a fishing boat they could steal after dark. They did better than that for they presently saw a ten-gun cutter which Bush instantly recognised as *Witch of Endor*, captured from the British Navy the previous year off Noirmoutier. She was in good order and ready for sea but with French colours still over

[1] It was demolished as part of a road-widening scheme in 1965. Only the stables remain and these have been turned into a garage.

British. Alongside the same quay were two American ships being unloaded by a gang of prisoners under a military guard—a chain-gang of criminals and deserters. The anchor watch on board the cutter comprised only a master's mate and two seamen. Going on board, Hornblower had no difficulty in securing all three together with a pilot from aboard another American ship which had just arrived. When these four had been tied helpless in the cabin, Hornblower ordered a sergeant to bring his chain-gang on board. When the sergeant had been secured in turn, the ten prisoners were promised their freedom in England and were then released. Then the cutter was cast off and the prisoners made to hoist the mainsail and jib. By moonlight the voyage began on the ebb tide with the pilot on deck and assured of death if the vessel so much as touched a sandbank. Well piloted, the cutter was off Noirmoutier at daybreak but there she lost the wind and was intercepted by three gunboats. The alarm had been given and acknowledged by telegraph and this attack was the result. Hornblower kept steerage way by putting his prisoners on the sweeps and then engaged the rowing boats with a six-pounder gun. Two of the pursuing boats were sunk and the third fled to safety. The voyage continued and a breeze that night carried the cutter out to sea where she presently fell in with the *Triumph*, commanded by Sir Thomas Hardy, a unit of the Channel Fleet led by Admiral Lord Gambier, in the *Victory*, to whom Hornblower made his report. 'Dismal Jimmy', as the pious Commander-in-Chief was called, was suitably impressed. He decided that Hornblower's report dated May 5th, with his own covering letter, should go to England in *Witch of Endor* navigated by Bush with the acting rank of Commander. A cutter was merely a lieutenant's command and this one had still to be retaken into the service but Bush's promotion, deserved in itself, was also a compliment to Hornblower; a sign of official approval. At almost the same moment Hornblower heard for the first time that Rear-Admiral Leighton had died of his wounds at Gibraltar and had been buried in St Paul's. Later the same day the Admiral's secretary broke the news to him that his wife, Maria, had died at Southsea while giving birth to a son, on 7th February, 1811. The son had lived and Maria, in a cutting from the *Morning Chronicle* was described as 'widow of the late Captain Horatio Hornblower, Bonaparte's martyred victim'. There is no means of knowing what Hornblower felt about this tragedy, for which he felt partly responsible. Might she not have lived had she known, somehow, of his survival? Was he not with Marie, and in her arms most likely, on the very day Maria died? Could he not have been kinder to her? To cap his present misery was the knowledge that the *Victory* was to sail for England in a fortnight and that he would be tried by court-martial almost as soon as he landed. He was the first captain of a British ship of the line to have struck his colours since the *Hannibal* was taken at Algeciras in 1801. . .

When Hornblower stepped ashore, however, at Portsmouth on June 6th he suddenly found himself famous. There was no other naval hero at the moment and the public fancy has been caught by the story of his heroism in battle, his imprisonment and escape, his reported death and his sudden return on board a recaptured prize. For the moment at least he was the idol of the populace and the press. Among the parcels awaiting him was one containing the hundred-guinea sword which he had left in pawn with the prize-agents—pledge for payment without which he would have had no captain's stores in the *Sutherland*. It was now returned to him as a mark of esteem and with it came a mass of letters, as also the news that *Witch of Endor* had been bought by the Navy for £4,000 of which two thirds would go to him as captain and no less than £400 to Brown as the only representative of the lower-deck. Most welcome letter of all was from Lady Barbara Leighton, dated from 129 Bond Street on 3rd June. She explained that she had taken charge of Maria's child, believing him to be an orphan, and that the boy had been christened Richard Arthur Horatio with her brothers, Lords Wellesley and Wellington, as godfathers. The letter ended kindly with the words 'You will be very welcome should you care to call here to see your son, who grows in intelligence every day. It will give pleasure not only to Richard, but to your firm friend, Barbara Leighton.' At the moment Hornblower had to keep his emotions in check. He remembered, and reminded himself daily, that he still had a court-martial to face.

He was acquitted of course (June 14th) and the Admiral President went out of his way to emphasise that Hornblower was 'deserving of every praise the country and this Court can give'. The problem of Leighton's signal was discussed but finally dismissed as irrelevant; as it would not have been had Leighton and not Hornblower, been on trial. The defending officer submitted and the Court agreed, that Hornblower acted properly in obeying the signal and would still have been acting properly had there been no signal at all. The verdict was greeted with cheers throughout the fleet and when Hornblower left the *Victory*, where the court-martial had been held, the yards of the ship were manned in spontaneous demonstration. By what must seem a remarkable coincidence, Hornblower had been condemned to death (in absentia) by a French court-martial held on June 10th, its sentence confirmed by the Emperor on the very day of his acquittal at Portsmouth. He knew nothing of this at the time and would have cared less had he known. It was enough for him to have been exonerated, and indeed highly praised, by seniors and contemporaries in the Service.

There was more cheering on the quayside and the dazed Hornblower found himself in a post-chaise racing to London. It reached London after dark and Mr Hookham Frere, who had been sent to fetch him, rushed him successively to Number 10 Downing Street, to the War Office and so at 10.0 p.m. to Carlton House. Before he knew what was happening the Prince Regent had knighted him, investing him with the insignia of a Knight of the Bath and telling him, for good measure, that he had been appointed a Colonel of Marines—a sinecure which would bring him another £1,200 a year. He ended that bewildering day in a room that had been engaged for him at the Golden Cross, his fortune made and his fame established.

Sir Horatio Hornblower, K.B., called at Lady Barbara's town house on June 15th and was so fortunate as to find her ladyship at home. Here it was that he first met Richard, his only son, aged four months and a picture of health. Sentimentalists would suppose that these two, Horatio and Barbara, would have rushed at this point into each other's arms sobbing that every obstacle to their happiness had now been removed. It was not quite as simple as that. Both were in mourning, for one thing, and no marriage was socially possible until Leighton had been dead for a twelvemonth. In all decency, a date in October was the earliest possible, with no talk of an engagement before September 12th. There were certain conventions to be observed in the meanwhile but we may assume that they understood each other well enough. The outcome of their vigil was foreshadowed, moreover, by the fact that the baby remained with Lady Barbara. To avoid scandal, however, Sir Horatio went out of town, deciding that his first task would be to provide himself with a country estate. It was inconsistent with Barbara's dignity, or with his, that they should spend their honeymoon in what had been Leighton's town house. He ought to have a place of his own and it ought to be in Kent. With his thoughts going automatically to Smallbridge Manor, he wrote on June 18th to Mr Hodge and received the surprising reply that old Mr Barnett had died in 1809. If he still wanted the property he would be well-advised to come at once. Fuming at the man's stupidity, Hornblower set off for Maidstone and was there on June 25th. The earliest surviving of his letters to Barbara was dated from there on the 27th.

> Royal Star,
> Maidstone.

My dear Lady Barbara,

I think I was never destin'd to be a landowner for I am daily vexed over the conduct of Mr Hodge who tells me at one time that the property I am interested in must already be sold and then again, changing his mind, that the present owner, Mr Barnett's cousin, is unlikely to sell at any price. His partner, meanwhile, keeps telling me of other bargains on offer, near five hundred acres for £1300 near Tunbridge, so cheap, he says, that there must be some objection to it, or that I should do better to purchase £200 p.ann. in the Long Annuities, whatever they may be. I am so cross and teazed by attorneys that I have resolved to visit Shropshire and make the purchase for myself. I was able to see Smallbridge yesterday and must acknowledge that some little effort has been made to remedy the neglect of a half century or more but the chief result is no more than a horrid smell of paint. I leave for Bridgnorth to-morrow and am only sorry to think that each day's drive will take me so much further from those dear to me. Please give my love to Richard and assure him that my present campaign is directed to his interests as well as mine— or dare I say ours? The post is come and brought me your charming letter of yesterday, in answer to which I can assure you that the rooms here are clean and that I breakfasted well on tea, bread, butter and eggs. I will write again to-morrow, perhaps from St Albans and will resist the temptation of travelling north by way of Bond Street. I must somehow settle this business one way or the other and am resolved, when I see you, to report my success.

Believe me your affectionate friend,

Horatio Hornblower.

The cousin and heir to Tom Barnett seems to have been almost as eccentric as Tom himself had been. It appears, however, that he had served briefly as a midshipman and had retained ever since a certain partiality for the Navy, if only perhaps as a topic of conversation. Perhaps for this reason, perhaps because of Hornblower's fame, or perhaps because he wanted the money for his mistress, he was persuaded to sell Smallbridge on the spot. The agreement was signed at Bridgnorth and the conveyance drawn up in Maidstone for completion in London. The problem was then to make the house habitable by October, which would certainly have been no mean feat after so long a period of virtual disuse. Hornblower had several victories to his credit but this was a battle he was destined to lose.

The unfortunate fact about Smallbridge Manor is that the place no longer exists. That it should have been accidentally destroyed by fire in 1884 is not especially remarkable; the odd thing is that nothing remains and that no one who was questioned seemed even to know where it stood. The problem is discussed in Appendix II and its position, as ascertained is shown on p. 252, an enlargement of the Ordnance Survey of 1819. It is represented in a coloured engraving of 1845, from which we learn that it was a Georgian house of some dignity, approached by a drive and surrounded by a small park. Its coach-house and stables were separate and the lodge used to be just south of Nettlestead Court. The house took its name from the small bridge which used to cross the River Medway between Nettlestead and Bowhill. The adjacent church and village have always been called Nettlestead, however (not Smallbridge), even when the bridge still existed. The farmland which Hornblower bought stretched westward to the boundaries of Mereworth Castle and Royston Hall and may have comprised up to a thousand acres. The whole place was on the modest side for a man of any consequence, as he evidently came to realise. He returned there, nevertheless, in old age, and there is ample proof that he loved the place. No descendant of his ever lived there, however, and it was tenanted by a certain Major

Perrin at the time of the fire. There was never any plan for re-building it.

Defeated by the plasterers and paperhangers, Hornblower finally rented a house in Tunbridge Wells. His marriage to Lady Barbara took place very quietly in London on October 9th, 1811, the Marquess Wellesley giving the bride away at St Margaret's, Westminster. Their first months were spent at Tunbridge Wells but with frequent visits to Smallbridge. By dint of coaxing and bribery the builders were dragged out of the house by the middle of March, 1812 and the carpets laid and furniture moved in by the end of the month. After countless delays and vexations they were able to fix their official arrival for April 10th, their introduction to the tenants for April 12th. All went well on the day with the vicar making a speech, the villagers singing 'See the conquering hero comes', Hornblower making his reply and the affair being rounded off by three cheers for Her Ladyship and as many for Sir Horatio. The person who most enjoyed the occasion was undoubtedly young Richard, who now for the first time had a garden of his own in which to play. With a typical lack of tact, however, their Lordships of the Admiralty chose the 10th for addressing to him a summons which reached him on the 12th. He was to proceed as Commodore, with a Captain under him, on a service which would be explained to him in due course. After six months of married life ashore, Hornblower was to go to sea again, no longer as captain of a single ship but in command of a squadron. He was being treated with some respect now, partly as a popular hero, partly as a member, by marriage, of the Wellesley family. After all, he had one brother-in-law who was Secretary of State for Foreign Affairs and another who was Commander-in-Chief in Spain and arguably the greatest general that Britain had ever produced. Hornblower was evidently a coming man.

There was no such rank as Commodore at this time. It was merely an honorary and informal title bestowed on a senior captain who had several ships under command; an office and title which he lost again when he went ashore. It was similarly used in the East India Company's Service and it is still the usage of the Merchant Navy. But the Royal Navy had Commodores on two levels, the junior having only a distinguishing pennant, the senior (with a different pennant) having a captain under him.

Relieved of the routine duties which went with the command of a ship, the Commodore in this category was more of a flag officer. It might have been thought simpler to make him a Rear-Admiral and have done with it. That this was impossible was due to the fact that all promotion on the captain's list and upwards went by seniority. To have promoted Hornblower Rear-Admiral at this stage, when he was merely halfway up the list would have meant promoting all the captains senior to him. It is true that few of those promoted would have been employed, but their services would thus have been lost. Retaining his basic rank of captain, Hornblower was now to be given the sort of responsibility which went with a flag. The system, inconvenient in many ways, had at least the merit of providing for failure. Were he to prove unsuitable he could once again be given a ship-of-the-line.

When Hornblower reached the Admiralty he was told that his station would be in the Baltic. He was to lead a squadron which would comprise the *Nonsuch* (74), the sloops *Lotus* (20) and *Raven* (18), the bomb-ketches *Moth* and *Harvey* and the cutter *Clam* (10). The Commander-in-Chief in the Baltic was Vice-Admiral Sir James Saumarez but Hornblower was to have something like a free hand, his task a vague co-operation with any potential opponents of Napoleon. The Baltic situation was extremely complex, with Denmark and Norway occupied by the French, Sweden ruled by a French General whose loyalty to Napoleon was doubtful, and Russia expecting a French invasion which might or might not materialise. There was no certainty about what he would have to do but Hornblower was the sort of man who might be useful in any situation which might arise. His squadron was to assemble in the Downs and he would embark at Deal—so near to the place where his childhood had been spent. The chief difficulty at the outset arose from Hornblower wanting to have Bush as Captain of the *Nonsuch*. It was pointed out to him that Bush had only just been promoted Commander and that his first command as Captain—when he was made post—would be a sloop not a ship-of-the-line. The compromise reached in the end was for Hornblower to have the nominal command of the *Nonsuch* and for Bush to be posted as supernumerary with the rank of captain. This allowed Bush to command the ship—except for the purpose of signing documents—while creating much jealousy among other Commanders. Here was a one-legged man commanding a seventy-four who had never so much as commanded a frigate! There could be no more shameful example of partiality and interest. All that can be said in Hornblower's defence is that Bush justified his promotion, which might have come sooner had he not been Hornblower's follower.

The new Commodore embarked off Deal on May 4th under a salute fired by each ship in the squadron. Sailing immediately with a fair wind for the Skaw, Hornblower led his ships into the Sound on May 10th at daybreak. He was fired on from Salthola and again from Amager, the squadron's guns replying, but came off with little damage. Only the *Harvey* lost her mast, having to proceed jury-rigged. Hornblower's next task was to report his arrival to Vice-Admiral Sir James Saumarez whose squadron was at Wingo Sound near Gothenburg. The Admiral showed no excess of cordiality, resenting the extent to which the Commodore had been given a free hand. He ordered Hornblower, however, to proceed to Kronstadt with despatches addressed to the Tsar of Russia. He was further instructed to offer the Tsar his co-operation in the event of war between Russia and France. Hornblower sailed from Wingo accordingly on May 14th and headed eastwards.

Soon afterwards Hornblower's squadron re-took an English merchant vessel, the *Maggie Jones*, prize to a French privateer called *Blanche Fleur*. This led Hornblower to look for the privateer herself which he caught and destroyed off Rügen. He soon afterwards learnt that Napoleon's armies were being concentrated between Dresden and Warsaw. He learnt still more from the British military attaché at Stockholm, who came on board off the Swedish coast and asked for a passage to St Petersburg. Agreeing to this, Hornblower arrived off Kronstadt on May 22nd and was invited to dinner with the Tsar at Peterhof. Another guest on this occasion was Bernadotte, the King of Sweden. The sequel was that the Tsar, Alexander, came on board the *Nonsuch*, but incognito as the 'Comte du Nord'. Hornblower did his best to impress the Tsar with the discipline and high morale of his men, considered as possible allies, but it is doubtful whether his diplomacy had more than a marginal success. He sailed again from Kronstadt on May 30th, having received orders from Sir James Saumarez to strike a blow against the French communications in the vicinity of Königsberg. Between that port and

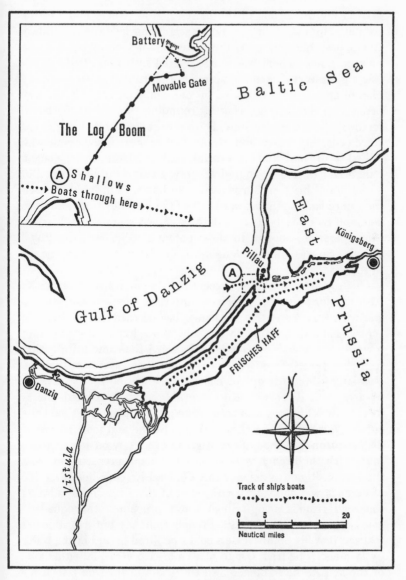

Chart of the Frisches Haff

Danzig lay the lagoon of the Frisches Haff, where much of the coastal shipping, many of the vessels being laden with military stores, had collected under the protection of a strong boom at the only entrance, which was itself covered by coastal batteries. It was a place very difficult of access but Hornblower worked out a plan of attack. Four boats led by Captain Vickery of the *Harvey* penetrated the Frisches Haff by rounding the end of the boom on the night of the 25th June. During the next day they destroyed eleven coasting vessels and twenty-four barges. The defenders all rallied to prevent Vickery's withdrawal and Hornblower made a feint attack on Pillau, enough to draw attention to that area. But Vickery and his men burnt their own boats, as ordered, crossed the spit of land on the seaward side of the Frisches Haff, and were taken off by other boats sent in to an agreed rendezvous. It was a neat operation, enough to show potential allies that the Royal Navy's arm was long and longer certainly than Napoleon was apt to suppose.

On July 8th Hornblower received a despatch from the British Ambassador to Russia, informing him that Napoleon had gone to war with Russia and that his armies had crossed the frontier, the central column heading towards Moscow but another column towards St Petersburg. He later received the same information from Sir James Saumarez with the further assurance that the Russians would attempt to check this more northerly advance by a resolute defence of Riga. Hornblower was ordered, therefore, to do all he could to co-operate in the defence. He sent the cutter *Clam* with despatches to Wingo Sound and took the rest of his squadron into the Gulf of Riga. Off that city on July 25th he found that the French were already there and preparing to cross the Dvina. Riga was defended by General Essen, whose first line of defence was at Daugavgriva, west of the river and straddling the road from Danzig. Shoal water prevented the squadron coming within range of the French trenches but Hornblower realised that his bomb-vessels could be lifted higher in the water by 'camels'. The trick was to place a loaded vessel on either side of the ship to be lightened. All three would then be lashed together and the outer vessels emptied, raising the centre ship further out of the water. Thus lightened, the bomb ketches came within range and did some damage. They were inevitably driven off again by the French artillery and once more withdrew out of range. The French parallels crept up to Daugavgriva and the village itself was reduced to a heap of ruins. Hornblower now offered to use his boats, with other craft commandeered for the purpose, to land a Russian force at night, choosing a point from which the French parallels could be attacked from the flank. This plan was accepted and the landing arranged for the night of August 11th. The operation took place as planned but coincided with a French night attack. There was a confused battle in the darkness and daybreak showed that the besiegers' trenches had been largely destroyed. More time had been gained but news came simultaneously of the fall of Moscow. Hornblower began to wonder whether the next news might not be of the Russian surrender and a peace treaty which would leave Napoleon master of the world. The news of the fall of Moscow probably reached the French at the same time for they now launched a full-scale assault on Daugavgriva, accepting heavy casualties in an attempt to shorten the siege. Hornblower was ashore at the time and became involved in the fighting, at one moment having his horse killed under him while leading a counter-attack in person. In conversation with generals he met in later life Hornblower was mischievous enough to pretend that he had won a battle on land —which was often more than could be claimed by the man to whom he was talking—and had practically saved St Petersburg from capture by the French. The fact is that his intervention, gallant in itself, was one incident in a confused battle with many such successes (and failures) on either side. He was luckily unhurt and the Russians continued to hold Riga, checking the French advance in that quarter. Elsewhere the Russians had been less successful but the vital fact was that they did not surrender. The story ended, as we know, with Napoleon's retreat from Moscow.

The Russian and Swedish alliance left Sir James Saumarez with little further to do in the Baltic, from which he was now anxious to withdraw before the coming of winter. Hornblower received orders dated August 15th to sail for Hano Bay, as it was too late in the year for the *Nonsuch* to remain in her insecure anchorage off Riga. His two bomb vessels were allowed to remain until the end of the month but Hornblower was presently ordered, with the *Nonsuch* and his two sloops, to proceed with convoy to England. He left the convoy in the Downs and took the *Nonsuch* to Chatham where his broad pennant was struck and where the ship was paid off on October 9th. Sir James Saumarez returned to England soon afterwards, struck his flag and ended his active career. Operations in the Baltic had almost ceased with the defeat of Napoleon and only light forces were needed there for the remainder of the war. It appears that Hornblower was a sick man when he landed, partly from exhaustion but more from typhus, a disease he caught during the defence of Riga. He joined his wife at Smallbridge Manor and spent the winter there, not fully recovering until the spring of 1813. There is reason to think that he was a bad patient, peevish, irritable and anxious to be back at sea. To add to his irritation were letters from Captain Bush, now commanding a frigate and from Jonathan Hornblower, serving in a flagship, who had just passed his examination as a prospective lieutenant. Napoleon was on the defensive that winter with his armies weakened and his satellites, Austria and Prussia, turned against him. Having lost the war in Russia, he had been no more successful in Spain where Wellington had fairly driven King Joseph out of his capital. It looked, therefore, as if the next year would see his downfall. Hornblower wanted to be in at the kill, rounding off his twenty years of active service with some final and dramatic achievement.

His ambitions were, unfortunately, rather difficult to satisfy. The Admirals of the day, like Saumarez, were first commissioned when Hornblower was born. They had all seen service in the previous war, being captains when Hornblower first went to sea. For a man originally without influence he had done very well to gain post rank by 1805. Aged only thirty-seven, with seven years' seniority, he was halfway up the list but unlikely to become Rear-Admiral until about 1820. His service as Commodore in the Baltic had been highly creditable to him but the assignment he was given belonged properly to a junior flag-officer. We know, indeed, that the appointment had aroused protest and we may suspect that any further preferment would have created bad feeling among officers of long and distinguished service. As against that he had now experienced the duties of a Commodore and could not readily revert to the command of a single ship. Granted, moreover, that he were willing to do so, would a Commander-in-Chief want to have him? He might be thought too ambitious, restless and critical; not disloyal, of course, but at least silently opinionated. A possible post for him would have been as Captain of the Fleet or even as Flag-Captain to an Admiral and this was the idea which occurred to him. He was encouraged in it by the knowledge that his old chief, Sir Edward Pellew, was Commander-in-Chief in the Mediterranean. He wrote to him, it would seem, in January, 1813 and received a kind but negative reply.

Caledonia
7th March, 1813.

Dear Sir Horatio,

It afforded me great pleasure to hear of your doings in the Baltic and I am glad to hear that you contrived to remain on reasonably good terms with Sir J.S., who is not everyone's *beau ideal* of a Commander-in-Chief. If our affairs continue as prosperously as they have been doing we should bring this Tyrant down at last and I hope before the year 13 passes over our heads. My fleet here is generally in good heart but the captains grow tired and some do little, I often think, but make plans which will excuse their going ashore. We none of us get younger and there is no sign of the Toulon fleet seeking to do battle. They absolutely outnumber us but are undermanned since Boney took many of their trained gunners for his artillery in the field.

I am truly sensible of the honour you do me in expressing a wish to serve under me but you have already proved yourself so equal to the command of a squadron that no one would approve your being placed in any inferior situation. As for the Mediterranean, it is well provided with Rear-Admirals, my brother being Captain of the Fleet, Sir Sidney Smith on detached service, King my second in the *San Josef* and as many again in search of preferment. There are no fewer than seventy-six Rear-Admirals in the list, some gone ashore for good no doubt but more active than are wanted and some having served with credit. I would urge you to be patient and confident that a further opportunity will be given you before the war ends. When that time comes no one is more confident than I that you will more than justify any responsibility that may be accorded you. My own services, I believe, are very nearly at an end but I console myself with the knowledge that many younger men are coming forward and you most certainly among them. It seems a lifetime since we were shipmates in the old *Indefatigable* and the thought occurs to me that

when youngsters I remember as midshipmen have become
Knights of the Bath I must myself be getting old.

Believe me, dear Sir Horatio,

Very faithfully yours

Ed. Pellew

In philosophical mood, Pellew might have remembered
receiving a very similar letter from Lord Nelson in 1804. Pellew's
first sentence must be read in the light of the fact that he and
Saumarez had not been on speaking terms for the last twenty
years. It is probable that Hornblower applied in other directions
without success. Seeing his restlessness, Lady Barbara persuaded
him to visit Ireland in May, 1813. She had inherited a small
estate there in County Sligo and the time had come, she maintained, to visit it. She had herself been brought up in Ireland
and she did not want to be classed with the absentee landlords.
The income derived from the estate was small but she felt a duty
towards her tenants and indeed towards the place itself. Horatio,
still in fact far from recovered, might have resisted all Barbara's
persuasions, preferring to spend the season in London where he
could pester the Admiralty for employment, but he was intrigued
by the fact that Barbara's inheritance included a castle. His day-
dream as a boy had never extended to the ownership of a castle
and his plans before 1811 had rarely gone beyond the acquisition
of a cottage. It seemed now that he and his wife were landowners
and that Drumcliff Castle (for that was its name) was the symbol
of their position. He agreed, though at first reluctantly, to
Barbara's scheme for paying the place a visit. They set off,
without Richard, on May 11th.

They travelled by road from London to Bristol where they
spent several days before boarding the packet for Dublin on May
18th. The Irish capital was full, as it seemed, of Lady Barbara's
relatives and of folk who had been acquainted with her parents
and brothers. Sir Horatio duly called on Lord Whitworth, the
Lord Lieutenant and made himself known to the other great men
of Dublin Castle, Lord Manners, Mr Robert Peel and Mr W.
Fitzgerald. It was during this visit that he began to master the
basic facts of the Irish problem. They were presented to him by
different people in a very different light. He found, moreover,
that his own sympathies were divided. As a disciplinarian he

agreed that maintenance of law and order was the first essential, without which no improvement was possible. As a liberal in politics he had to agree that the Irish peasantry had real grievances which demanded redress. As a freethinker, finally, he could find no justification for exacting tithes from the Catholics for the support of the Prostestant Church in Ireland. Hornblower had first considered the Irish problem back in 1799 when, as a lieutenant, he had carried out the execution of Barry McCool (see page 59). He had had on that occasion the opportunity to send over fifty Irishmen to the gallows and his decision had been to throw the incriminating list overboard. The memory of this had remained with him and he was more than predisposed to hear what the Irish had to say. What influenced him still more, however, was a chance meeting with Mr Justice Fletcher who was later to attract so much attention by his Charge to the Grand Jury of the County of Wexford in 1814. It was from Fletcher that Hornblower heard of the enlightened work done by the Earl Fitzwilliam in Wicklow and by the Marquis of Hertford in Antrim. He was also made to realise that many of the great landlords were permanent absentees, drawing an income from estates upon which they spent nothing. He was glad to be able to explain that he was on his way to Sligo and that only his service afloat had prevented him going there before.

The Hornblowers reached Sligo early in June, visiting several country houses on the way, and were met there by Mr Wylie, the land agent for Lady Barbara's estate. Drumcliff Castle stands on a headland which projects into the Atlantic but is built on the landward side, facing up the estuary towards Sligo town. It was then, and is still, the remains of a strong fortification, some part of which was then theoretically still habitable. The surrounding estate was quite small but the property included a number of farms further inland along the riverside. On most days the waves from the Atlantic pounded on the rocky shore and miles of the coastline seemed to be almost without population. As compared with other counties the recent history of Sligo had been relatively uneventful, perhaps from mere lack of inhabitants. All we know of the first visit is based upon a letter addressed by Lady Barbara to her old friend, Mrs Fancourt, their next door neighbour in Bond Street.

Sligo, June 16th (1813)

My dear Margaret—You will be wondering what our fate has
been in this remote country, and whether indeed we have survived the journey hither. After a stay in Dublin, meeting friends
and making ourselves known, we travelled across Ireland by easy
stages, enjoying the hospitality of the various houses at which we
stayed. Our own castle needs repair and alteration before we can
even discuss its furniture but we were offered hospitality by
Mr McDermott at this house on the outskirts of the town and
fronting on Lough Gill. The weather has been delightful but I
have taken the opportunity of a wet afternoon to write you the
news, which will seem dull indeed in comparison with the reports
which come in daily from the continent. It was a proud day for
me when I heard the splendid news of Arthur's victory at the
Battle of Vittoria, with Spain lost to the Tyrant and only the
Pyrenees between France and an actual invasion. Horatio is fret-
ful to be without employment but he is not yet recovered from
the effects of the fever to which he nearly fell victim at Riga. This
visit to Ireland is doing him good, reluctant as he may be to
admit it. As for me I had nearly forgot how beautiful this country
is with its hills and lakes, no whit inferior to those in Westmore-
land so much praised by Mr Wordsworth. I am partial to his
works, as you know, and am also an admirer of Lord Byron (for
his poetry, I mean, not his character) so that you must suppose
me an amateur of high cliffs and romantic waterfalls. Horatio
says that he would rather see a prospering agriculture and some
neat cottages for the labouring poor. Secretly he loves wild
scenery as much as I but talks as he does to tease me. His object
has always been to appear taciturn, surly and prosaic, all quite the
opposite of his real nature as known to me and perhaps to no-one
else. He has kept a diary during this visit to Ireland, I think
because he was used to keeping a log-book when at sea. He thinks,
as I do, that our agent here is none too honest and that our
tenants have not been treated fairly. We plan to build some new
cottages to begin with and make the castle at least habitable
against our next visit. Our return is fix'd for July and we shall
spend the autumn at Smallbridge, where Richard will be missing
us and where there is much still to do. My hope is to keep Horatio
ashore for the winter but doubt whether I shall succeed for he
longs, I know, to play some part in the Tyrant's downfall. We

shall hope to see you when we pass through London and will tell you more then of our travels. Do please give my love to your sister Jane and our kind regards to our other neighbours, Mr Watkins, Mrs Nettley and old Sir James.

Believe me always your firm friend
Barbara.

P.S. Do you remember Mr Briggs whom we met at the Fentons? I saw him again in Dublin, there I believe for a lawsuit. I was glad that Sophie would not marry him.

It is tantalising to learn that Hornblower kept a diary at this time, for no such record of travel has so far come to light. We know more of his later visits to Ireland, however, especially that of 1817–18. After this first glimpse of their Irish estate the Hornblowers made a leisurely journey to Belfast and sailed from there to the Clyde. It was there that Horatio had his first introduction to the steamship. The *Comet*, the first boat to be powered by a steam engine (of three horsepower) had appeared on the Clyde in 1812, and a service had since been established between Glasgow and Greenock. The *Elizabeth*, a more suitable vessel than the *Comet*, had first appeared on the Clyde in March and she was now the more popular ship, carrying up to a hundred passengers at a time. The commercial success of this venture was still in doubt but the story was already being told that she had once covered the twenty-six miles in two hours and a half. That was admittedly with the help of wind and tide but the wonder was that a voyage *against* the tide was at all possible. Hornblower took passage several times and spent hours in the engine-room. With his mechanical bent he was (like Nelson) an early convert to steam and believed from this first experience, that the Royal Navy should make use of it. The invention had come too late, he realised, for the war against Napoleon, but he had no doubt of its importance. While he did not expect to see steamships on the ocean, he foresaw their value in harbour. He lived, in fact, to see them everywhere: though not, of course, to the exclusion of sail.

From Glasgow the Hornblowers travelled south, crossed the border and made their first visit to the Lake District. In a letter from Windermere to her sister Anne, Barbara refers to the yacht race recently won on that lake by the schooner *Peggy* from the Isle of Man, dragged overland for the purpose. The *Peggy* still

exists, ashore in Castletown, and is our chief remaining link with
the yachtsmen of this period. From Kendal the Hornblowers
travelled south to Bath, where they briefly took the waters, and
so to London and eventually back to Smallbridge. They were
there in early September and soon afterward heard of Napoleon's
victory at Dresden. By now completely recovered, Hornblower
began again to ask the Admiralty for employment. Fearing that
his sense of frustration might make him ill again, Barbara now
began to second his efforts, using her far greater influence at a far
higher level. She was told that it was merely a question of time
before the right command fell vacant. There was no question of
Hornblower being forgotten or neglected. He could have the first
ship-of-the-line which became available. Barbara pressed for
something better, alleging that it was Sir Horatio who had persuaded the Prussians around Riga to turn against Napoleon. This
legend has often been repeated since, although there is little
evidence to support it, but the story, in any case, did little for
him at the time. It was not a diplomatic post for which he was a
candidate. What he wanted was a command at sea and for most of
the opportunities which offered he was either too senior or (more
often) not nearly senior enough.

In the last week of September the Hornblowers moved to their
town house in Bond Street, from which base Barbara was prepared to bully the Ministry at short range. She seems to have had
no scruple at all where her husband's career was concerned and
Horatio was fortunate in knowing very little about the sort of
pressure she was prepared to exert. By his talents and courage
Horatio had made himself a country gentleman, too proud to beg
for favour. His wife came of a noble family which had been
demanding favours for the last hundred years. How else had her
grandfather secured a peerage? How else had her father turned it
into an Earldom? As compared with the gentry, the real aristocrats had never scrupled to ask for anything, nor to go on asking
for it until mere persistence had worn down the opposition into a
wearied consent. The Wellesleys were not at their most influential in 1813 for Richard was out of office, having failed to form
a government the year before. They had friends, however and
relatives, and Richard's jealousy of Arthur was latent, at this
time, rather than obvious. If the Ministers of the day were to keep
Hornblower out of the House of Lords they would prove them-

selves better men than had ever so far held office. There was small risk of that but the immediate problem was the smaller one of finding him a command at sea. The marriage which had given Hornblower some powerful friends had as certainly made for him some highly-placed enemies. His next appointment could easily have ended his career and there is reason to believe that it was meant to do exactly that. The task presented to him, which he could not refuse, offered him (as it seemed) the choice between disgrace and death.

CHAPTER NINE

Peerage

The Britain of Hornblower's time came nearest to disaster when the Fleet mutinied in 1797. It was a moment of appalling danger, the situation being more immediately saved by Richard, Earl Howe. After persuading the government to redress the main grievances, the old Admiral then persuaded the seamen to return to duty. The next task was to restore discipline and this fell to Sir John Jervis (Earl St Vincent), the great teacher of the fleet which Nelson was to lead. The morale of the Navy rested thenceforward on the victories that had been won. The danger, however, of 1797 had never been quite forgotten and there were occasional reminders of it, minor uprisings in ships that were badly officered. Now, in late September, 1813, came news of a mutiny which might be extremely serious, if only by example. The brig sloop *Flame* (18), on blockade duty in the Bay of the Seine, had mutinied against her officers, holding them as hostages. A master's mate and four loyal seamen had been turned adrift in the gig, entrusted with an ultimatum addressed to the Admiralty. The gig made Bembridge and the ultimatum reached their Lordships, accusing Mr Chadwick (Lieutenant commanding) of tyranny and murder and ending with this significant sentence: 'We want to fight on for England's liberties for we are loyal hearts and true like we said but France is under our lee and we are all in this together and we are not going to be hanged as mutineers and if you try to take this vessel we shall run him up to the yardarm and go in to the French.'

Considering this document, the naval members of the Board knew or suspected that Chadwick had been unjust and cruel, an embittered man passed over for promotion. The crew had been driven to mutiny and any other crew, given a resolute ringleader, would probably have done the same. As against that, mutiny was mutiny and could spread by example. In this instance, however, any attempt to capture the *Flame* would merely encourage the mutineers to take her into Havre. The loss of a sloop was not significant in itself but Napoleon would see its propaganda value. In the *Moniteur* the *Flame* would be at least a frigate and her surrender would be proof that the British morale was cracking. News of the incident would be broadcast and exaggerated for the benefit of countries which might or might not be turning against Napoleon. His empire might be on the point of collapse but this was the moment for a final decisive effort, not for a last minute sign of weakness. What was to be done? Were an Admiral sent to reason with the mutineers he would have only two alternatives. He could offer them the amnesty which they demanded, thus undermining the discipline throughout the fleet. He could, on the other hand, refuse their demands and watch the *Flame* enter Havre under French colours. The mere sighting of any superior force would produce this result, which was inevitable, in any case, when her provisions had been expended. A surprise attack would almost certainly fail because *Flame* would be in shoal water, placed where she could sail into a French port at the least sign of danger. There was no obvious solution to the problem which had nevertheless, somehow, to be solved. Their Lordships decided to send for Hornblower.

There were several good reasons for making this choice. In the first place, Hornblower was not an Admiral, which would make his probable failure less of a setback. In the second place, he was something of a popular hero—the sort of man to whom the seamen would (possibly) listen. In the third place, he had been asking for employment—his relatives had been pestering everyone from the Prince Regent downwards—and he could not, therefore, refuse what was offered him. It was this last point which was vital. Offered this almost impossible task, the more senior officers would say 'Hardly an Admiral's command, is it?' Others less senior might plead their poor state of health: 'But for the gout, I should have been glad to accept. . .' Hornblower could make no such excuse. He could admittedly reject the command of a ship but not, clearly the command of a squadron. He must therefore be offered his broad pennant again as Commodore, with some sort of detachment from the Channel Fleet. Nor was there any likelihood of this particular appointment causing jealousy, for the task was one which nobody could want. If the officer chosen were miraculously successful the whole inciden would be hushed up, with credit to no one. If he failed, by

contrast, there would be pitying comments on board the flag-
ships: 'Poor Hornblower! That task was a little beyond him.
He'll be less cocky another time. It all comes of marrying
money!' Hornblower knew very well the penalty of failure but
there was no escape from the trap. Offered a detachment with one
ship-of-the-line, two frigates and a sloop, he had to accept it. His
first stipulation was that the sloop should be of the same tonnage
as the *Flame*, able to go wherever the mutinous vessel went. He
was promptly given the *Porta Coeli* (18), an actual sister ship,
commanded by Freeman who had served under him in the Baltic.
His second stipulation was that he should be given full powers to
deal with the situation, even to the point of granting pardon; and
this too was confirmed in writing. He was to be allowed no excuse
for changing his mind.

Hornblower left his town house early on October 13th, 1813,
saying goodbye to Richard, who shook hands like a man and
asked 'Are you going back to fight, Father?' Hornblower had no
very concise answer to that, having no idea what he meant to do.
Barbara came with him to Portsmouth, where he embarked in the
Northumberland (74) and hoisted his broad pennant as Commodore on the evening of October 14th. Sailing that night, with the
frigates *Glenmore* (36) and *Cerberus* (32) he shifted his pennant
almost immediately to the *Porta Coeli* brig. Leaving the other
ships out of sight but within call, he took the *Porta Coeli* into the
Bay of the Seine. He sighted the *Flame* there on the morning of
the 16th. When *Porta Coeli* approached her she set her course for
Honfleur. When *Porta Coeli* hove-to, *Flame* followed suit. She
clearly intended to remain out of range. Nor was Hornblower
successful when he went on board the *Flame*, rowed over in a boat.
An old seaman, Nathaniel Sweet, was in effective command and had
already been in contact with the French at Le Havre. He merely
re-stated the crew's ultimatum; Chadwick to be tried by court-
martial and the mutineers to be pardoned. There was nothing to
be gained by argument but the almost identical appearance of the
Porta Coeli and *Flame* had given Hornblower an idea. The
distinctive thing about the *Flame* was a patched foretopsail,
giving the effect of a light cross against a darker background.
Hornblower gave orders to patch the *Porta Coeli*'s foretopsail to
the same pattern, making the two brigs virtually identical, their
resemblance made perfect by a change of name as painted on the

stern. Ignoring the *Flame* for the time being, Hornblower told Freeman to take the *Porta Coeli* into Havre, the officers to hide their uniforms and the men to cheer. The approach was made in failing light on the evening of the 16th, the brig being met successively by the pilot lugger and by the cutter which carried the reception committee. The pilot and the officials were successively made prisoners and the *Porta Coeli* hove-to near an anchored West Indiaman, a French blockade runner recently arrived with cargo. In gathering darkness the merchantman was boarded and brought out astern of the sloop, both under a belated and ineffective fire from the shore batteries. Any attempt by the apparently double-dealing *Flame* to enter Havre would now be met by gunfire. Hornblower had cut off her retreat.

The moment had now come to deal with the *Flame* before the mutineers had the chance to explain their innocence. Before the *Porta Coeli* could act, however, on the 17th, the *Flame* was attacked by a lugger, the *Bonne Celestine* and four gunboats under the French flag. Hornblower intervened, the *Porta Coeli* sinking two of the gunboats and then coming alongside the lugger. Hornblower himself led the boarding party which swept over the French vessel and so into the *Flame*, which was quickly recaptured. He himself shot Nathaniel Sweet as that mutineer tried to escape by swimming to a surviving French gunboat. By the 18th Hornblower had withdrawn from the French coast with his four sail, reached his rendezvous with the *Northumberland* and sent his report to the Commander-in-Chief. The report was sent in the Indiaman, with Chadwick in command, and it concluded with a request for reinforcements. News had come of Napoleon's defeat at the Battle of Leipzig and one of the prisoners—an official from Le Havre—had told him that the town was ready to rise against the Emperor, if properly encouraged, and declare its support for Louis XVIII. The result was the arrival of the *Nonsuch* (74) and the *Camilla* (36) with three hundred marines above establishment. Captain of the *Nonsuch*, just appointed, was none other than his old follower, Bush. As for the *Flame*, Hornblower issued a pardon to the surviving crew, redistributing them and keeping both the *Flame* and the French lugger for further service, each commanded by an acting lieutenant. With his squadron thus strengthened, Hornblower returned to Le Havre, sailed into the port and was received as an ally. A little uncertainly, the citadel hoisted the white standard of the Bourbons and Hornblower assumed office as Governor of Le Havre. He was soon informed, however, that the Duc d'Angoulême—nephew of Louis XVIII—was on his way and would be treated as royalty. These orders were duly observed, and with every proper ceremony, but the fact remained that Napoleon was still in France and that his forces were likely to react. News came of a column, with artillery, sent by river from Rouen to recapture Le Havre. Rather than wait for this threat to develop, Hornblower decided to meet it half-way, sending a raiding party up the river to meet Napoleon's artillery at Caudebec. Bush was given the command, seven boats manned by seamen and marines, and the raid was a success in that the siege train was duly intercepted and largely destroyed but only two boats returned and Bush was in neither. Reports made it clear that he had been killed in action, drowned most probably when his launch went down. The threat from Rouen died away and troops began to arrive from England. With them came the Duchesse d'Angoulême, the brightest and most attractive of the French royal family and with her came Lady Barbara Hornblower to take her place by Horatio's side.

These events, and the subsequent occupation of Rouen, took place during the winter of 1813–14. With the spring came news of other victories, including those of the Duke of Wellington—as he shortly became—in the south of France. Then, at last, in April, came the news that Napoleon had abdicated and that the war was over. Almost at the same time came the astonishing news that Hornblower was to be ennobled as a Baron of the United Kingdom, Lord Hornblower of Smallbridge in the County of Kent. There was practically no precedent for such an honour being accorded to any seaman under the rank of Rear-Admiral, nor indeed to an officer who had not commanded nor taken part in a victorious battle. To all appearances it was Hornblower's reward for his part in restoring the Bourbons but the campaign to gain him a peerage had evidently begun before that, having behind it the whole weight of the Wellesley clan. Hornblower knew nothing of the pressure that had been applied, and it is doubtful if the whole story will ever be known. What we do know is that Hornblower entered the House of Lords at the same time as Sir Edward Pellew, now Lord Exmouth, and seventeen

The Battle of Algiers, from the coloured aquatint engraved by J. C. Stadler after the oil painting by P. H. Rogers

Boxley House, from a recent photograph in the present owner's possession

Admiralty House, Kingston, Jamaica, from a photograph taken in 1910 and published in the West Indies Chronicle. This house, often called 'Admiral's Pen', was acquired by the Admiralty in 1774 but has since been sold and is now all but derelict

years ahead of Sir James Saumarez, under whom he had lately served in the Baltic. His elevation created a great deal of jealousy among officers senior to him and had much to do with his having no command at sea between 1816 and 1821.

After Napoleon had departed for Elba the allies assembled in Paris: Louis XVIII, the Tsar of Russia, the Emperor of Austria, the King of Prussia and all the Marshals from Wellington to Blucher, from Platow to Ney. When the Duke of Wellington was made Ambassador to France it was natural that he should ask to have Hornblower as his naval attaché. This was how they first met, with respect on either side, and this was how the Duke first experienced Barbara's usefulness in diplomacy. The truth is that he had seen little of his youngest sister since 1808 and was pleased to find her an accomplished hostess, a great lady in her own right, a poor linguist but a genius for remembering people. It was in the midst of this glittering society of post-war Paris that Lady Hornblower moved with the greatest assurance, a reluctant husband in tow. And it was here, among the returned emigrés that Lord Hornblower came across the Comte de Graçay and with him his daughter-in-law, Marie, the Vicomtesse. Introducing Marie to Barbara gave Hornblower a difficult moment but they parted with civilities, Barbara wondering afterwards why the Vicomtesse had never remarried. Late in 1814 the arrangement was made for the Duke of Wellington to leave Paris, going as Ambassador to Vienna, where the peace conference was being held. He invited Hornblower to accompany him but Horatio had suffered much and would suffer no more. Diplomacy was not for him but he agreed finally that Barbara should go, knowing that Wellington genuinely needed her to act as hostess. The plan finally agreed was that Barbara should go with the Duke and that Hornblower should rejoin Richard at Smallbridge. The parting took place in January, 1815, and the circumstances were not very favourable to the further success of their marriage.

After six weeks of Smallbridge and boredom, Hornblower left for France. There can be no moral excuse for his conduct and there is little that a biographer can say in his defence. It may be urged that his wife had deserted him, choosing for preference the gaiety of Vienna; and this is indeed the truth. But what of Marie? What had Hornblower to offer her? Taking her love, which was his (as he knew) for the asking, what could he give her but misery? He returned to her inevitably of course, and their love affair was resumed. Brown, his former coxswain and present valet, similarly resumed his relationship with Annette, daughter of the Count's cook, Jeanne, but with the difference that he was free to marry her, which he now proceeded to do. The wedding was celebrated, with all the village present. The date was March 6th and the news came next day that Bonaparte had left Elba and landed in France. Conflicting reports and rumours followed but the news was finally confirmed that Napoleon was in Paris and had declared himself Emperor. The King had fled, the troops had gone over to the Emperor and the Bourbon regime had collapsed. The Count, Marie and their guests were now plainly in the greatest danger. It was decided that they should ride for Rochelle and try to embark there for Britain or Spain; and this was certainly the wisest plan. It was not, however, carried out. Riding through Nevers (the five of them, with Annette) they found there the Duchesse d'Angoulême whom Hornblower had known at Le Havre. That spirited woman was prepared to fight Napoleon and was going to rally Gascony against him. She appointed the Count her Lieutenant-General in the Nivernais and Hornblower agreed to help him. Thus began the guerrilla war on the Upper Loire, a handful of Royalists against Napoleon's regular troops.

This sort of war could not last for long. There were a few successful skirmishes, some less successful, and then the survivors were being hunted through the forest. They were finally trapped between the hussars and the Loire, Marie being killed and the others taken prisoner. A court-martial was assembled before which the Count was quickly condemned to death as a rebel. Hornblower was tried next and the prosecuting officer, having established the prisoner's identity, submitted to the Court the verdict passed on Hornblower on 10th June, 1811. He had already been condemned to death for piracy and it was only necessary now to carry the sentence into execution. The Court agreed and ordered the prisoner to be shot at dawn the following day, which was June 22nd. It so happened that Napoleon had already been defeated at Waterloo on the 17th, the news of which reached General Clausen during the night of the 22nd. He decided that the two executions should not take place, after all. Neither was Hornblower released at that time for Clausen wanted more certain news of Napoleon's fate. This he presently received in the form of a report that the Emperor had abdicated. It was not, however, until July 16th that Hornblower was allowed to leave and that was the day after Napoleon had gone on board the *Bellerophon*. With the Count, with Brown and Annette, Hornblower went back to Graçay. The Count's first care was to recover Marie's body and arrange for her proper burial. With what feelings Hornblower attended that funeral we can never know. That he blamed himself for her death is probable. That he blamed himself for much else is certain. But for his folly in coming to France the Count and Marie might have remained safely at Graçay. But for that mad escapade, Hornblower might have been at sea when the war finally ended. It might even have been to him, not to Maitland, that Napoleon had surrendered. He could do little, at the moment, to resume his naval career. He could do nothing to repair the damage he had done to his friends. The question remained whether he could make good the damage he had done to himself, to his wife, to his child. There is reason to believe that the Count had known all along of Marie's attachment to Hornblower. Even if he had not, the truth must have come out during Hornblower's last days at Graçay. The Count was, in some ways, the closest friend Hornblower ever had. When they parted it was with full understanding and, on the Count's side, with forgiveness. They were never to meet again.

In attempting to follow Hornblower's next and most difficult campaign, one is bound to ask two questions at the outset. First, was it Hornblower's intention to leave Barbara in 1814 and begin a new life with Marie? The answer must be that he had no such intention. Granted that he had drifted apart from Barbara in Paris, she loving the social life which he came to detest, he was still wedded to his career. There was no future in 19th Century Britain for a naval officer who had openly deserted the Duke of Wellington's sister. There was no future, even, for an officer who preferred to live with his mistress in France. In a choice to be made between Barbara and Marie, the scales were weighted, therefore, on Barbara's side with the whole mass of service and official opinion. The second question, arising from the first, concerns his correspondence. Did he write to Barbara during the first half of the year 1815; and if so, to what effect? How did he explain his decision to leave Smallbridge? What was the ostensible object of his journey? It is perhaps significant that no letters of this period have survived, perhaps because he and Barbara wanted no reminder of their estrangement. Our only clue is contained in a letter written by Barbara from Vienna to her brother Richard and printed in volume III of the *Wellesley Papers*. It is dated from the British Embassy on February 23rd and the last sentence reads thus: 'Horatio has soon tired of the country and has accepted an invitation to visit the Duc d'Angoulême, his friend from the days of his governorship of Le Havre. He has not remembered to tell me at which of his châteaux the Duc is presently to be found but his next letter will no doubt enlighten me.' Whatever coldness there may have been between them, the conventions were not too openly flouted. Whether Barbara believed his story is another matter but he had at least provided her with an explanation she might choose to accept. It accounted for his being at Nevers at the commencement of 'The Hundred Days'. There was no immediate cause, therefore, for public scandal.

The actual rift between the Hornblowers was more basic, we may suspect, than a mere disagreement over party-going. Horatio, aged thirty-nine, had strong emotional and sexual needs. Barbara, at thirty-four, was at least outwardly more stately, more poised, more cold. In the literature of today we hasten to expose all marital discord to the light of our supposedly scientific expertise. That was not the custom under the Regency, an age far from puritan during which some aspects of life were treated, nevertheless, with some reticence. Our conclusion about the Hornblowers must be based, therefore, on guesswork, not upon any revelations dating from the period in which they lived. Writing with modern frankness, then, but with perhaps less confidence than is now fashionable, we might guess that Hornblower's love was on two levels, one higher and one lower. Barbara was his (high-level) ideal of a great lady, the sort of dignified woman he had once admired from afar. From the point of view of a married lifetime, hers was the sort of affection which would last. From the point of view of a wild weekend she probably offered less than could many a (low-level) chambermaid or shopgirl. If Horatio Hornblower had a weakness which could possibly lead even to a momentary neglect of duty, it was on this lower level. And while his naval career largely saved him from temptation in this form, he was perhaps the less capable of resistance when the oppor-

tunity arose. Earlier in his career (in 1801, for instance) he may
well have had affairs of the heart and we may suspect that they
were on the lower, perhaps on the lowest, level. Marie, remember, was of peasant origin and extremely pretty, offering much
and demanding, apparently, nothing. Compared with her,
Barbara might have seemed like a marble statue, beautiful, cool
and remote. This, if true, is no proof that a marriage with Marie
would have been a success. She too had her limitations—just as
he, heaven knows, had his—and there was at least one aspect of
his life which he could never have discussed with her, and that
was the professional aspect. He was a naval officer before he was
ever a lover and he would remain one after his passions had
dwindled. That was something which Barbara could understand
and Marie, never. Lucky is the man whose high and low level
affections can converge, in the end, on a single girl. This was not
Hornblower's good fortune in the year of Waterloo.

When the Duke of Wellington was summoned back from
Vienna in March, 1815, it was to take command of the allied
armies which concentrated, finally, round Brussels. Many British
visitors to the continent collected in that same capitol and some
were still there when the Duke won his final victory. Lady Hornblower was not among them for she had chosen to remain in
Vienna. She was still there, moreover, in August, a fact which
suggests that the rift between her and Horatio was serious. How
much had she heard of his doings in France? There is no means
of knowing, but there is a shred of evidence to suggest that her
own conduct was not utterly above reproach. Among the British
left in Vienna was the Hon. Archibald Hammond, who held
some junior appointment at the Embassy and whose letters from
abroad[1] were afterwards published by his niece, Sophia Mitchell.
In one letter, addressed to his uncle, Lord Reigate, and dated on
May 4th, 1815, there is the following reference to Barbara:

'Yesterday I attended the Imperial Opera House for the
purpose of seeing (or should I say hearing?) *Le Nozze di Figaro*.
There was talk during the interval of a new work by Herr Lud-
wig von Beethoven called *Wellingtons Sieg in der Schlacht bei
Victoria* but nobody has yet heard it performed altho' it was

[1] *The Life and Letters of a Diplomat* by the Hon. Sir Archibald
Hammond, H.M. Ambassador to Sweden, London, 1868.

acclaimed last February at Drury Lane. Apropos, I had an unexpected meeting there with Lady Hornblower, Wellington's sister, who was on the arm of a rather handsome man whom I took to be her present husband, Captain Lord H. of the Royal Navy. She greeted me merely in passing but I was surprised to learn, by subsequent inquiry, that her escort was none other than the Baron Franz Alexander von Neffzer, an officer, as I understand, in a Hungarian Cavalry Regiment. He has a name for gallantry among the ladies and fought a duel last year with the jealous husband of one of them, the Freiherr von H-B, neither bullet taking effect. As the Baron had been similarly challenged not so long before by a Major in the Pavlograd Regiment of Hussars, his reputation is none of the best and I feel that the Ambassador would do well to give her a word of warning. During the same evening I also met Colonel Herzen, who is Aide, I believe, to the Archduke Rudolf'. . . etc., etc.

Such gossip as this could be untrue but it seems not unlikely that Barbara should have found consolation when apparently deserted. How else can we account for her lingering behind in Austria after Wellington had left? She had gone there to play hostess for him and his departure left her free to resume her country life at Smallbridge. That she did nothing of the sort is significant. Nor did she and her husband meet until September when they met in Brussels. By the end of the year Hornblower was at Smallbridge but Barbara was in Dublin and the breach between them must have been obvious to their relatives and friends.

So far as we can judge from this distance of time, our conclusion might be that they were two proud people, easily hurt and none too easy to reconcile. Had Richard been Barbara's child he would have been a bond between them, but they were childless, as a couple, and were so to remain. Hornblower's response to the situation was typical of him: he wanted to go back to the sea. When things had gone wrong he was out of his proper element, playing the part of Governor at Le Havre, pretending to be a diplomatist in Paris or acting like Robin Hood in the Nivernais. Were he to return to the quarterdeck, with the salt spray in his face, he would be himself once more, a seaman and an officer. After even a peacetime cruise he would feel clean again, ready to take Barbara in his arms. The man she had loved had been a naval captain, coming ashore with tales of adventure and prize-money. The woman he loved had been the one who had met him on the quayside, relieved to see him unhurt and glad to see him promoted. All would be well if they could regain that old relationship of the sailor and his girl! If these were his thoughts—as they must have been—Hornblower was frustrated again by the knowledge that the war was over. It had ended while he was ashore, a fool on a fool's errand! He might never have a command again. The crews were being disbanded, the ships were being laid up and there might be no more active service for a lifetime. He was not yet forty and his chosen career was already ended! Early in 1816 came news from the Mediterranean, Lord Exmouth was dealing with the Barbary States, using at least the threat of force. He would soon be on his way home, however, when his ships too would be paid off. There seemed to be no future in the Navy for anyone. As for Barbara, she had left Dublin for Drumcliff Castle. Her brief letter from County Sligo assured him that she was perfectly well, but mentioned no date for her return.

On June 27th, 1816, the miracle happened. Hornblower received what he never expected to see again; a summons for him to report at the Admiralty. He reached Charing Cross as fast as his horses could travel and was at once shown in to the office of Sir Thomas Byam Martin, a naval member of the Board. Hornblower recorded the conversation afterwards in a letter addressed to Sir Charles Penrose:

Martin: I am authorised to offer your Lordship the appointment of Captain of the Fleet to Lord Exmouth.

Hornblower: I am happy to accept but more than a little surprised at receiving the offer. His Lordship's brother has usually held that post and there are other followers of Lord Exmouth whom I should have expected his Lordship to prefer. I last served with him in the rank of midshipman and that was in 1796.

Martin: Of those facts I am aware. During the recent negotiations at Algiers Lord Exmouth had around him the officers whose service has been mainly under his flag. He is now to revisit Algiers but with different orders which make hostilities almost certain. Knowing that his own life will be in danger, Lord Exmouth has rejected the idea of endangering the lives of his closest followers. His brother will not be with his fleet, nor will either of his sons. He regards this service as particularly hazardous.

Hornblower: His friends will be disappointed. What others are to go?

Martin: Admiral Penrose will be second-in-command, Rear-Admiral Milne will be third, Captain Brisbane will be his Lordship's flag-captain in the *Queen Charlotte*, Captain Brace with Milne in the *Impregnable*. Penrose is in the Mediterranean now and is ordered to join his Lordship's flag at Gibraltar.

Hornblower: It will be an honour to serve with these officers. This last opportunity of active service may well be followed by ten years of peace.

Martin: By twenty years, more likely, my Lord. There may be no other battle in our lifetime!

This last guess was incorrect but it remained true that Europe was to be at peace, more or less, for years to come. Every officer in the service wanted to sail with Lord Exmouth, whose difficulty in rejecting them was more than equalled by his difficulty in manning his lower decks. Seamen were entitled to their discharge when war ended and most of them had seen all they wanted of the Navy. For Hornblower, whose carriage was racing to Portsmouth, the irony of the situation lay in the fact that he had been chosen for the wrong reason; not because Lord Exmouth liked him but specifically because the Admiral refused to risk the lives of men he liked a great deal more. The further irony was that Hornblower, after twenty years of active service, had never taken part in a general engagement. This was common enough, as he knew. There had been twenty-seven sail of the line at the Battle of Trafalgar out of a hundred and seventy-two warships in all. Men who had fought at St Vincent or the Nile were a fortunate minority, able to brag about it for ever. Now, at the last moment, he, Hornblower, was being given this unexpected chance. There would be a battle, so much was certain, and he would be on board the flagship. If he fell—and he realised that this was not unlikely —his problem with Barbara was solved. If he came back a hero, as he had in 1811, the problem might be solved in another way. She could not stand aside (could she?) while he was being acclaimed by everyone else. If he could not return as a hero he would rather not return at all.

Why was there to be a battle at Algiers? The basic fact is that the Barbary States, as Hornblower had known since boyhood (see page 25), and had experienced since (see page 115), lived by piracy and habitually enslaved all the prisoners they took in a warfare directed against the smaller Christian States of the Mediterranean. During the French Wars the British Mediterranean Fleet was often without a single European ally and relied on Algiers, Tunis, Oran and other Muslim ports for its supply of food. While the war continued, the piratical habits of these allies had to be overlooked. When the war ended these pirates ceased to be of any importance and Britain came under pressure to deal with them. The British had abolished their own negro slave trade in 1807 and pressed at the Congress of Vienna for other countries to follow suit. Humanitarian arguments were met, however, by the cold inquiry as to why the British were concerned only about *black* slavery? There were *white* slaves in North Africa and the British had so far been content to leave them there. If the British were more consistent on this issue their arguments would carry more weight. The result was that Lord Exmouth, Commander-in-Chief in the Mediterranean, was instructed to visit the Barbary States and arrange for the release of the slaves. This he did in the spring of 1816, acting merely as mediator for such countries as could pay the ransom that would be asked. He thus visited Algiers, Tunis and Tripoli, concluding some sort of an agreement with all of them. He then sailed for England, dropping anchor at Spithead on June 24th. His departure from Barbary was immediately followed by a massacre of Italian coral fishermen at Bona in Algeria. Since the other European powers were far from satisfied with the treaties made, the Cabinet decided to send Exmouth back with new instructions. He was told to teach the Dey of Algiers a lesson—chiefly to impress the European Powers now assembled at Aix-la-Chapelle. The bombardment of Algiers was thus decided upon in London and would have taken place in any event; even, in fact, if the Dey had been abject in his apologies. The operation was a dangerous one, for the guns in wooden ships would be matched against guns mounted in stone emplacements. Exmouth's advantage, however, lay in the fact that he had recently studied the fortifications in detail and thus knew the problem backwards. His fleet was formed, therefore, and equipped for a particular task, defined in advance. Exmouth knew from the start what he intended to do. The Dey, less fortunate, imagined for a time that he was (more or less) at peace.

At the time of Hornblower's appointment Lord Exmouth was already in Portsmouth and trying to man his ships. Hornblower reported to him there on July 2nd and was plunged at once into a frenzy of activity. All sorts of special equipment had to be shipped and Exmouth left Hornblower to issue the orders while he himself went back to London for a further conference with Lords Castlereagh, Sidmouth and Melville. There was much to do and not the least of his effort went in rejecting applications for employment. In only one respect did he make a questionable use of his influence and that was in appointing Mr Hornblower to a staff vacancy as signal lieutenant. It is to him that we owe a description, written for his father, of the scene of activity into which Captain Lord Hornblower was now so abruptly hurled.

Queen Charlotte,
Spithead, 6th July, 1816

My dear Sir,

I hope you are all well at home as I am. I write this from Lord Exmouth's flagship, he having shifted his flag from the *Boyne*, and am glad to tell you that I have been confirmed now as lieutenant in a staff vacancy. I reveal no secret in stating that we are destined for Algiers, so much you could have learnt from the newspapers, which are loud against our Admiral for merely arguing and not fighting with the Dey on the occasion of his last visit. Our cousin, Lord Hornblower, is appointed Captain of Fleet and it is to him that I owe my present posting. It is amazing how much there is to do before the fleet can sail, special attention being given to the guns, for gunnery is the old Admiral's hobby-horse and nothing is to be left to chance. New gun-sights are being fitted, new carronades are being tried and chain cables fitted instead of hemp. We are to ship a supply of Mr Congreve's rockets, to be used by the Marines, and there are extra supplies of ammunition to be used in target practice. Lord Hornblower is in his element, dashing backward and forward between the ships and the dockyard, quick to see any defect and as quick to know the remedy. He is as terse as ever in giving his orders but we all know exactly what has to be done and by whom and when. I shall need to work hard if I am to justify my promotion and this is what I intend. My friends in the service or those of them I have met ashore in Portsmouth are envious of me because I shall have fought in a battle and they may have no such chance before they retire. Do not worry about the danger for these Arabs know nothing about gunnery and will miss more often than they hit. Remember me to Penelope, Sarah and John. I am sad indeed to think that poor Rover is dead so soon after Grandfather. With my love to Mother and sisters,

I remain, dear Father,

Your affectionate son,

Jo. Hornblower

Lord Exmouth finally sailed on July 24th, coming into Gibraltar Bay on August 9th. Instead of finding Admiral Penrose there, he found five Dutch frigates and a corvette under the Baron Van de Capellan, who offered to co-operate and whose help was accepted. As from that point Exmouth's fleet comprised *Queen Charlotte* (100), *Impregnable* (98), *Superb* (74), *Minden* (74) and *Albion* (74), with *Leander* (50), four British frigates and six sloops, four bomb-vessels and five gunboats; to which force the Dutch warships could now be added. This force was sufficient for the tasks assigned: to frighten the Dey into submission, to destroy the Algerine Navy in its harbour and to silence most of the shore batteries. Exmouth sailed in to attack Algiers on August 27th and fire was opened at about 3.0 p.m. It was a tremendous bombardment, lasting until nightfall, the last gunfire not ending until after midnight. The Dey's fleet was burnt, his batteries mostly destroyed and his town riddled with shot and shell. The expenditure of ammunition was almost incredible (50,000 rounds in nine hours) and the casualties were proportionately heavier than in the Battle of Copenhagen. The Dey submitted next day, released all slaves, repaid all sums received in ransom and agreed never to enslave his prisoners again. It was, and beyond question, a notable victory.

Hornblower's place was at his Chief's elbow and he came under heavy fire during the battle. On only two occasions did he have an independent role, so far as is known. The first was when he took the flagship's launch to dislodge some snipers from the head of the breakwater. At other times he climbed to the mizzen top and reported to Exmouth what he could see from above the level of the smoke. His luck holding in one respect, he never received so much as a scratch, although there were men killed or wounded all round him. It was under his direction, in the second place, that the diversion was made which covered the withdrawal of the mishandled and battered *Impregnable*. Exmouth gave him full credit in his gazette letter but Hornblower's part in the battle gained him no further honour; probably because he had been too highly rewarded already. He had become K.C.B. when the Order was extended in 1815 and he received no further honour for years. Lord Exmouth, by contrast, became a Viscount, Milne a K.C.B., six of the captains received the C.B. and most of the first lieutenants were promoted Commander.

The fleet dropped anchor at Spithead on October 5th and Lord Exmouth struck his flag on the 8th, going ashore for the last time after forty years' service. Hornblower's reward, having no other, was to find Barbara to meet him at the Sally Port when he landed there on the 6th. There can be no doubt of the completeness of their reconciliation. He had written to her before he sailed, warning her of the battle that was to take place, and she had wondered whether he would live to tell her about it. Had he been killed she would have been left with the knowledge that she had given him little to live for. More than that, she would never have known whether he had not risked his life deliberately, as a far more famous sailor had done in 1805. Her relief at his return unhurt was wholehearted, as we know from the note she sent him on the 5th; a scrap of paper he afterwards carefully preserved:

The George Inn, October 5th.
Sweetheart,—You are safe and that is all that matters in the world. I am here with Richard and we have looked for your sails this week past ever since we heard the news. Each day since you have sailed I have blamed myself for the foolish pride which had kept us apart for so long. The fault was mine in the first place to have left you alone and then again I was at fault. If you had fallen I must have died of shame to think what little encouragement I had given you. My hope is now to ask your pardon and seek to make amends with love more ardent than any you have yet had from anyone. This I promise and will not fail, knowing now where we went wrong. When you land to-morrow you will

see us at the Sally Port and you will know that I am yours more than ever before—With dearest love, Barbara.

It might be allowable to guess that each of them had matured during their period of estrangement. Hornblower had learnt something from Marie and came back to Barbara with a greater knowledge of what he had to offer, as also of what he had come to need. As for Barbara, we are not to know the extent of her Viennese romance. It could have been the mildest flirtation but our guess—in a matter where all is guesswork—must be that her Hungarian Baron was not satisfied with kisses. While a platonic friendship might have been all that she intended, it would not have been very consistent with the Baron's reputation so far as it is known to us. Our surmise would be that she learnt more from von Neffzer than her husband learnt from Marie de Graçay and that the love affair between Horatio and Barbara was more successful after 1816 than it had ever been before. There must always have been something wrong, surely, in the relationship of a great lady and her socially naïve husband. As from this point they must have been more on a level, each more experienced and neither in a position to reproach the other. As from this time they would seem to have been more than ever in love.

It would be tempting to end this chapter with the sentence which concludes the nursery tale 'And they all lived happily ever after.' That would not, however, be true to the life we have to live. If our ordinary observation is any guide we must suppose that their marriage, like any other, had its ups and downs. Where it differed from the marriages we know was in their ages as compared with ours. The Duke of Wellington's age at Waterloo was forty-six and that battle marked the end of his active service. Horatio Hornblower, the Duke's brother-in-law, was aged forty at Algiers and, while he did go to sea once more, he was never again in battle. For each, therefore, their later career, in the role of elder statesman, was relatively longer than would be our own period of retirement. Having fought for twenty years, Hornblower was to be a dignified public figure for another forty. During all this later and less eventful period Barbara was the perfect wife, a woman who aged gracefully, who looked and behaved well on every occasion. To judge from her portraits, she was more strictly beautiful in 1848 than she had ever been before

1820. Commenting upon the fact that 'incompatibility' is said to be a ground for divorce in the United States, a great author once expressed surprise that all Americans are not divorced, for while he had known many happy marriages, he had never observed one which could be called compatible. In this sense Horatio and Barbara could never have been without reason to differ. As against that, they were clearly devoted to each other and the more so perhaps as they grew older. Fortunate in so many things, though not in all, Horatio Hornblower was especially fortunate in his marriage.

CHAPTER TEN

Rear-Admiral

In the years of peace which followed the Battle of Algiers the Royal Navy had little to offer a captain who had gained a peerage as Commodore. There were too many candidates for too few appointments and Hornblower would not be promoted until about 1820, depending upon the demise of those senior to him. What commands were available went, very properly, to officers of flag rank. Since the Navy List of 1816 showed no less than seventy-five rear-admirals, together with not a few captains posted before 1805, Hornblower could expect no immediate employment. He and Barbara went, therefore, to Ireland in 1817, where they found that Drumcliff Castle had now been made habitable. Of their stay there we know all too little but Barbara's letters to the Duke of Wellington refer to a sailing boat in which young Richard, aged six, was given his first lessons in seamanship. There are other references to a pony called Trooper and to a project called, mysteriously, 'the Citadel'. Further study has now established the fact that 'the Citadel' was a miniature earthwork designed by Horatio to teach Richard the basic principles of fortification. These had been studied by Horatio himself as a boy (see page 25) and he evidently believed that Richard's education should not be inferior to his own. The possibly unexpected result was that Richard decided upon a military rather than a naval career. It may be that the pony was the deciding factor, or else perhaps an early experience of seasickness. The choice was sensible in any case, for the nephew of a Field-Marshal (or, any-way, *that* Field-Marshal), would have a greater advantage in the Army than would Hornblower's son in the Navy. Some trace of 'the Citadel' remains to this day at Drumcliff, relic of a lesson which succeeded all too well.

The Hornblowers were in Ireland long enough to prove that they were not absentee landlords. It was a country, moreover, which they loved and for which they were determined to do what they could. On a small scale their estate became a model of its kind, with the tenants well housed and the land sheltered, where possible, by belts of trees. Horatio never took to hunting or shooting and was too impatient for fishing, but he was keen on planting trees, very much as Lord Collingwood had been. He had a keen eye, moreover, for broken fences or blocked gutters. As for Drumcliff Castle, it was never quite as impressive as its name, being no more than a small Regency house with a picturesque setting of battlements and towers. Its position was dramatic, however, with wide views over the estuary, and, in the opposite direction, the great waves could be heard crashing in from the Atlantic. Fond as he might be of Sligo, however, Hornblower toured the rest of Ireland and came to know something of its people and its problems. Beginning with some knowledge of the Irish Rebellion of 1796–99, his first instinct was probably to see the maintenance of law and order as the chief task of government. Responsibility for this had been placed directly on Britain by the Act of Union in 1800 and Hornblower, a member of the British Legislature, was no lover of treason. He soon came to realise, however, that the Irish question was more complex than one of merely keeping order. Its complexities became apparent to him when he attended the Meath Assizes in 1817. His role at Trim, the county town, was merely that of an interested spectator, accorded a seat in court by Mr Justice Daly. He was present, therefore, for the trial of Mr Roger O'Connor on a charge of highway robbery and we know that this case made a deep impression on him.

The events which led to this trial may be traced back to the year 1803 when Roger O'Connor took up residence at Dangan Castle,[1] near Trim, the home of the Wellesleys during the period before Arthur, the future Duke, was born. This O'Connor, nephew of Viscount Longueville, was the great friend of a certain Baronet and Member of Parliament, whose love affair with Lady O— was about to become the subject of a lawsuit in October, 1812. The letters which were the evidence in the case were to be sent by the Galway Mail to an eminent King's Counsel, a fact which became known to the Baronet. He accordingly persuaded O'Connor to waylay the coach and recover the documents. O'Con-

---

[1] Reputed birthplace of the Duke of Wellington, who was actually born in Merrion Street, Dublin.

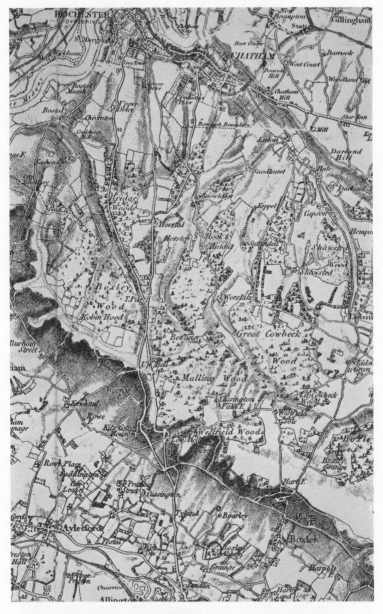

Map of Kent showing the relative positions of Boxley House and the Royal Naval Dockyard at Chatham

The *Comet* steamship as seen on the River Clyde, from a lithograph engraved by Schenk & Macfarlane published in 1846

nor assembled eight men for this purpose, ambushed the coach, killed the guard and removed the mailbags. For this service O'Connor was given an annuity of £300 a year, which was paid until his death in 1835. As it happened, however, the mails contained large sums in banknotes which were shared between O'Connor and his men. O'Connor's character for this and for other crimes was fairly notorious at the time but there was no case against him until Owens, one of the men who took part in the robbery (and who received £530 for his share) made confession in 1817 while under sentence of death on another charge. Owens' information was taken down in the presence of a police magistrate and a warrant was issued for O'Connor's arrest. He was duly arrested by a police officer, with the help of a troop of dragoons, and so was brought to trial. Hornblower was interested to the extent that Dangan Castle had belonged to Barbara's family and had been mostly destroyed by fire in 1809 after O'Connor had heavily insured it. He had no doubt of O'Connor's guilt and was only sorry that the prosecution had not added a further indictment for arson.

Unfortunately for the Counsel briefed by the Port Officer, O'Connor was a patriot as well as a criminal. He was known to have been a rebel in 1798, even to the point of fortifying Connerville against the King's troops. The result was that the jury, like the populace, were on his side. Sir Francis Burdett had come over from England for the trial but his influence was hardly needed. Without even allowing Mr Justice Daly to summarise the evidence, the jurymen brought in a verdict of 'Not guilty', which was greeted with loud applause by the crowd assembled in the street. O'Connor's acquittal was regarded as a political triumph, as indeed it was, and it foreshadowed the career of his son, Fergus O'Connor (1794–1855), who was to lead the more violent section of the Chartists. While feeling no sympathy for Roger O'Connor, Hornblower came to see that the Irish case could not be dismissed as mere sedition. He doubted, however, whether the Irish could ever succeed in gaining even a measure of emancipation and self-government. They would always fail, he thought, because of their inability to agree among themselves. There were always some of them ready to betray the rest, as Hornblower pointed out in a letter written to Richard, his brother-in-law, on 7th June, 1818:

'I have come to like the Irish and to respect them for many good qualities of head and heart and not least for their intelligence and courage. From the story of Mr O'Connor's trial and acquittal, plainly against the evidence, one might conclude that they are all in league against us. But the whole story of the late rebellion points to the opposite conclusion that they can seldom rely on each other. There was Francis Higgins, a friend of the great O'Kelly,[1] who is said to have accepted £1,000 and a pension of £300 a year for betraying Lord Edward Fitzgerald. There was the case of the Rev. William Jackson, who came to Ireland on some treasonable mission but was accompanied by a Mr Cockayne who had been in government pay from the beginning. There was Brennan, once editor of the *Evening Press*, who was on both sides, and there are a dozen others one could name all ready to betray their associates and friends. The United Irishmen were penetrated by government agents from the outset, one being Armstrong and another the very clerk who made out the list of men who were in the conspiracy. While informers are so easily recruited no future rebellion seems likely to succeed. It is widely believed among the Irish that the British Ministers secretly encouraged the rebellion in order to justify the Act of Union on which they had already decided. I know this story to be false but its currency is the proof of the influence which our agents are believed to possess among the disaffected. From careful inquiry I begin to understand the nature of the question, which is not to say that I have as yet any notion of the answer.'

This letter is an indication of the thought Hornblower gave to Ireland, which would justify the speeches on the subject he was later to make in the House of Lords. He became more lucid when his views began to crystallise and especially during the years in which Richard, the Marquess Wellesley, was in a position to influence British policy. It could never be said of Hornblower that he neglected to study his brief.

As on the occasion of their first visit to Ireland the Hornblowers travelled home by way of Belfast and the Clyde. It so happened that they reached Donegal during the first week in July, 1819, and were twenty miles from Londonderry on July 10th. They found themselves approaching a village which was

---

[1] This O'Kelly was the owner of the celebrated racehorse 'Eclipse'.

surrounded by troops and guarded by cannon. Nearby was an encampment full of men, and further off were gathered still larger numbers, all armed with sticks or cudgels. On inquiry, they discovered that it was the Orangemen who were encamped there in preparation for the great event of their year; the procession to commemorate the Battle of the Boyne on July 12th. The other crowd converging on this place were Roman Catholics, intent on spoiling the procession. The military, seemingly too few for the purpose, had been called in to keep the peace and seemed to have an unenviable task. Horatio had seen fighting enough in his day but was appalled to think that bloodshed might be caused by anything so trivial and that British soldiers might have to intervene, using grape-shot and fixed bayonets as a means of telling Pat and Tim to be friends again. Barbara took it all as a matter of course, not indeed as something she had experienced before but as something of which she had heard in the nursery. Why people should be so excited about something that happened in 1690 was a mystery to Horatio, who was mystified again when the expected riot failed to take place. There was much about the Irish he had still to understand.

On his second visit to the Clyde (August, 1819), Hornblower met the builder of the *Comet*, Mr John Wood,[1] who was already planning the *James Watt* steamship, to be launched in 1822 with engines made in Birmingham by Messrs Boulton & Watt. Mr Wood was to build thirty-three river steamships in all, besides sailing vessels, and it was he who later built the *Acadia* for Samuel Cunard. From Hornblower's correspondence at this time it is evident that the development in which he was really interested was that of the steam tug. First of the breed was actually named *Tug* and had been built in 1817 for the coasting trade but (proving unsuitable), had been used since for towing other vessels. This example had inspired William Denny & Co. to build the *Samson* of 53 tons at Dumbarton, powered with two engines of no less than 24 horse-power each. It would seem that Hornblower saw her nearing completion and realised how useful such a craft would be at (say) Portsmouth. He also realised and pointed out that a steam tug could have rendered invaluable service at the Battle of Algiers; as for example in rescuing the

[1] This was the younger Mr John Wood (1788–1860). The elder, his father, had died in 1811.

becalmed *Impregnable* from the dangerous position into which Milne had led her. It is interesting to observe that this point was actually proved by the French when they captured Algiers in 1830. Their fleet on that occasion included no less than seven steamships (one, the *Sphinx*, of 780 tons) and it was partly to these that the success of the operation was due.

The Hornblowers came back to Kent in 1819 and decided at about this time that Smallbridge Manor was not sufficiently impressive for a Peer of the United Kingdom. After looking at various other properties they finally bought Boxley House on the other side of Maidstone but without selling Smallbridge, which was eventually let furnished to General Crabtree, a veteran of the Peninsular War. There was some delay in gaining possession of Boxley House and Hornblower was not resident there himself until after his return from the West Indies in 1823. Boxley House still exists and may be found outside the village of Boxley which is two and a half miles from Maidstone. It is sheltered by the North Downs and is within easy reach of Chatham. The Manor of Boxley is mentioned in Domesday Book as belonging to Odo, Bishop of Bayeux. In 1189 it was given by Richard I to the Cistercian Order, who established an Abbey there which passed, at the Reformation to Sir Thomas Wiat, or Wyatt (1503?–1542), a Yorkshireman who had acquired Allington Castle in 1492. The Wyatts lost this estate when the younger Sir Thomas (1521?–1554) was executed for treason but recovered some of it during the reign of Elizabeth I. The Manor thus came to Sir Francis Wyatt, at one time Governor of Virginia. From him the Manor and Abbey passed to Lady Selyard but Edwin Wyatt, a lawyer, brought a successful lawsuit against her as a result of which he obtained part of the estate. This comprised the lands above the church and an old building which is said to have been tenanted by Thomas Vicary (died 1561) who was surgeon to Henry VIII. This building was called Boxley House, as distinct from Boxley Abbey, and remained in Edwin's possession until he died in 1714 (aged 85). It is clear that Edwin levelled all but a fragment of the older house and built the 17th Century parts of the buildings which remain. He was succeeded by Francis, who died without issue and left the estate to his brother, Richard, who again was childless. His heir, Lord Romney, was never resident but leased and later sold the property to a Mr Styles, who added the Georgian windows and modernised the interior before his death in 1818. It was then that the estate came on the market and was bought by Lord Hornblower, in whose family it was to remain until 1953. In that year the Sixth Viscount sold the property to Mr Marr-Johnson, a barrister and gentleman farmer, soon after whose death the house and its 20-acre park was acquired by the present owner, Mr T. J. Knowlden, who restored the building and turned it into the Boxley House Country Club, complete with swimming pool, tennis courts, lounge bar and restaurant. Apart from these modern improvements, the house is externally the building which Horatio Hornblower knew; a 17th Century house with Georgian additions. Although neglected for many years, the house and park are now in good hands, giving pleasure to the Club members and to other visitors as well. The day for large country houses would seem to have passed but Boxley House has found a new and contemporary role; nor is Hornblower forgotten by the present owners and their guests.

While in residence at Boxley House, Hornblower often took occasion to visit the Dockyard at Chatham. He was thus able to keep in touch with the Navy and indulge in arguments about the value (if any) of the steam engine as a means of propulsion at sea. His own attitude was progressive, as we have seen, but other senior officers were mainly concerned about vibration and the risk of fire. On one occasion, however, his argument with an admiral was about fencing. He had been taking lessons, at first merely for exercise, but had become interested in the mathematics of sword-play. Whereas naval tradition centres on the use of the cutlass, essentially a cutting weapon, the user of the small sword relies on the point. Hornblower argued that the superiority of the point was a mere question of applied geometry. The tip of the blade, he maintained, went to its target by the shortest route. After the dinner at which this discussion took place Hornblower walked back towards the Inn at which he was staying the night. His way led through some rather shabby streets near the dockyard entrance and there he was attacked by a footpad armed with a cudgel. Hornblower's only weapon was his walking stick but he proceeded to demonstrate the principle he had been defending. He lunged in classic style and the footpad took the point on his throat. He was quickly overpowered and could have been hanged for the offence. Hornblower decided otherwise, however, and asked the Captain of the Dockyard to enlist the man in the guardship. In telling the story afterwards Hornblower was always careful to emphasise the superiority of the point over the edge.

In February, 1821, Hornblower was at last promoted Rear-Admiral of the Blue Squadron. This could only happen through the death of those above him in the list. Once he had his flag, however, the Wellesley interest was quite sufficient to secure him a command at sea. He was appointed Commander-in-Chief in the West Indies and hoisted his flag in the *Phoebe* frigate at Plymouth on March 12th. This ship, with two other frigates, *Clorinda* and *Roebuck*, and fourteen smaller vessels, sloops and schooners, was to constitute the squadron. No very suitable flagship was included but his station, as Commander-in-Chief, was at Admiralty House, Kingston, Jamaica. It was originally planned for Barbara to join him there but she was reluctant either to bring Richard or desert him. She knew that yellow fever was endemic in the West Indies and she was anxious, besides, not to interrupt Richard's schooling. The result was that her coming to Jamaica was continually postponed, her visit finally taking place at the end of his three-year tour of duty. Some of Barbara's relatives may have concluded that the Hornblowers were on bad terms but the truth is that she was faced by the dilemma which has faced a thousand Englishwomen in each generation, the dilemma of whether to go with their husbands or to stay with their children. Barbara's case was peculiar to the extent that there was only one child and that she was not his mother. It is clear, nevertheless, from her correspondence that she was a devoted mother to Richard, especially after 1816, and genuinely at a loss to decide between the claims of her husband and her stepson. When he agreed to Richard's staying in England, Hornblower may well have been influenced by the fact that he had no other heir. Still childless in 1821, Barbara (aged forty) was likely to remain so. Hornblower had no such scruples, however, over taking his young cousin to the West Indies and the young Jonathan Hornblower was posted, therefore, as third lieutenant in the *Roebuck*. But Jonathan was not the heir to a peerage and an estate; all he inherited was the name.

As Hornblower soon discovered, the command in the West Indies was no sinecure. The Spanish South American territories were about to win their struggle for independence, with every variety of problem arising or likely to result. The slave trade, now illegal, was still in existence. All sorts of strange characters were engaged in everything from gun-running to piracy. Although there was no glory to be won there was no lack of opportunity for making mistakes or causing an international incident. The first problem to present itself centred upon an 800-ton vessel called the *Daring*, built as a privateer during the War of 1812, and chartered at New Orleans by Napoleon's General, Count Cambronne, who led the Old Guard at Waterloo. The General's ostensible purpose was to ship home five hundred of the Old Guard who had joined in a scheme to colonise a part of Texas, then part of Mexico. The colony had been a failure and it was reasonable the survivors should be given a passage to France. What worried the British Consul-General was the possibility that Cambronne had some other destination. He reported his doubts to Hornblower, who arrived in the schooner *Crab* on May 11th, 1821. Hornblower and Cambronne met that evening at dinner with the Consul-General but the French General made an excuse to leave early. When Hornblower left it was to find that the *Daring* had sailed in a hurry. Those set to watch her reported that her cargo, shipped at the last moment, had consisted of muskets and uniforms. She was to pick up her human cargo on the coast of Mexico and would then sail under the American flag for whatever port Cambronne might choose. Hornblower followed down the river in the *Crab* and guessed the *Daring*'s destination. Cambronne would head for St Helena in an attempt to rescue Napoleon, who would then try again to supplant the Bourbons in France. Acting on this wild guess, for it was nothing more, Hornblower told Harcourt, the *Crab*'s commanding officer, to sail the *Crab* to Tobago Channel, a point of interception for a ship on course from Mexico to St Helena. By good fortune the *Crab* was in the Tobago Channel ahead of the *Daring* and Hornblower was able to go on board, sure at last that his guess had been correct.

The interception had been cleverly brought about, the *Crab* being in fact much slower than the American ship. The problem was what to do next. Hornblower could not fire on the flag of the United States. He had no proof that Cambronne was planning an act of war or that he had five hundred armed men on board the vessel he had chartered. Even granted that Cambronne's purpose could be assumed, what could the *Crab* schooner do with her six-pounders against the dozen 12-pounders mounted in the *Daring*? What could her sixteen men do against five hundred? Taking a painful decision Hornblower informed Cambronne that Napoleon had died and that an official report to that effect had reached Port of Spain in Trinidad. He could have called there two days before but had not done so for lack of time. He told the lie convincingly, giving his word of honour, and knowing that he could not interfere in any other way. Cambronne believed him and told his American captain to steer for France. Hornblower then took the *Crab* into Port of Spain, where he received the news that Napoleon *had* died at St Helena on May 5th. This was evidently a great relief to the Admiral whose conscience had been tried over the deception to which he had been driven. He told his son in later years that this had been one of the most difficult decisions he had ever had to take.

Looking back on this incident one may feel that Hornblower may have made too much of it. The *Daring*, with Cambronne's five hundred men, could never have rescued Napoleon in any case. St Helena was regularly patrolled by men-of-war and no ordinary merchantman might even approach the island, let alone anchor in the roadstead. When the *Willwood*, an American ship in distress, called at Jamestown in 1816, she was boarded at once by a boat from H.M. Brig *Julia*. When she tried to move to a more sheltered area, the *Willwood* had accurate shots fired across her bows by the shore batteries.[1] Of the Navy's vigilance there can be no doubt at all. Once ashore, moreover (supposing that a landing proved possible), Cambronne's seasick veterans would have been faced by four battalions of infantry and a brigade of artillery. In the circumstances, one can imagine a confused affair in which Napoleon might well have perished. One cannot picture his being rescued by as small a force as Cambronne had available, and some doubt must remain as to whether the attempt would ever have been made. If Hornblower took it too seriously it may have been because he had heard of a similar plot in Ireland. The Lady O— on whose behalf Roger O'Connor robbed the Galway Mail (see page 208)—a clever and beautiful woman—was said to have planned Napoleon's escape with the assistance of Lady Holland. Whether true or false, this was a rumour that Hornblower had certainly heard and may well have believed.

[1] See *St. Helena*, Philip Gosse, London, 1938, pp. 272–4.

The more normal concern of the Commander-in-Chief, West Indies, was with the suppression of the slave trade. British ships were prevented from pursuing this business by the Act of 1807 and other countries were slowly and reluctantly following suit. In 1821 the Spanish government had signed a preliminary convention which allowed the British Navy to capture slavers at sea but not in Spanish territorial waters. When the complex negotiations ended, these ships would be liable to seizure in port by the Spanish authorities themselves. In the interim the slave traders were running cargoes in as quickly as they could, with prices rising as the day of prohibition approached. For slaves freed on the high seas men-of-war were paid five pounds a head in prize money; a useful bonus in peacetime when no other prize money could be earned. Hornblower deployed a part of his squadron with a view to intercepting this trade, hoisting his own flag in the frigate *Clorinda*, commanded by a rather dull officer, Sir Thomas Fell. The main slave market was at Havana but Spanish slavers coming from Africa would make their landfall at Puerto Rico, calling there for water and possibly to sell a few slaves. It was off Puerto Rico that *Clorinda* was accordingly stationed and it was there, on December 11th, 1822, that a topsail schooner was sighted. She was presently identified as the *Estrella del Sur* (or Southern Star), a slaver designed to load four hundred slaves on each passage. The *Estrella* easily escaped the pursuit of the *Clorinda*, a much slower ship, and reached San Juan, where she dropped anchor under the protection of the shore batteries. The *Clorinda* followed her in but could do nothing more and Hornblower took the opportunity of paying an official call on the Spanish Captain-General. He ascertained in advance that the *Estrella* would be sailing early next day for Havana. While ashore at a reception, Hornblower met Gomez, the captain of the slaver, and told him that *Clorinda* would leave on the same tide. As the slaver would clearly be far ahead before the limits of territorial waters were reached, the *Estrella*'s captain was perfectly happy about the situation, knowing that he could outsail this pursuer on any point of sailing.

While the reception took place a guard-boat circled the *Clorinda* and a sailmaker's gang was hard at work manufacturing a large canvas drogue or sleeve with a length of chain attached. Captain Sir Thomas Fell's order was to make such a device and then, after he and the Admiral were on board again, a boat's crew under a lieutenant's command would silently approach the *Estrella*'s stern where two swimmers would attach the drogue by its chain to one of her lower rudder pintles. The final touch was to attach a length of spun yarn to the tail of the drogue and lead it forward, keeping the drogue out of sight and relatively ineffective at the time when the slaver would get under way, the assumption being that the spun yarn would part after she had gathered speed, which would not be until she was well clear of the harbour. The drogue was duly attached under cover of darkness with no alarm given and the *Estrella* duly sailed at first light with the frigate about a mile astern. Both ships had the land breeze at first, which died away as the sun rose. Then they picked up the trade wind and the slaver increased her distance until, at midday, she was hull down. Then the time came for her to alter course and set her topsails and topgallant. A moment later she was taken aback with her foretopmast gone. So, of course, was her rudder but that, at the moment, was known only to her pursuers. Even after the *Estrella* had surrendered, with over three hundred slaves aboard, Gomez was never to know what trick had been played on him, nor was there any word of it in Fell's or in Hornblower's report. What was difficult for Hornblower was to give all the credit for the capture to the captain when the original idea was his own, suggested to Fell by Spendlove, the Admiral's secretary (at the Admiral's instigation) and then proposed to the Admiral by Fell himself, who had finally convinced himself that the plan was his own. Hornblower had already learnt, however, to give credit to those whose careers might depend upon it; he needed none while his command was in good order, with smuggling and piracy reduced to a minimum. It was at this time, incidentally, that a pirate sloop, *Blossom*, one of the last of these pests, was driven ashore at the mouth of the Sweet River, her captain killed and her now leaderless crew hunted but not caught by the troops which had been sent after them. Even if they survived, these last pirates were no longer in business. Order was being well maintained.

Hornblower was at Admiralty House, Jamaica, for the early months of 1822 and played his part in the social life of the island. It was while doing this, attending a ball given by Mr Hough, a leading planter, that an astonishing thing happened. He and his secretary, Mr Spendlove, were kidnapped in the garden by a gang of desperate men, who led them on mule-back to their lair, a cave halfway up a sheer cliff with a river at its foot, approached only by a rope ladder from the bottom. When morning came Hornblower found himself a prisoner in this inaccessible place, some miles from Kingston but within view of Montego Bay. He was plainly in the Cockpit Country, a wild area to which British rule had never been effectively extended. He then discovered that his captors were the crew of the *Blossom*, hunted men whose counter-stroke was to capture him and hold him to ransom. They at first ordered him to write a letter to the Governor and state that a free pardon for the whole gang was the price of his own life. No one of the pirates could read what he had written, however, and their leader, a man called Johnson, changed his mind and decided to release Hornblower and keep Spendlove as hostage—evidently believing that Hornblower was well placed to influence the Governor so as to save Spendlove's life. When Hornblower reached Government House he found the Governor, Sir Augustus Hooper, utterly opposed to any idea of pardoning the pirates. Next morning, however, Spendlove appeared in time for break-fast. He had escaped from the cave by jumping into the river—a sixty-foot drop in the dark—and had managed to reach Montego Bay, where he was provided with a horse to bring him back to Kingston. Hornblower was free now to deal with the pirates and the Governor agreed that the task should be left to the Navy.

Hornblower went straight to the dockyard and ordered two punts and a boat mortar to be sent on board *Clorinda*, with two hundred mortar shells and as many fuses. The frigate sailed before sunset and anchored at dawn in Montego Bay. A landing party went ashore with Spendlove as guide, the marines as advance guard and the punts, with mortar and ammunition, dragged by seamen. Each time the punts ran aground a tem-porary dam was built, allowing them to float over another stretch of the river. And so, with infinite labour, the landing party came near the pirates' lair that afternoon and halted just out of small-arms range. The mortar took up position and the gunner found the range of the cave, his shell bursts creeping nearer until two direct hits were scored. There were a few survivors to capture and these were hanged later, after trial. The little campaign was over and so was all piratical activity in Jamaican waters. This was just as well for Hornblower was nearing the end of his tour of duty. More than that, his successor had been named, Rear-Admiral Henry Ransome, C.B., who would be coming out in the autumn of 1823. It was Hornblower's pride to leave everything in good order and such was his success that he received from the merchants of Jamaica a valuable piece of plate, presented to him in recognition of his services in the protection of trade. A smaller piece of plate was presented at the same time to Mr Spendlove, who had certainly earned it.

The most interesting event of 1823 was the arrival in the West Indies of a brig called *Bride of Abydos*, flying the ensign of the Royal Yacht Squadron, and commanded by her owner, Mr Charles Ramsbottom, who brought letters of introduction from Lord Liverpool, Bishop Wilberforce and—still more significantly —from Lady Hornblower. It appeared that Mr Ramsbottom's father had made a large fortune in Yorkshire wool and army clothing contracts. Such was now the son's inherited wealth that he moved in the best society and had bought the *Bride of Abydos* from the Navy to use as his yacht. She was manned and armed very much as she had been in the service but with a great deal of added luxury for her fortunate owner. At first somewhat prejudiced against Mr Ramsbottom, Hornblower nevertheless asked him to dinner and was favourably impressed. Asked in his turn to dine on board the yacht, with the Governor among the guests, Hornblower enjoyed an excellent dinner at which the conversation turned upon the civil war in Venezuela. The Spanish were seeking to maintain their authority over a country in revolt. The coast they largely controlled but news had come that Maracribo had revolted and that Bolivar, the rebel leader, had now a better access to the sea. It transpired in conversation that their host's mother had been Venezuelan. He denied having any interest, however, in South American politics and said that his cruise would not take him to the mainland. His brig left Jamaica two days later and Hornblower took his squadron to sea for a fortnight of concentrated training.

When Hornblower returned to Kingston the Governor sent for him and asked his authority for blockading the coast of Venezuela. Hornblower replied briefly that he had not been within five hundred miles of it. Spanish and Dutch officers were produced who said that the blockade had been instituted by a

British man-of-war, the brig *Desperate*. As there was no such vessel in the Navy, Hornblower had no difficulty in concluding that Ramsbottom was the man responsible. He was then told that the *Desperate* had captured a Dutch ship, the *Helmond* laden with artillery for the Spanish army; two batteries of field artillery, now almost certainly delivered to Bolivar, whose forces were marching on Caracas. There and soon the whole fate of Venezuela was about to be decided. Hornblower decided to sail at once for La Guaira, the port for Caracas, and the *Clorinda* sailed next morning. At La Guaira Hornblower learnt that the crucial battle was likely to take place at Puerto Cabello and that the '*Desperate*' had gone in that direction. When he arrived there he could hear the sound of cannon ashore and there, at anchor, were the vessels he sought, the *Bride of Abydos* and the *Helmond*. The former was practically unmanned, for Ramsbottom—now described as Admiral—had taken all his men ashore. The Dutch captain and crew were in the *Helmond* and Hornblower told them they were free to go. The *Bride of Abydos* he seized and put a prize-crew aboard.

Going ashore at Puerto Cabello, Hornblower found that the battle was over. He presently identified the field artillery and with it was Ramsbottom, mortally wounded. He could do nothing for him, however, because two strange sail were sighted and he had to re-embark at once and tell Sir Thomas to clear for action. The strangers were two frigates, one Spanish and one Dutch, but Hornblower would not give up the captured brig to either of them. The legal position was almost unbelievably complicated, the problem centring not upon the eventual verdict but upon the nature of the court which might claim to have jurisdiction. Although competent as ever, Hornblower did nothing decisive one way or the other but merely kept out of trouble. As for Ramsbottom it can be said that his intervention on the side of Bolivar was probably vital and that the guns he landed were enough to tip the scales and turn defeat into victory. In this and in other struggles for independence in South America the sympathy of the British government was clearly on the side of the rebels. Hornblower was thought to have done well in turning a blind eye on the *Bride of Abydos*, and the more so in that Ramsbottom's intention had been known to some of his friends in London. We know in fact that Hornblower was innocent of any such duplicity and was genuinely surprised as well as pleased when the notification came of his being gazetted Knight Grand Cross of the Order of the Bath. Heaven knows that he had earned all the honours that came his way. On this occasion, however, it is arguable that his reward was due to a misunderstanding; the sort of thing that may still occasionally happen.

Lady Barbara finally arrived in the packet *Pretty Jane*, the same vessel that was to take them both back to England. They met on October 4th, 1823, after more than two and a half years of separation. Hornblower's successor was expected to arrive by the frigate *Triton* and that would be the moment when Horatio would cease to be Commander-in-Chief. In point of fact Barbara had only two weeks to enjoy the hospitality of Kingston before the *Triton* was sighted. Rear-Admiral Ransome was on board and the official ceremony was arranged for the following day, October 20th. On that morning, with the ship's company assembled, with the band playing and the captains of the other ships present, Hornblower's flag was hauled down to a salute of thirteen guns. A minute or so later as many guns saluted Ransome's flag as it was broken from the mizzen peak. Hornblower left the ship, no longer a Commander-in-Chief but merely a Rear-Admiral on half pay, a guest with his wife at Government House. For a few days there was little to do, then the news came that the *Pretty Jane* was ready to sail. Sail she did on October 26th with Hornblower and his wife as the only passengers. With some difficulty, owing to a headwind, the packet passed the Windward Channel and fairly entered the Atlantic. At that time it became apparent that they were in for a gale. It blew so hard on November 7th that Captain Knyvett decided to heave to. It was not a gale, it seemed, but a hurricane.

There was no reason to expect a hurricane at that time of year, two months before the proper season, but all indications pointed to the conclusion that they were faced by one. Were they right in its path or on its fringe? The wind soon gave them the answer as it rose beyond gale force. There was little anyone could do but Hornblower saw that the deckhouse which had been assigned to him and to Barbara was unlikely to stand for long the waves that were bursting over the ship. He brought Barbara away from it and tied her and himself to the mainmast. The deckhouse went overboard shortly afterwards but it seemed unlikely by then that the ship would last much longer. She was only afloat, it seemed, because her cargo was mostly of coir or coconut fibre, a buoyant substance which would prevent her sinking so long as her hull held together. But how long would that be? When the main-topmast staysail went and the deckhouse followed, the ship was no longer head to the wind and sea but broadside on and rolling heavily. To bring her head to the wind again the only possible means was to cut away the foremast. Hornblower tried to suggest this idea to Knyvett who was too stupified even to understand, and his men were in no better shape. Unable to find an axe, Hornblower took a knife from one of the crew and managed to reach the weather shrouds of the foremast. He sawed desperately at the first shroud, cutting a few of the fibres at a time. It finally parted and whirled out of sight and he began work on the next, now submerged by the waves and now able to breathe again. After he had severed all the shrouds within reach from the after end he found that the knife was losing its edge. The problem was solved for him, however, for the four remaining shrouds parted and the mast went over the side. The effect was immediate in two ways for the ship came round with her bows to the sea and the foremast, still attached by the lee shrouds, acted as a sea anchor to steady her as she made sternway. Hornblower made his way back to the mainmast where he tied himself next to Barbara and did all he could to keep her warm.

For a night they endured, feeling the wind die away to a gale and finally to a breeze but with the sea still violent. They suffered from thirst but rain fell towards morning and Hornblower managed to catch some water in his shirt, enough to save Barbara and himself. Revived by this and finding that Knyvett was dead, Hornblower took command of the waterlogged ship and what remained of the crew—nine of the sixteen who had sailed from Kingston. Another rainstorm brought them strength enough to tackle the problem of how to reach the Antilles, the nearest land to leeward. The only spar remaining was a spare jib-boom which was fished to the stump of the foremast. A sail was then impro-vised from the sacking in which the coir bales were wrapped; and later another sail was set on what remained of the mainmast. The ship was under way and Puerto Rico was sighted on the following day. Then they fell in with a fishing boat and Hornblower and Barbara went aboard her so as to fetch help from San Juan; a port where Hornblower was already known. There they were kindly received and Hornblower woke next morning for long enough to see the *Pretty Jane* creep into the harbour. They rested for days while new clothes were made for them and they were lucky that the Captain-General had apparently forgiven Hornblower for his capture of the *Estrella del Sur*. News had been sent meanwhile to Jamaica where it was arranged that the next man-of-war should sail for England by the Mona Passage and call at San Juan on the way. It was in February, 1824, that they sailed again and the voyage on this occasion was mercifully uneventful. The sloop *Seahorse* made a good passage and came into Portsmouth on April 9th. The Hornblowers went at once to Smallbridge and were soon busy with the move to Boxley House which took place in June. Hornblower was to be at sea again and even in action, but not as Commander-in-Chief. It was the deaths of those senior to him raised him to the rank of Vice-Admiral in 1825. He had many years still to live and his seniority brought him eventually to the highest rank of all.

We have seen in earlier chapters that Horatio and Barbara had been sometimes estranged by personalities and events. There had been misunderstandings, quarrels, and some infidelity on either side. There is no hint of this after 1824 and we are probably right to think that they were united as never before by the dangers they had undergone in the *Pretty Jane*. Here was an experience which they had faced together, each fearing most that the other would be lost and each coming to know what the other had to offer in terms of fortitude, courage and hope. Before this time Horatio had been jealous to the extent of wondering whether Barbara had loved her first husband more than she would ever love her second. He never felt that sort of jealousy again, seemingly because Barbara had told him—when they were both apparently on the point of death—that she had never loved any other man. In the same way Barbara had wondered, inevitably, whether Horatio had loved Marie more deeply than he now loved his wife. She never had that feeling again, not after that dreadful danger they had shared and would never forget. That she owed her life to him was only perhaps a minor factor. What mattered was that they had been tested together and passed the test, not merely in the face of danger but afterwards in fatigue and pain when neither uttered a word of complaint. In terms of mountainous

The Castaway. Oil painting which belonged to Hornblower in youth, now in the author's possession

The Battle of Navarino, from the coloured lithograph by G. P. Reinagle

seas and shrieking wind they had been through hell and back. They never doubted each other again.

Richard was now aged thirteen and went to Eton that autumn, still intent on a military career. Jonathan Hornblower remained in the Navy and was stationed at this time at Chatham. He was a frequent visitor at Boxley House and was as welcome as if he had been an adopted son. In point of fact his parents were both very much alive but they still had their home in the industrial midlands and were disappointed that Jonathan was not an engineer. He lived, as we shall see, to become a very technically-minded officer but the days of the engineering branch in the Navy were still to come. As for Lord and Lady Hornblower they came to London for the season of 1825 and it was then that Horatio made his maiden speech in the House of Lords. He seems to have avoided strictly naval topics, knowing that he might have a command again, and preferred instead to speak on the subject of steam navigation between Belfast and the Clyde. He was no orator but he showed a familiarity with the problems both of Ireland and of steam. He received congratulations afterwards, from Lord Sidmouth among others, and the suggestion was made to him that he might some day hold ministerial office. In point of fact there was nothing less likely. He was a seaman and he could have been an engineer. He was a sound administrator and he was becoming a good landowner. Nothing, one may suspect, would ever have turned him into a politician. As against that, he had rivals who did not scruple to say that he was married to one.

CHAPTER ELEVEN

Admiral

In the history books the brilliant career of Richard Wellesley reached its climax in his appointment as Governor-General of India in 1797. He was finally recalled from India in 1805, by which time he had become the Marquis Wellesley. He was Ambassador to Spain, then Foreign Secretary (1809–12) and was even asked by the Prince Regent to form a government, which however he failed to do. As from that point there was anticlimax and his next and almost his last public appointment was as Lord-Lieutenant of Ireland in 1821–28. After a last and brief appearance as Lord Chamberlain (a very minor office) he withdrew from public life in 1835. As from 1812 he was not merely out of the Cabinet but eclipsed in every way by his younger brother, Duke of Wellington from 1814. As Lord-Lieutenant of Ireland Richard was less important than he had been twenty years before and the post itself had lost something of its significance since the Act of Union. He took his work seriously, nevertheless, and tried to solve the different problems with which he was faced, famine being one (in 1822) and sedition being another. He saw little of Hornblower until 1826, the year in which the Admiral returned to Ireland. On this occasion the Hornblowers spent more time in Dublin, as might have been expected, and Horatio had the chance, no doubt, to express his views on Ireland. When he spoke on that subject in the House of Lords he would be thought to be expressing the views of the Lord-Lieutenant, as indeed he probably was. Their views, moreover, were similar, especially on the need to remove unsuitable magistrates.

Of more definite importance was Hornblower's contribution to the development of steam navigation. He had made himself familiar with the early experiments on the Clyde and he had watched the later efforts which centred upon the triangle of sea between the Clyde, Belfast and Dublin. It was in these relatively sheltered waters that the early steamships made their uncertain voyages, gradually extending their field of enterprise to Liverpool, to Holyhead, to Bristol and so to London. Only short voyages were possible and those only where there was coal at either end. Among the most enterprising of the pioneer companies was the Dublin and London Steam Packet Co., which was already in existence when Hornblower came to Dublin in 1826. The directors quickly invited him to join the Board, probably to give the Company an added air of respectability. After some hesitation and after consultation with both Dublin Castle and the Board of Admiralty, Hornblower accepted the offer. But if the directors had merely wanted his name on their notepaper they must have been grievously disillusioned. He showed from the beginning a close interest in the Company's affairs and quickly made himself an expert in steam navigation. At this period the Company's ships went back and forth between London, Plymouth, Falmouth, Dublin and Belfast. Pride of their fleet, to be launched in 1829, was the *William Fawcett* of 206 tons, powered by engines of sixty horse-power. She was rigged as a topsail schooner with a gaff topsail on the mainmast and a square topsail and topgallant on the foremast. Between the two masts rose a tall smokestack and on either beam were the paddle wheels. She had been built by Caleb Smith and engined by Fawcett & Preston of Liverpool, being employed at first as a ferry-boat on the Mersey. Bought by the Dublin Company, she was chartered by Willcox and Anderson whose ships provided a service to Spain and Portugal. It was through this connection that Hornblower came also to join the Board of Willcox & Anderson, a firm which gained the mail contract to Oporto and Lisbon. They took the name of the Peninsular Company in 1837, which became the Peninsular and Oriental Steam Navigation Company in 1840, with Hornblower still a member of the Board. His directorship of the P. & O. became more important to him in later life. His more immediate interest was in the technical side and in the economic progress of Ireland.

Technically, the argument centred upon the future, if any, of the paddle wheel. The early engineers were basically millwrights, whose ideas developed from the windmill and watermill. The paddle wheel steamship was no more than a waterwheel in reverse, the wheel driving the water instead of the water driving the wheel. The paddle wheel was a fairly efficient device for river work, found unsuitable at the outset for use in canals (where the disturbance damaged the banks) and adopted with some caution by vessels designed for anything that could be called a sea voyage. An effect of the paddle wheel was to provide the ship with a 'bridge', a catwalk between the two paddle-boxes. This was esssential because the officer of the watch could now see nothing from his old position near the helmsman. That problem was easy to solve. More difficult was the problem created by the ship's heeling and rolling. With sails set and a wind on the beam the one paddle wheel would be buried deep while the other would be revolving in the air. With the ship rolling, on the other hand, in any sort of sea, the motion would bury and raise the two paddle wheels alternately, setting up a severe strain on the engine. The opposite principle of the propeller or screw was as well known as the principle which governed the paddle wheel, being no more than an adaptation of the windmill in reverse with water instead of air. This idea encountered the objection, however, that an underwater propeller must involve making a hole in the ship's hull below the waterline, much against the shipbuilder's instinct and quite contrary to every dictate of common sense. When the Lords of the Admiralty looked dubiously on the early steamships they had some reason on their side. After all, the paddle wheels which might be useful in harbour and in peacetime would be horribly vulnerable in battle.

As compared with other naval officers, Horatio Hornblower had this advantage that he came of a family of engineers. He was never one of the fanatics for seamanship who looked upon a steam engine afloat as a sort of sacrilege. It was admittedly the tug that he advocated at first, as an auxiliary to the sailing ship, but he went on from there to see a future for the steamship proper, more especially for passengers and mail. And while he dismissed the paddle wheel as useless in a man-of-war he could never see that this was the only way in which steam power could be applied. While no one would claim for him that he invented the screw, he was one of those who instantly saw in it the answer to the marine engineer's central problem. Among the *Hornblower Papers*, Vol. II[1] there are frequent references to experiments and discussions and not a few diagrams and calculations made by Hornblower himself, some of them surprisingly in advance of his time. From a still earlier period (see page 91)

[1] Navy Record Society Volume for 1948, edited by Nathaniel Parker.

he was convinced that naval artillery would eventually fire shell as well as shot. Nor would he dismiss the Congreve rocket merely because it had been useless at the Battle of Algiers. He was rather convinced that it had great possibilities, depending only upon some means of improving its accuracy, and here again events were to prove him right. There were many unimaginative and obstructive officers in Hornblower's generation but he was clearly not one of them.

An advantage which Hornblower had over many flag officers of the day was in being relatively young. He was thus aged forty-nine when he became Vice-Admiral in 1825 and well able to appreciate the merits of the steam engine. He had the further good fortune to reach old age and with it the highest naval rank. As against that, he was junior in 1825 to officers of great distinction who would be active for years to come. He was junior, for example, to Sir Edward Codrington, who was appointed Commander-in-Chief, Mediterranean, in 1827. Sir Edward, born in 1770, had entered the Navy in 1783 and was Commander when Hornblower was a midshipman, Rear-Admiral in 1814 when Hornblower was only a Captain, Vice-Admiral in 1821 when Hornblower at last achieved his flag. As Codrington was a veteran of the Battle of Trafalgar—one who had been an officer, for that matter, at the Glorious First of June—he and others of his generation were entitled to high command in 1827. Hornblower's turn would come in about 1840, a period so remote that several of his contemporaries, losing patience, took service with the newly independent countries of South America. This was easier, perhaps, for men of high birth whose social position was secure, or again for bachelors whose social position was non-existent. It was a temptation, anyway, which Hornblower had to resist and the result was that he had no sort of command in 1827, not even in Bolivia, and had to use all his influence even to secure employment for his young cousin. In this, however, he succeeded and Jonathan Hornblower was appointed third lieutenant in the *Genoa* (74) under Captain Bathurst. There was no promotion involved but the Mediterranean offered the best chance of active service. This was because the Greeks had risen in revolt against their Turkish rulers. Gaining a measure of success from 1820, the Greeks were finally confronted with the combined fleets of Turkey and Egypt. They suffered several reverses and Athens fell again to the Turks in 1827. For a number of different reasons the Turkish advance was unwelcome to Britain, Russia and France. Squadrons provided by these three countries assembled in the Aegean on the basis of a treaty signed 'for the pacification of Greece'. The aim of the Ottoman fleet was to follow up the capture of Athens by a re-conquest of the Morea, for which purpose the Ottoman fleet was off the Greek coast. Sir Edward Codrington hoisted his flag in February 1827 and eventually reached agreement with Ibrahim Pasha on September 25th, providing an armistice between the Greek and Turkish forces. In accordance with this agreement the Ottoman fleet was allowed to enter the port of Navarino. The Turks then landed, breaking the agreement, and proceeded to the Greek town, driving the inhabitants into the mountains, where they starved. On October 18th the three European Admirals decided to interfere, entering the harbour of Navarino for that purpose. On the 20th they did so, all three squadrons under the command of Sir Edward Codrington. The Battle of Navarino was the result.

Among the British of this period there was a sharp divergence of opinion about Greece. It was no part of British policy to weaken Turkey, for it was the Turks who opposed the entry of Russia into the Mediterranean. As against that, many people had a lively sympathy for the Greeks, some because they had undergone a classical education, others because the Greeks were fellow-Christians subject to the oppressive rule of Islam. If, there was an agreed policy it would be one of gaining freedom for the Greeks without extending Russian influence in the Balkans. Hornblower's contemporary, Admiral Cochrane, was the theoretical commander of a Greek Navy that included some steamships armed for war, practically the first of their kind, but he could collect no seamen able and willing to fight. As for Codrington, he had been ordered to intercept all supplies intended for use against the Greeks while adopting a policy of conciliation towards the Turks. These impossible orders were amplified, no doubt, by verbal instructions which would not appear in the record, the legend being that H.R.H. the Duke of Clarence advised him to 'Go in, my dear Ned, and smash those bloody Turks.' Codrington's decision, like that of Lord Exmouth at Algiers, was to create a situation in which the relatively undisciplined Turks would open fire. This would enable the Allies to fire in self-defence, bringing on a general action. The freedom of Greece was to be a by-product of an incident for which Britain could afterwards apologise.

The allied fleet which entered Navarino comprised three squadrons. The first, under Sir Edward Codrington, was led by his flagship, the *Asia* (84), followed by the *Genoa* (74) and the *Albion* (74), these three sail of the line being supported by four frigates and four brig sloops. The second, under the French Rear-Admiral de Rigny, was led by his flagship, *Sirene* (60), followed by *Scipion* (74), *Trident* (74) and *Breslaw* (74), supported by one frigate and two schooners. The third, under the Russian Rear-Admiral Count de Heiden, was led by his flagship *Azov* (74), followed by *Gargoute* (74), *Ezekiel* (74) and *Alexander Nevsky* (74), and supported by four frigates. There was thus an effective total of eleven sail of the line and nine frigates, the Russian contingent being actually the strongest. The combined Turkish and Egyptian fleet comprised three sail of the line, four two-decked frigates, thirteen ordinary frigates, thirty corvettes, twenty-eight brigs and over forty transports for the army, making a total, with small craft, of a hundred and thirty vessels. Strong as they might be in total numbers, the Turko-Egyptians had only three sail of the line against eleven and these were the only ships that counted in battle. The Turks lacked nothing in courage but were relatively ill-trained and without operational experience. It was one of the Egyptian ships which fired first, the French flagship replied and then the engagement became general. The battle continued for about four hours, at the end of which time the enemy fleet was very largely destroyed.

The Battle of Navarino might be called the swan song of the old sailing ship Navy. Its interest, however, from the biographical point of view, must centre upon Lieutenant Jonathan Hornblower. Unable himself to be present, Hornblower was well represented there by his young cousin, whose letter written after the battle gives a good impression of the part he played:

> *Genoa*
> Port of Navarin
> October 21st, 1827

My dear Lord,
    Yesterday there was a general engagement between the allied

squadron and the Ottoman Navy and you will I know be glad to hear that I sustained only a scratch and a bruise and am little the worse after four hours under heavy fire. Our Admiral led in the *Asia* and was well supported by the *Genoa* and *Albion*. I commanded the upper deck battery and cannot sufficiently admire the coolness and intrepidity of the seamen who fired just as steadily as in a practice with no foe to return their fire. I had always believed that much would depend in battle on the care with which the guns were laid but there was little or no wind and the smoke after the first broadside was so thick that we could see nothing of our opponents. I tried the experiment of ceasing fire in the hope that the smoke would clear but it did not answer and we continued to fire in the same direction as when we began. The position of the enemy was known only from viewing his masthead from ours. We were at anchor and used springs on our cable to bring the broadside to bear on new opponents after the first were silenced. In all our battle against the French we read of ships striking their colours in token of surrender. Perhaps in part because of the shore being adjacent, this the Turks never did. They fought very bravely while they could and when beaten they fairly set fire to their ships and took to the boats, cheating us of any prize-money. Our Admiral's report lists no ships taken but enumerates the ships that were destroyed, being driven ashore, wrecked and burnt. The Turkish loss in men must amount to many thousand and their fleet is no longer a fleet at all. What is sad indeed to report is the loss on our side which included our own Captain Bathurst, than which no better officer could be found, and several other of my messmates, making twenty-six killed in all and thirty-three wounded. What saved us from heavier loss was the fact that few of the Turkish shot pierced our ship's side. Our losses were mostly on the quarterdeck and forecastle and were caused many of them by falling wreckage and flying splinters of wood.

I feel fortunate in having escaped injury and am more fortunate still in having been present for the battle. So long is it since the war ended against Napoleon that there are already officers in the service, some even commanding ships, who have never been under fire. All the senior captains and some of the lieutenants have been in action, though not all in battle, and have the more authority over youngsters who entered the navy after 1815.

Others, less fortunate, have less idea of active service than many of the lower deck men, for only a few were in Burma and of those that were a proportion did nothing but wait around, eat curry, and curse the mosquitoes. I was actually under fire more than once in the late war, was at Algiers and now again in the Battle I am trying to describe. So if there should be twenty years of peace I shall count as a veteran and will persuade myself that I deserve promotion. I am not many years junior to our First, who will be made Commander for a certainty and am not five years younger than one of the Commanders who will as certainly be made post.

My belief is that the next battle whenever it occurs, will not be fought under sail alone. The story goes in this fleet and I believe it to be true that Admiral Cochrane originally planned to equip the Greek Navy with six steamships armed each with four 68-pounder cannon, enough, he said, to destroy the whole Turkish Navy. Your old friend Lord Exmouth is said to have observed that such a force could destroy any other Navy, ours included. Only one such vessel in these waters has actually appeared in these waters, the *Karteria* and she recently used her 68-pounders—with red hot shot—and her 45-pound mortars— against Turkish ships in the Gulf of Corinth. Cochrane could accomplish little because his Greek sailors are cowardly, un-disciplined and untrained, but the fact remains that this one ship, if properly manned, could probably destroy any ship we have. In a dead calm more especially a steamship like the *Karteria* could choose her own range and silence the *Asia*, our flagship, with guns just three times as powerful as anything we possess, afterwards closing to finish her off with mortar fire. I remember being told that you once tried something of the sort a lifetime since[1] and with a measure of success. This makes me the more concerned to think that the Greek Navy, of all absurdities, should be in some respects, superior to ours. I do trust that you may have the opportunity to make this fact known to their Lordships. It is unfortunate, perhaps, that the mere mention of Lord Coch-rane's name is enough to turn them against any scheme, however judicious, with which he has been even remotely connected.

We sail presently for Malta[2] where our wounded can be landed and our rigging repaired and I shall not be sorry to have leave ashore when the opportunity offers. In the meanwhile you will be

[1] See page 91.   [2] October 25th.

glad to know that the British seamen of to-day is as intrepid as any who fought against Napoleon and not inferior to those who fought in the last war under your own command.

I am yours sincerely,

Jonathan Hornblower

It is the extraordinary fact, which the young Hornblower perceived, that there was already in 1827, a steam warship afloat which made every other ship obsolete. The *Karteria* had the means to revolutionise naval warfare; mechanical propulsion, guns of heavy calibre, to contrast with the 32-pounders which were then the largest guns mounted in ships-of-the-line, and weapons capable of firing a bomb instead of a solid shot. Lord Hornblower saw the logic behind these developments and there is reason to believe that he discussed the subject with Lord Exmouth. The weakness of the *Karteria*, as they must have agreed, lay in the vulnerable position of the paddle wheels and indeed of the engine. After a single well-aimed shot a paddle steamship might be going round in a tight circle—unless indeed her boiler were to blow up. The future of the steamship, considered as a man-of-war, must depend, they saw, on applying steam-power in some different way. No one could deny the usefulness in war of a seagoing tug—so much was obvious—but some further step was needed to perfect the warship of the future. Basic to their thinking was the fact upon which young Hornblower commented, that the oak hull of a ship like the *Genoa* was her crew's best protection, and that her means of propulsion needed to have at least the same protection if she was to close with the enemy in battle. It was easier to state the problem than to solve it.

The young Hornblower remained with the Mediterranean Fleet in 1828 and it was only by correspondence that he could convey the ideas he had formed on the basis of his recent experience. His letters went not merely to Lord Hornblower but also, of course, to his father. Jeremiah Hornblower was still active as an engineer and there can be no doubt that he took the question up with his contemporaries in the vicinity of Birmingham. There were men there who knew a great deal about steam engines but they were less familiar with ships. No promising new idea came from that direction but Horatio, paying another visit to Ireland in 1828, broke his return journey at Belfast and there met with a retired sea captain called John Hogan. It was Hogan who first explained to Hornblower the principle of the Archimedian screw. It was Hornblower who first explained to Hogan that the paddle wheel, acceptable for river navigation in peacetime, was not really suitable for propelling a warship. This exchange of ideas proved fruitful in the end but led to no immediate solution of the problem. Returning to Kent that autumn, moreover, Hornblower's thoughts were led in another direction. He was asked whether he would accept the Governorship of Malta in 1829.[1] This post had been associated with the Navy from the time of the island's capture from the French. Hornblower already knew the island and was known there. He therefore accepted the appointment without much hesitation, he and Barbara landing at Valletta on March 12th, 1829. He must at the same time have accepted the fact that he was no longer being considered for a sea-going command. He resigned his directorship of the P. & O. Company at this time but was reappointed in 1836.

Hornblower's arrival at Valletta was during the aftermath of the Battle of Navarino. The British government, pursuing its ambiguous policy, had recalled Sir Edward Codrington in a despatch dated June 4th, 1828. Lord Aberdeen's excuse was that the Admiral had gone beyond his instructions. In his reply, dated from the *Asia* off Corfu on June 22nd, Sir Edward welcomed the appointment of another officer 'more competent to understand the language' of the instructions he might receive.[2] With still greater irony he hoped that his successor 'will be better informed by your Lordship previous to his leaving England than it has fallen to my lot to be'. The fact was, of course, that the policy pursued was to destroy the Turkish Fleet and then apologise afterwards. The apology took the form of recalling the Admiral, who was thus made a sacrifice at the very moment he was arranging for the Turks to evacuate the Morea. His successor, Sir Pulteney Malcolm, hoisted his flag and relieved Sir Edward on 21st August. Codrington, back in London that autumn, was greeted in the street by a country gentleman who took no interest

---

[1] This offer was made at a time when the Duke of Wellington was Prime Minister (1828–30).

[2] *Memoir of the Life of Admiral Sir Edward Codrington.* Ed. by Lady Bouchier, 2nd ed. London, 1875.

in anything but agriculture and sport. He greeted Sir Edward with the words, 'How are you, Codrington? I haven't met you for some time. Have you had any good shooting lately?' The Admiral admitted that he *had* and went on his way, reflecting on his countrymen's ingratitude. There can be no doubt that Hornblower was considered as a possible successor to Codrington and that the governorship of Malta was given him as a consolation prize. There can be as little doubt that the command in the Mediterranean, had he been offered it, was one which could have brought him more vexation than credit. It is true that Codrington was later given a short spell in command of the Channel Fleet, but the fact remains that he had been discarded as an act of policy and cheated of any reward for his distinguished service. Other admirals, and Hornblower among them, may well have thought that half-pay was preferable. More fortunate than many, Hornblower was given a shore appointment at least suitable for his rank. His only stipulation was that he should have his young cousin as his naval aide-de-camp. This was agreed and Jonathan was already at Valletta when the guns saluted his own arrival there.

In the present century some governorships carry little more than ceremonial duties. The governorship of Malta in 1829–31 was a more active post than that, for the Mediterranean was anything but tranquil. Eastwards there was the situation created by the Battle of Navarino, the Turks falling back on Alexandria and the Greeks bewildered by a new sense of freedom. Westward, the Barbary States were indulging (like the Greeks) in piracy, enjoying what was to be their last fling before the French invasion. There would have been no real co-operation between Hornblower and Admiral Malcolm—for they seem to have disliked each other at sight—but there was much to do for the defence of the island and for the protection at sea of its inhabitants. Apart from that, Hornblower was delighted with his reception there and liked both Malta and the Maltese. Barbara, moreover, was in her element as the Governor's wife, more beautiful than she had ever been and active in her social and charitable duties. Once again, our best account comes from young Jonathan, who was evidently pleased with his appointment:

Grand Master's Palace
Valletta, Malta
March 17th, 1829.

My dear Sir,

I trust you will have received my last letter in which I told you that our cousin Horatio had asked for my services here as Aide-de-Camp, and that I had hastened to accept the appointment and say goodbye to the *Genoa*. I was not sorry to quit her when the time came because various promotions and postings had put me in the way of being First Lieutenant, which post was finally denied me. As the man chosen had seen no active service and was as much a seaman as my Aunt Rebecca, I was heartily glad to be off and the more so in that the experience I am now gaining might help towards gaining me an appointment as Flag Lieutenant which is always a step towards promotion. I was here a few days before his Lordship's arrival in the *Neptune* and was able to meet him on the quayside and tell him in a whisper who all the notabilities were who had come to meet him. It was hard work to memorise what I had found out about them but the General's A.D.C. came to my rescue the day before. Lord Hornblower looked and behaved splendidly and I could have fallen in love with Lady Hornblower had such a plan been consistent with the duties I have to perform! I remembered from my first service in the Navy that our cousin has no ear for music. I told him, therefore, when the National Anthem was being played as also the general salute. I have to be careful, though, for he hates the idea of being managed or protected in any way and will obstinately do the wrong thing just to spite anyone who seems too officious. All went well, however, on the day of his arrival and there was a particularly moving scene when some Maltese were presented to him whose release he had arranged from slavery.[1] He bids fair to be popular here and will certainly be so if he can suppress piracy in this part of the Mediterranean.

As for Malta, I only wish that my powers of description were equal to describing what there is to describe! Imagine an island which centres upon one of the finest harbours in the world with deep blue water in a number of adjacent inlets. On all the cliffs and headlands around there rise great ramparts in honey-coloured stone, pierced for many hundred cannon; Fort St Elmo,

[1] This was in 1806. See page 117 et seq.

Fort St Angelo and many more. Behind the ramparts there is not one city but a number of them, Valletta being the chief, crowned with its citadel, and entered by a fine gateway from Floriana, another city, which centres upon the finest street I have ever seen. As for Valletta, it is a city of palaces, all of them bearing the stamp of the Knights of Malta. In all the fortifications and buildings of this island I find the same character, the impression left by pitiless men of tremendous resolution whose aims were to be achieved without regard to the labour, the pain, the time or the cost. They meant to have it as they had planned it and nothing would be suffered to stand in their way. While each Grand Master left some trace of his determination the total effect is that left by the Order itself. Our cousin, Lord Hornblower, takes the place of the Grand Master in so far as anyone can in this our present age, and I can think of few officers who would be as little out of place.

I have written at such length about Malta that I have left myself no time or space in which to inquire about our several relatives and friends. I shall make amends in my next but must now content myself by assuring you that I am most fortunate in my present appointment and will be sorry indeed when it comes to an end in 1831.

> With kind remembrance to all our friends, I am
> Your affectionate son
> Jo. Hornblower

To follow Lord Hornblower through all the multifarious duties which fell to him as Governor and Commander-in-Chief of Malta would be to write a whole volume on that alone. The only alternative is to pursue some one line of interest, chosen from many as possibly the most significant. The theme to choose, if one has to be chosen, is clearly that of steam propulsion as applied to men-of-war, for this was the subject to which Hornblower's mind continually returned. On the first occasion when he could fairly take a holiday, he thus went to inspect the *Karteria*, lying useless and unmanned at Volos. While finding her of the greatest interest and learning a great deal from the way her big guns were mounted, he saw that she was too vulnerable. Granted that she might be used (and had been used) with surprise effect, he doubted whether any civilised opponent would be caught a second time with the same device. Back in the Malta dockyard he ordered some experiments to be made with the Archimedian screw. A small boat was used for this purpose, the carpenters fitting her with two false keeps between which a sort of cork-screw was to revolve. The difficulty was to transmit power to the screw without admitting water into the boat. The final solution was to enclose the cork-screw in an iron tube to which it was welded and drive by means of a chain connecting two gear wheels, one fixed to the after end of the tube and the other worked manually over the boat's stern. There were no engineering works in Malta and this simple machinery had to be made by a blacksmith, who made a copy in iron of a model constructed in cardboard and wood. First experiments proved that a boat *could* be propelled in this way, though at no greater speed than it could have been rowed with oars. At a second attempt the boat was given an inboard vertical shaft in which the chain could work, thus eliminating the need to work over the boat's stern. The third step was to do the same thing on a bigger scale, using a small coasting vessel and placing the machinery below the top deck. With six men at a sort of windlass, the vessel, re-named the *Archimedes*, could make up to three knots in calm waters; but only of course for an hour or two, until the men tired. It only remained to replace the men by a steam engine but none was readily available and the Maltese had, in any case, seen a use for the vessel as she was. They were still troubled by the Barbary pirates and it seemed to them that a vessel moving mysterious under her own power might be used with considerable effect. The *Archimedes* was armed, therefore, with a single 32-pounder gun in the bows, well concealed, and put to sea as a novel sort of decoy.

Was the *Archimedes* a success? We know all too little about her. The trouble is that she was never commissioned in the Navy and had, in fact, no official existence. Hornblower wisely said nothing about her and we only know of her existence from papers left by Jonathan, who probably commanded the *Archimedes* on her first cruise. Young Richard, now at Trinity, Cambridge, came to Malta for a holiday during the summer of 1830. And he too went to sea in *Archimedes* on at least one occasion. By then, however, the day of the corsairs was practically over. The French captured Algiers on July 4th, 1830, and while Tunis remained independent, the Tunisian pirates were in a less aggressive mood. The interest of the *Archimedes* lies not in her effectiveness as a decoy ship, but in her means of propulsion. Hornblower and his friends had virtually invented the modern warship. It is true that there was no need for a cork-screw as long as the vessel's keel. A shorter length, a propeller in fact, was all that was required. As against that, it is arguable that the *Archimedes* had one useful feature which later steamships were to lack. By building the screw into a tube which itself revolved, Hornblower had ensured that the whole thrust was made directly aft. The appearance of a ship's wake where the disturbance of the water fans out sideways would seem, at first sight, the indication of wasted effort. In at least this one respect Hornblower would seem to have been ahead of his time.

Hornblower's period of office ended in 1831 and he went directly to another appointment, which was to be his last. He might have expected to hoist his flag at Portsmouth or Plymouth but his preference was for the less important post of Commander-in-Chief at Chatham. He wanted this for no better reason than its proximity to his home in Kent. If he were in Chatham Dockyard during the week he could be at Boxley, if he chose, for the week-end. He succeeded to the Chatham command in 1832 and retired from that and from active service in 1835. This was a period of drastic, if belated, reform in the administration of the Navy. Sir James Graham was the First Lord responsible for this and the reorganisation extended of course to the dockyards. Hornblower carried out the orders he received, but there is no evidence that he took much personal interest in Sir James's great work. Nor, unfortunately, were the great reformers, like Sir John Barrow, as keen on the technical progress in which Hornblower specialised. Experiments apart, however, Hornblower was now able to devote more personal attention to his family.

His first care at this time was to remove Richard from Cambridge, where he had been wasting his time, and secure for him a commission in the Lifeguards. There were some regrets about Richard's choice of a career but no military door could be closed against a nephew by marriage of the Duke of Wellington. He was to be promoted, in fact, with indecent speed and at considerable expense. Although resembling his father in some ways—in expression, in colour and height—Richard lacked the same driving ambition and had no special gift for mathematics or

Singapore in 1851, from the painting by J. Turnbull Thomson

The Harbour at Balaclava, from the print by William Simpson, as published in a book entitled THE SEAT OF WAR (1885)

mechanical invention. He was to prove himself a brave man and a useful and popular officer, but he had no ability which would justify his promotion beyond the rank of Colonel. He rode to hounds regularly, incurred some gambling debts and probably kept a mistress in Maida Vale or Kilburn. He could not marry, of course, until after he had reached the rank of Captain.

So far as the Navy was concerned, Horatio's successor was Jonathan, who at this time became First Lieutenant of the *Dartmouth* frigate (42), attached to the Channel Fleet. There was never any doubt of his ability but his was, from this point, a relatively dull period of naval history. The interest of the next twenty years was to centre more upon technical development than upon sensational events. He saw no further active service until he was on the point of retirement but was a model naval officer throughout the intervening period. Both his parents were dead by 1834, from which date he was resident, when ashore, at Boxley House. He did not marry until after he was promoted Commander in 1837, but his engagement—to Gertrude, the eldest daughter of Rear-Admiral Hugh Fitzmorris—was announced in 1834. During the period of this long betrothal he acquired, improved, decorated and furnished a small country house at Aylesford, not far from Boxley. It was called Aylesford Lodge and it still exists as the home and surgery of a medical practitioner. When ashore, the Commander was an active magistrate, a keen sportsman and a director at one time of the South Eastern Railway Company. He and his wife, Gertrude, had seven children in all, five of them survived and two of his sons entered the Navy. Of his three daughters, one, the youngest, married Captain Barton of the Royal Marines. It was a family in which the naval tradition was strong for the rest of the century.

While at Chatham, Hornblower was visited by John Hogan of Belfast, and they went more deeply into the problems of screw propulsion. Another model was built in the dockyard and this time with a steam engine. They were not alone, however, in pursuing this line of experiment and it would be difficult to prove that any one man invented a device on which so many had worked. In the words of an eminent maritime historian 'experiments to discover the means of applying the screw as a motive power to ships were at different periods spontaneously and independently made in various places by inquiring minds, who frequently were perfect strangers to each other. . .'[1] Mr Robert Wilson thus demonstrated in 1833 a screw which he had invented in 1827. Almost simultaneous was the work of the Frenchman, Fréderic Sauvage, whose screw was perfected in 1832. John Ericsson of Sweden produced a working model in 1836, and so did Mr Thomas Pettit Smith. Hogan's model, therefore (of 1835) was merely one of a series and intended by Hornblower to convince their Lordships of the Admiralty that the screw-driven steamship was the warship of the future. The Navy had included one steam tug since the year 1819 but Hornblower's demonstration at Chatham, though successful in driving a boat at ten knots, was insufficient to convert their Lordships. There was to be no screw-driven warship until the *Rattler* was launched in 1843.

When Horatio Hornblower finally hauled down his flag at Chatham on October 27th, 1835, handing over to Vice-Admiral Sir Henry Digby, K.C.B., he had been in the service for forty-one years. Aged sixty, he had given of his best since he first embarked in 1794, rising from midshipman to Vice-Admiral. He was far from worn out, however, and he was quickly re-elected to an honorary membership of the Board of the Peninsular Steam Navigation Company. He was to take an active interest in this enterprise for years to come, retaining his directorship until 1850. It was a subject for regret among some of his contemporaries that Lord Hornblower never joined the Board of Admiralty. It was thought by some that the Navy's technical progress would have been faster with a man of his type appointed, if only to battle against conservatism. While there is something in this argument, we have to remember that he might also have broken his heart and achieved nothing. One of the most important reforms of the time was the establishment in 1832 of H.M. Ship *Excellent* as the naval gunnery school. A great work was done there by Sir Thomas Hastings, but Hornblower did no more than express approval. He did not count as a gunnery specialist, and the steamship, in which he did specialise, made slower progress in the Navy than in the merchant service. It was as well, therefore, that he gave his time and energies to the P. & O. Company, as it would soon become, and had one last adventure in their service.

[1] *A History of Merchant Shipping*, W. S. Lindsay. In 4 vols. London, 1876. See Vol. IV, pp. 102–18.

It was his regret, on retirement, that he had never been posted to the East Indies. When the chance came, he made good this gap in his experience and could claim afterwards that he was, in every sense, a man of the world. He was urged at this time to write his memoirs but he rejected the idea with impatience. The most he would undertake to do was to arrange his official papers in some sort of order. This was as much as he would promise and more (far more) than he ever performed.

Hornblower spent the summer of 1836 in Ireland, making up for his long absence in Malta and Chatham, but was back in England the following year. It was in 1837 that King William IV died, to be succeeded by Queen Victoria. Whether as Duke of Clarence or as King, William had always been a keen supporter of the Navy in which he himself had served. He was, it was said, 'a just and upright King, a forgiving enemy, a sincere friend, and a most gracious and indulgent master'. All this was true and he had spoken kindly to Hornblower on a number of occasions, notably at the funeral of Admiral Sir Richard Keats in 1834. Admiral Lord Saumarez was to have been one of the pall-bearers but was unable to be present, his place being taken, at short notice, by Hornblower. He was thanked by the King at the next levée and some mention was made of his good service at the Battle of Algiers. Most flag officers had similar memories of King William and some, like Keats, had been shipmates with him. The King's death marked the end of an era for all whose services had begun in the War of American Independence. The period which had ended was also that of the Regency, an age of loose morals and riotous behaviour. William's known mistress had been the actress, Dorothea Jordan—who was also mistress at other times to Richard Daly and Sir Richard Ford. Like George III's other sons, William had enjoyed life to the full, more especially before his marriage in 1818. Of the Regency roisterers he had certainly been one.

With the accession of Queen Victoria the court atmosphere changed abruptly, much to the regret of her older courtiers. The new reign was to be more staid and sober, more earnest and more bent on improvement. Into this new pattern Hornblower fitted rather well. Granted that there were wild episodes in his past, he was not—except in his agnosticism—an 18th Century character. His habits were almost ascetic, his reading austere, his outlook progressive and his private life, latterly, beyond reproach. The Wellesleys, incidentally, were far from raffish and Richard while in India 'openly patronised religion' and 'paid a strict regard to divine worship on the Sunday'. Many families were Victorian before the great Queen's reign began and the Hornblowers might be said in this way to have been ahead of the age. The previous reign had begun while Hornblower had been in Malta, so that the Coronation of 1838 was his first. He no longer held office but he was entitled, as a peer, to his place in the Abbey. It was a day which Barbara after described to younger people as an experience she would never forget. More significant, in fact, was the part played by Captain the Hon Richard Hornblower. It was his squadron of Lifeguards which formed the Sovereign's Escort and he was afterwards thanked for his services by the Queen herself. When the great day came to an end he made the occasion still more memorable by announcing his engagement to the Lady Harriet Mountstuart, elder daughter of the seventh Earl of Glenshiel. She was an outstandingly beautiful girl aged twenty-two and the match was approved by both families. She had no great fortune, having no less than four brothers, and Richard's lack of ancestry was saved by the fact of his being an only son and well-connected. Their marriage would seem to have been successful in every way and their children were to number four in all; Maria (1839), Augusta (1840), Horatio (1842), and Alice (1845). Their home was at first in London but Lord Hornblower vacated Boxley House in 1847, saying that the children should be brought up there even if Richard's duties kept him mostly at court. He and his wife then took up residence again at Smallbridge Manor, the tenant's lease of which had expired. He explained at the time that this arrangement—the opposite of what Richard and Harriet expected—was due to the completion in 1844 of the South Eastern Railway Company's branch line from Paddock Wood to Maidstone. The track almost skirted the Smallbridge Manor park and there was every likelihood (he said) of the children's ponies being frightened by the noise of a locomotive, with possibly fatal results to Horatio, the sole heir to the title. The argument must have seemed unanswerable but the truth was that the Admiral really preferred Smallbridge. As for the horses and cows, they were accustomed to the trains after a week or two and scarcely bothered to look at them. If anyone took any notice of the railway it might have been the Admiral himself and he—though he would never admit it—was a train enthusiast. He was only annoyed when the expected train was *late*.

CHAPTER TWELVE

Admiral of the Fleet

The Peninsular Steam Navigation Company gained its mail contract in the year of Queen Victoria's accession. Their ships sailed on a regular schedule from London, calling at Falmouth before going on to Oporto, Lisbon, Cadiz and Gibraltar. From Gibraltar the mails were carried by H.M. Post Office Packets to Malta, Corfu and Alexandria. Letters for India might be entrusted to Mr Waghorn, who forwarded them via Suez to Bombay. Gibraltar however, was the furthest place served by the Peninsular Company itself. It was the directors' ambition to extend their service to Alexandria and Hornblower was among those who advocated doing this. He and his friends on the Board worked hard at this project and their efforts were crowned by the decision in 1840 to form a new Company to be called the Peninsular and Oriental Steam Navigation Company. A Royal Charter was obtained, moreover, which authorised the Company to operate a service between Egypt and India. The new chairman was Sir John Larpent and he had now to organise what was virtually a new trade route to the East, superseding the route via the Cape that had been in use since the 16th Century. The P. & O. service began officially in 1841 but the *Hindustan*, first ship to operate between India and Egypt, did not sail until 1842. Other ships followed and the Cape route, at least for passengers, began to go out of fashion.

The P. & O. directors had to look ahead and did so, realising from the outset that the logical sequel to their new venture, the overland route to India, was an extension of the route to the Far East. A demand for this was inevitable and the directors had to decide in advance whether they were ready to provide it. Steamships operating to Alexandria and Suez had an immense advantage in distance over ships which had to round the Cape. To the Straits of Sunda the alternative routes were not as unequal and the merit of the 'overland' passage would depend very largely on the cargoes that might be available locally as between India and

China. There was a further problem about security, for the Straits of Malacca and the China Seas were frequented by pirates, both Malay and Chinese, and there had been a local conflict with the Malays as recently as 1831. There was a market for Malayan tin in China but it was a question whether the supply could be relied upon. Singapore had been founded as recently as 1819 and seemed to be flourishing, but there had once been as great hopes of Penang, hopes which were mostly disappointed; and who was to know whether Singapore would not fail in the same way? There was said to be trouble there with the Chinese Secret Societies. It was a question, incidentally, whether there would be a wharf on which cargo could be landed or warehouse space in which goods could be stored. It was decided, therefore, to send a director out to make inquiries. Hornblower promptly offered to go and his offer, after some hesitation, was accepted. He was not the ideal man to send, for his knowledge of commerce was small. As against that, he was not the sort of envoy that the local authorities could ignore. He was also quite sufficiently expert in all problems of navigation and defence. What probably clinched the matter was the fact that the managing directors—Mr Willcox, Mr Anderson and Mr Carleton—were all frantically busy in London. They were planning new ships, raising capital, appointing agents and trying to build up coal supplies at all the ports their ships would frequent. At moments of crisis Mr Anderson had visited Egypt and argued with the Pasha and Mr Waghorn, but a visit to the Far East was another matter. The result was that Hornblower and his wife took passage to Singapore in the corvette *Diana* (of 18 guns and 740 tons) as guests of Captain Ashworth. Sailing in December, 1841, the *Diana* reached Simon's Bay on March 11th, 1842, sighted Java Head on April 20th and sailed into Singapore on May 4th. Preparations were being made there for the expedition to China which would involve the capture of the Woosung forts and *Diana* sailed again on May 8th. The Hornblowers went ashore, however, and were hospitably received by Governor Bonham. They were presently lent a house, however, and set up an establishment of their own.

First problem to study was Britain's relations with China. The conflict in which the *Diana* was to take part has been termed the Opium War because its basic cause was the Chinese action in making the opium trade illegal. The war was of brief duration and the Treaty of Nanking, which marked the end of hostilities, provided for the cession of Hong Kong to Britain. This was an important acquisition from the point of view of international trade, for Hong Kong had been a pirate lair and was now to become a naval base. Piracy continued, nevertheless, with advantage perhaps to the larger steamships which were least likely to be attacked. Hornblower paid a visit to the new colony in the winter of 1842-3, partly to assess its commercial possibilities and partly to enjoy a change of climate. The steamship he was in was actually attacked by pirates and he saw for the first time how such assailants could be discouraged by a hosepipe connected with the ship's boiler. The jet of steam wiped them off the deck in a matter of seconds, leaving the other pirates in a mood of alarm and despondency. Hornblower reported that Hong Kong was highly suitable for the Company's purposes and that piracy, while it made vigilance necessary, was only a minor hindrance to trade. He collected some facts about the goods, apart from opium, which might be exported to China, laying special emphasis on the products of south-east Asia.

Back in Singapore, and reunited with Barbara, Hornblower met with Captain Henry Keppel of H.M. Sloop *Dido*, at whose table he was placed next to Mr James Brooke, who had only recently made himself the ruler of Sarawak, a territory in Borneo. From Brooke it was easy to learn about Malay piracy, a separate problem in the waters of south-east Asia, as also about Keppel's plans for dealing with it. Whether Hornblower was actually in the *Dido* when the attack was made on the pirates (June, 1843) there is at present no means of knowing. He certainly visited Sarawak on one occasion for he referred to it in later life. He was also friendly with Brooke and discussed with him the possibility of finding coal in Brunei or Labuzu. To find a coal supply would make a big difference to the cost of re-fuelling ships on the way to Hong Kong, as also to the cost of supplying Hong Kong itself. There was no immediate solution to that problem but Hornblower collected a great deal of information about trade among the islands. While he wrote his reports, Barbara enjoyed the life of Singapore. At the end of 1843 they went for a holiday at Penang, took ship from there to Calcutta and were just in time to catch the *Hindustan* and make the homeward voyage in her to Suez. From there they went to Alexandria, where they embarked in the *Iberia* and sailed for Malta and Britain with Thackeray, the novelist, as a fellow passenger and a worthy opponent at whist. They reached London again in April, 1844, having neatly dodged the English winter.

It was largely on Hornblower's advice that the Company extended its service to Hong Kong in 1845. The steamship *Lady Mary Wood* inaugurated the route when she reached Singapore from the Red Sea on 4th August carrying mail which had left London forty-one days before. A second ship, *Braganza*, came into service soon afterwards and the *Canton* (of 400 tons) extended the route to Canton and became the first of a series of ships similarly named. The route to Australia was not opened until 1852 and Hornblower had no more to do with it than any other director. His special responsibility was for the extension of the service to Singapore and Hong Kong and he clearly did much to prepare the way for it. His visits to Singapore, Hong Kong and Penang were, from his point of view, however, a reward in themselves and an experience he would have been sorry to miss. He was sixty-eight when he returned to England and he never went to sea again. Although he remained a director of the P. & O., his active career was finished. The Board of the P. & O. had only one way of recognising their debt to him and they paid it when they launched and named the *Hornblower* in 1849, an iron ship of nearly 2,000 tons and the first screw-driven ship of the P. & O. fleet. She was built on the Thames but engined by Napiers of Glasgow and was a popular ship for many years, being finally sold to the government as a troopship in 1855.

When Hornblower returned to England, it was to find himself a full Admiral, having been promoted to that rank in 1843. Officers senior to him were mostly dead and he had reached that age at which even his contemporaries were no longer numerous. Richard was now a Major and Harriet the proud mother of a male heir named after the Admiral himself. For a season or two Hornblower continued to appear in London and was addressed by the Queen on several occasions. He was promoted to Admiral of the Fleet in 1847 and attended a levée for what was to prove the last time. By that year the Hornblowers were tired of London. They handed over their town house to Richard, who had more need of it, and retired to Smallbridge. There they remained except for periodic visits to Boxley House. On these occasions,

Barbara would lecture Harriet (as grandmothers will) on the upbringing of children and Harriet would smilingly agree before doing exactly what she thought best. By modern standards they neither of them knew anything about it for children of those days were brought up by nurses and displayed in the drawing-room for about half-an-hour each afternoon; provided, that is, that the parents were there at all. The Hornblowers never visited Aylesford Lodge, by contrast, but Jonathan and Gertrude were summoned periodically to Smallbridge. Jonathan was a Captain by this time but had no command until 1849. The annual pilgrimage to Smallbridge had also to be made by the Admiral at Chatham and by the Captain of the Dockyard. Other visitors were infrequent and Hornblower was content that it should be so.

That visitors were few made an event of 1848 all the more dramatic. It was a year of crisis in Europe, one grim event following another, and Hornblower's only consolation was that the situation called for no action on his part. 'Let them look out that has the watch!' he would say, adding that it was his watch below. So it was, and the collapse of the French monarchy in February was but one incident in the confused scene, a problem for Lord Palmerston but just a column in *The Times* for Lord Hornblower. The riots in Paris were reflected, moreover, in Rome, Vienna and Berlin, suggesting that revolution might be infectious. There was even the threat of a Chartist riot in London arranged for April 10th which was easily dealt with, however, by the Duke's strategy and the British climate. The troops were never called into action, least of all the 1st Lifeguards, now commanded by Lt-Col Hornblower and kept very properly in reserve. The steady downpour which discouraged the Chartists fell also, impartially, on Prince Louis Bonaparte, the Emperor Napoleon's nephew, who had appeared in the improbable role of a special constable. He had been in Paris but the Provisional Government of M. de Lamartine had asked him to leave, with the result that he was now resident in King Street, St James's. He was soon to be joined in exile by Prince Metternich of Austria, who came to stay at the Brunswick Hotel in Hanover Square. The situation in Europe was fluid and it seemed to Louis Bonaparte that his chance might come at any time. It could fall to him to save France from anarchy. His chance came with the announcement

The storming of the Great Redan, from a contemporary print published by Dickenson Brothers

The fall of Sebastopol, from a print made after the painting by William Simpson, published by Day & Son in 1857

that France was to elect a President of the Republic. Without losing a minute Louis Bonaparte set off for France.

The autumn of 1848 was unusually wet and Hornblower (aged seventy-two) was glad to stay mostly indoors. When he had occasion, however, to visit Maidstone, he found that the River Medway had risen so as to cover the road at several points between Bow Bridge, Teston and Barming. His coachman had, therefore, to abandon his usual route, covering a distance of five and a half miles, and take the longer way via Wateringbury and Ditton, which was eight miles if it was an inch. That autumn and winter Maidstone was for all practical purposes, eight miles away. Hornblower could admittedly have gone into Maidstone by rail, for the branch line from Paddock Wood had been constructed four years before. He would then, however, have lacked his coach at the other end, which would have been inconvenient as well as undignified. Apart from that, the heavy rains were apt to cause landslides in the various cuttings, blocking the line for hours. Hornblower used his coach, therefore, but went into Maidstone as rarely as possible. He liked to appear at Quarter Sessions though and occasionally on market day if there was a horse or cow to be bought. Lady Hornblower went into town rather more often, mostly in connection with some charity or other but sometimes in order to attend an auction. They were always back home before dark and the coachman was never wanted after that, not even when there was a full moon. There were gentlemen who would come home late after a race meeting or a gambling session but old Lord Hornblower was not one of them.

It was on a wet evening in 1848, that the unexpected visitor arrived. The Hornblowers had dined in comfort and Horatio was enjoying his glass of port while his wife had gone to read in the drawing-room, where coffee would presently be brought to them both. We may picture the contrast between the warmth of the dining room and the discomfort of the weather outside, for the rain was beating on the window panes and the wind was loud in the treetops. It was as rough an evening as anyone could wish to avoid, being windy, cold and wet. The doorbell rang, the footman answered it and Hornblower's former coxswain and present butler presently reported that there was a lunatic at the door. Asked what form the lunacy took, the invaluable Brown replied that the visitor had given his name as Napoleon Bonaparte.

What then was the object of the call? Mr Bonaparte wished to borrow a carriage and horses so as to catch the packet boat from Dover to Calais. Thoroughly mystified, Hornblower told Brown to show the visitor in. The man who now entered the room was

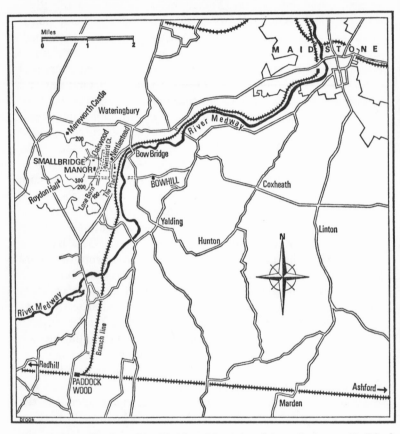

Map of Kent showing Smallbridge Manor and its relation to Paddock Wood and Maidstone

aged about forty, dressed in civilian clothes under a rain-soaked cape and spattered with mud from his boots to his knees. He had no resemblance to the late Emperor, wearing in fact a heavy moustache and a tuft of beard. Although clearly a foreigner, he was fluent in English and quickly explained the disaster that had befallen him. He had been travelling by rail from London to

Dover with a view to reaching Paris as quickly as possible. As a result of the recent downpour the railway embankment had given way at one point, burying the rails under hundreds of tons of earth. It might take days to clear the line—and there was not even an hour to spare! What the strange visitor wanted was a carriage to take him to Maidstone, beyond the point where the line was blocked. From there he could catch another train to Dover, and so board the steam packet for Calais which would connect again with the train for Paris. The whole future of France depended, he said, upon his arrival in time for the election.

At this point both Hornblower and Brown were convinced that they had to do with a lunatic, but each for a different reason. Hornblower had not been following the events in France with more than a passing interest. He saw it as a country in which society had been torn up by the roots, never to recover. Napoleon had been dead for a quarter of a century and more, and was without a living heir. That a lunatic should call himself Bonaparte was not improbable and that he should see himself as the saviour of France was a more or less logical corollary to his central delusion. It was merely a question of how to get rid of him! Brown was more immediately interested in the visitor's account of where he was travelling and why. The collapse of the embankment had blocked the branch line, it seemed, at a point near Nettlestead, bringing a train to a standstill—all this Brown had heard from another source and could readily believe, for it had happened before. But the train for Maidstone was not, in any case, a means of reaching Dover. The railway ended at Maidstone and there was no line from there by which anyone could travel farther in any direction. One was under discussion, maybe, but that was neither here nor there.[1] The right policy for a traveller bound for Dover was to head back for Paddock Wood and the South Eastern Railway Company's main line. Unless that were his final destination, only a lunatic would be wanting to reach Maidstone at all. If the man was insane, Brown was all for telling him to walk.

At this point Lady Hornblower intervened, returning to the dining room to see who the visitor was. The lunatic—as Horatio took him to be—kissed Barbara's hand and paid her a few compliments, with the result that she urged Hornblower to order the

[1] The line between Maidstone and Rochester was not constructed, in fact, until 1856, nor was the system completed until 1874.

carriage. He did so and the footman returned in ten minutes to say that the carriage was at the door. Taking his leave and protesting his gratitude, the visitor left the room but not the house. He was intercepted in the hall and asked why he wanted to reach Maidstone. It was only then that the problem of his movements was finally solved. He had been travelling on the main line, it transpired, from London to Dover via Redhill and Tonbridge. As a foreigner he was none too clear about the directions he had been given and believed, vaguely, that Maidstone was a station at which he would have to change trains. When the train stopped at Paddock Wood a porter there called the name of the station and added 'Dover train, Dover train, all change for Maidstone.' Still further confused, the foreign traveller had left the train with his valet and boarded the train which stood at the other platform. This was the small local train for Maidstone, which set off northwards at its normally unambitious speed. It pottered on in the failing light for about four and a half miles, passing East Peckham and Hale Street, Nettlestead Green and Smallbridge Manor. Then the driver found the line blocked at Nettlestead. While he was still contemplating the scene a further, if smaller, landslide prevented his return to Paddock Wood. Only half understanding the situation, the poor foreigner tramped off in the rain and headed for the only light he could see, which was a window in Nettlestead Rectory. From there a puzzled servant directed him to Smallbridge Manor as the nearest house where a carriage was kept. Once all this had been explained, Brown and the coachman decided between them that the coach should take the Frenchman back to Paddock Wood, where there would be another train in about an hour. This plan was carried out without reference to Lord Hornblower, who believed to his dying day that his strange visitor had been taken to Maidstone. The later train should not, by rights, have connected with the steam packet but on this night the vessel was delayed and the foreigner reached his own country without loss of time.

The odd sequel to this strange incident was the discovery that the traveller *was* in fact Napoleon's nephew. He was a candidate for the office of President and was duly elected to that office in December. He became Emperor as Napoleon III in 1852. In the meanwhile he was genuinely grateful to the old Admiral who had helped him on his way. Almost his first act as President was to confer on Hornblower the insignia of a Chevalier of the Legion of Honour, with a sapphire as a present for Barbara. He did more than that, however, asking Queen Victoria to confer some further honour on a man he described as his particular friend. Wanting at that moment to conciliate the new French government, Lord John Russell agreed (rather reluctantly) to make Hornblower a Viscount. There was some opposition to this, however, and the new honour was not announced until 1850. He then became Viscount Hornblower of Smallbridge, his son assuming the courtesy title of Lord Maidstone of Boxley. This last honour, the result of a fortunate accident, was not due to the Wellesley influence. He had owed much to that in the past, his peerage included, but the family was no longer so influential. Richard Wellesley, who had long since retired from politics, had died in 1842 and the Duke was last in the cabinet in 1841–46. He was an old man now and Viscount Hornblower, as we must now call him, went over to Walmer to pay him a brief visit in 1851. He and Barbara chose to go by rail and were scolded by the Duke for taking such a risk. It was not the same thing, he admitted, as Barbara travelling by herself—*that*, he trusted, was out of the question—but it was a risk they should never run if it were avoidable. He told them the story of how poor Mr Huskisson was killed by a railway locomotive twenty years before. He had never liked the railway since and always tried to discourage ladies from travelling in so dangerous a fashion. He asked after Richard, remembering his duty as Commander-in-Chief. The trouble was, he said, that none of these young men had been in action. He went on to ask Hornblower whether he had ever fought a duel and was told that he had. The Duke disapproved of duelling, especially in the army, but had to admit that his own example told against him. He had fought Lord Winchelsea back in 1829, and could still remember that morning at Battersea. . . . The two old men had a long talk but the Duke was somewhat deaf, compelling the others to shout. The visit came to an end and Lord and Lady Hornblower set off again (by rail) for Smallbridge via Paddock Wood.

They never visited Walmer again for the Duke of Wellington died in 1852. Hornblower was inevitably present at the funeral and described it afterwards for the benefit of Jonathan who was at sea, commanding a frigate in the Mediterranean:

Bond Street
November, 1852.

My dear Jonathan,

You will have heard by now that the Duke of Wellington is dead and you will have guessed that I would be at his funeral, from which indeed I am just returned. I attended as a relative rather than as Admiral of the Fleet and am rather exhausted after a long day which began, at least, with heavy rainfall. My good lady stayed at home, being rather unwell, and I was glad of it, for the fatigue of the day would have greatly hindered her recovery. All London was there just as if the death had been in the royal family and Richard looked the part very well at the head of his Regiment. He said to me just now, after his return from barracks, that the work that had fallen to him was more than any civilian could ever comprehend. Throughout the days of planning the man they missed was the Duke himself, who knew best of anybody how to regulate a State occasion like this. Nothing of the sort had been staged for a lifetime without his concurrence and advice and this made it the more difficult for others to decide on the points of procedure which had always been submitted to him. I then told Richard what he evidently did not know, that I was myself responsible, in part, for the funeral of Lord Nelson, and knew pretty well what had to be done.

Our loss in losing the Duke is past anyone's ability who never spoke with him. It would please me as an old seaman if I could say that the greatest man of my time had been an Admiral but this would not be true. Lord Nelson I met only on the one occasion but I have known many who served with him and I cannot doubt that he was a great tactician and a born leader of men—not outstanding as a seaman nor even nearly the equal in that line of Pellew or Keats, but an officer unequalled in battle. Having conceded all that I still look upon the Duke as the greater man. For we in the Navy had the easier task and for Lord Nelson it was easier than it had been for his predecessor in command. The Revolution in France deprived the French Navy of all its best officers, leaving their ships' companies leaderless, untrained and filled with false notions about equality and fraternity. They were beaten at the outset and driven into their ports. There was a moment of supreme danger when it seemed as if the revolutionary ideas had spread to our own fleet but the seamen were

brought back to their duty, lured by Lord Howe and driven by
Lord St Vincent, the one offering the carrot while the other
wielded the stick. When they were fairly disciplined again and
trained by a hundred captains whose names are already forgotten, Lord Nelson was lucky enough to be given the command of fleets which other men had prepared for battle, and
which were to be led against enemy fleets which had never been
exercised at sea. Fortunate in all that, Nelson was fortunate
again, from the point of view of fame, in being killed as he was in
the moment of victory. His further career, had he lived, might
have been spoilt by failure and tarnished by scandal. To hear
some people talk one would think that Trafalgar had marked the
end of the war just as the fall of the curtain may end the third act
of a stage play. But the war continued for another ten years with
the fleet still at sea and Admirals fairly worn out by further years
of service. Nelson died at the moment when his fame was secure.

The Duke of Wellington had no such advantages. His opponents were not discredited officers at the head of spiritless armies.
They were victorious and experienced generals whose troops had
never been beaten. His own armies were composed of men whose
previous service had been in withdrawals, humiliations and
retreats. It was Arthur Wellesley's task to equip, train and inspire
his men, gain the measure of his opponents and turn defeat into
victory. His final antagonist was among the greatest generals who
ever lived (despicable as he was in character). Nor did the Duke
fall at Waterloo but lived on rather to be the nation's leader and
the sovereign's adviser in one crisis after another, always calm,
always decided and nearly always right. I am proud indeed of the
family connection which made me his kinsman and allowed me to
regard him as a friend. During this long day of Arthur's funeral
my thoughts have gone to England's past and future and my
conclusion is that the great days are over. That, you will say, is
an old man's fancy, a sentiment expressed by the elderly in every
age. Think that if you will but we passed our zenith, as I believe,
between 1845 and 1850. We shall extend our influence yet in the
Far East and I have done a little to bring this about. There may
even be this canal at Suez, though I incline to believe that the
scheme will come to nothing, and such a canal, if made would
certainly extend our power. There is, however, a lack of direction
in our policy and the Duke's death would seem to mark the end

of a period. I am glad to have known him, glad to have lived through the great days and will be glad to go when my own time comes. It is strange to reflect that a lifetime's struggle against Napoleon should end with a Napoleon ruling France and the Duke dead and buried, stranger still that Napoleon's bastard son should have been at the funeral. I shall write again when I return to Smallbridge and give you the gossip for which I was not to-day in the mood. The whole business of Arthur's death has left me somewhat shaken.

With apologies for not writing more cheerfully and at greater length, I am

Yours most sincerely,
Hornblower

In his attitude towards Napoleon III, Hornblower was rather inconsistent. The Prince President had rewarded him generously for a small service and they would presumably have greeted each other, had they met, as friends. On the other hand, Horatio was utterly opposed to anyone called Napoleon and thoroughly distrustful of the French. Those he had respected (and indeed loved) were of the old regime and he liked a Republic no better for calling itself an Empire. When he heard in 1853 of growing friction between Russia and France he was instinctively on the Russian side. He had fought alongside the Russians in 1812. Another Hornblower, his successor in the Navy, had fought alongside them at Navarino. If the French were to quarrel with the Russians again, they would be defeated as before—and serve them right! Other naval officers may have thought the same but few, on the other hand, wanted to see a Russian fleet in the Mediterranean. The decline of Turkish power (hastened by the defeat at Navarino) was creating a vacuum into which other forces were being drawn, the British not excepted, and the final result was an alliance of Britain, France and Turkey against Russia. Without any real intention or purpose the British found themselves committed to a war with Russia in the spring of 1854 and war was actually declared on March 27th. It was not until the autumn, however, that the allies began their invasion of the Crimea, first step towards the capture and destruction of Sebastopol, base of the Russian Black Sea Fleet. Hornblower had misgivings about this plan and even made official protests, as an

Admiral of the Fleet was entitled to do. No such folly would have been attempted, he believed, had the Duke been still alive. In this belief he was almost certainly correct, the Crimean War being not Hamlet without the Prince so much as Waterloo without the Duke. The Cabinet coldly acknowledged the receipt of Hornblower's Memoranda and continued to plan the capture of Sebastopol. But the old Admiral had not really expected to have any influence on policy. All he had wanted was to place his objections on record and so disclaim responsibility for any of the consequences. He had no support, however, from Richard. Far from that, Lord Maidstone, Lt-Colonel of the 1st Lifeguards, was eager to begin his first campaign.

When the British forces embarked for the Crimea they numbered about 30,000 men; one cavalry and five infantry divisions. There had been no war of consequence for nearly forty years and the few and elderly survivors of that Peninsular War were to direct formations with no operational experience at all, led by unit commanders and staff officers who had never been under fire. The Lifeguards were kept in England but Richard quitted his Regiment and obtained a posting, as full Colonel, to the staff of the Cavalry Division, commanded by the Earl of Lucan. The two Brigade Commanders were the Earl of Cardigan and the Hon Sir James Scarlett, the former being Lord Lucan's brother-in-law. Richard, Lord Maidstone, was now aged forty-three, a conscientious but inexperienced officer, in a very difficult position. Commanding the British army was Lord Raglan, aged sixty-six, whose active service with the Duke of Wellington had begun in 1808. Lord Lucan, by contrast had been commissioned in 1816, Scarlett in 1818, Cardigan in 1824; all too late even for Waterloo. None, save Raglan, had seen service in the field and Richard was in no position to advise them. In September, 1854 he was among those who landed in the Crimea and presently advanced on Sebastopol. He was at the Battle of the Alma: in which, however, the cavalry played no active part. At Balaclava he was at one time under fire with the Heavy Brigade but was at Lord Lucan's side when the Light Brigade made its fatal charge. He was not among those who were blamed afterwards for the disaster. Nor was there much opportunity for the cavalry during the remainder of the campaign. Most of the horses died during the following winter, leaving regiments with an average number

of about sixty and none of them fit for battle. The siege of
Sebastopol was left to engineers, gunners and infantry.

The fleet, meanwhile, using Balaclava as its base, was asked to
co-operate with the allied armies by bombarding Sebastopol.
Among the men-of-war which took part in the bombardment was
H.M. Screw Vessel *Sealion* commanded by Captain J. Hornblower. She played a conspicuous part in the attack, suffered
some casualties but withdrew otherwise undamaged. Ashore
afterwards at Balaclava, Captain J. Hornblower had an unexpected meeting with Lord Maidstone. They arranged to dine
together on the following day and did so, drinking a health to
Lord Hornblower and sending him a joint letter to describe
the progress of the campaign. Jonathan was emphatic upon the
advantages of steamships with screw propulsion, as also upon the
dangers of shell-fire directed against wooden ships-of-the-line.
Richard explained that he was learning about siege warfare and
could have wished that he had known more about it beforehand.
Both were sure of victory and looked forward to reporting in
person when the war was over. As from this time they seem to
have met periodically, writing cheerfully to the old Admiral and
assuring him that no discredit had fallen, so far, on the family
name. Jonathan's contribution to the war was afterwards recognised by the award of the C.B. and Richard, for his part, was
twice mentioned in despatches.

On June 17th, 1855, the allies began their great assault on
Sebastopol with heavy fire from six hundred guns and mortars.
The attack followed but was repulsed with heavy loss. It was
renewed on the night of the 19th but still without success. At that
point Lord Raglan died, almost literally broken-hearted. At last,
on September 8th, the allies resumed the offensive but, while
the French captured the Malakoff Fort and held it, the British
failed at the Redan. In this last attack, Richard, Lord Maidstone,
led a depleted battalion of infantry, replacing a lieutenant-
colonel killed in the June assault. He was badly wounded as he
tried to rally a remnant of his men for a final and desperate effort.
The troops failed to respond, being exhausted and dispirited, and
they fell back under heavy fire, bringing their Colonel with them.
He was taken to a base hospital and there, while still unconscious,
his left arm was amputated. It was doubtful at this point whether
he would recover, such had been the loss of blood, but he rallied

on the 9th when told that Sebastopol had fallen. The loss of the Malakoff had convinced Prince Gortschakoff that the fortress was no longer tenable. He blew up the arsenal, magazines and docks, sunk or burnt all the warships, and withdrew from Sebastopol, into which the allies marched on the 9th. To all intents and purposes the war was over, and Captain J. Hornblower was at his cousin's bedside, congratulating him on having survived one of the bloodiest battles in history. The *Sealion* was ordered home, having sustained some damage, and Lord Maidstone went with her, a convalescent but on the way to recovery. Sailing on September 30th, and calling at Malta, the *Sealion* reached Portsmouth on October 17th. Lord Maidstone, met by his wife on the quayside, was taken to Boxley House, where Jonathan, whose ship was paid off, came with his family to visit him at Christmas. Old Lord Hornblower did the same and this was the last occasion that the whole family was together.

We should know nothing of this occasion had not Lady Hornblower written a letter from Boxley to her nephew, Henry Richard Wellesley, Lord Cowley. He was a diplomatist whose immediate task was to negotiate the Treaty of Paris, ending the war in which Richard had so nearly lost his life. He was at this time the British Ambassador at Paris, where he was presently to conclude the international agreement by which privateering was abolished.

Boxley House
28th December, 1855

My dear Henry,

We all wish you could have been here for this family party, soon to be celebrating the New Year, but we all know what important work you have to do, ensuring that we do not lose in negotiation all that we have gained in battle. As you know, Horatio was always opposed to this campaign and convinced, moreover, that Arthur, had he been alive, would have prevented it. The great thing is, however, that the fighting is over and that both Richard and Jonathan are still alive. Richard gets on amazingly with his one hand, luckily his right, and even talks of being able to shoot again. He will not go back to his Regiment but will be given a desk at the Horse Guards until his promotion comes through as Major-General. Both he and Jonathan have been nominated for the C.B. and both are regarded as heroes by all the neighbourhood. It is odd to think that Horatio, who was twenty years at war, had scarcely a scratch, ill as he was in 1812 and lucky so often to survive at all.

You would have been proud, I think, had you seen the company at dinner here on the 25th. Horatio was made to sit at the head of the table, and very rightly, even though Richard was host. Behind his chair and above the fireplace was his portrait by Sir William Beechey and opposite me was that picture by Clarkson Stanfield of the Battle of Algiers. The silver candlesticks were a gift to Horatio from the directors of the Peninsular and Oriental Steam Navigation Company and the candles were reflected in the polished mahogany of the long table. Richard looked every inch a soldier and is happier now that he has been in action and proved his courage under fire. Jonathan begins to look distinguished too and sometimes a little like Horatio but without quite that air of decision—I cannot see him as an Admiral. At the opposite end of the room was the portrait of Arthur, looking down appreciatively at Harriet, who is still quite lovely, and even sparing a glance at Gertrude whose looks have lasted very well. On this occasion some of the older grand-children were present, Richard's Maria and Jonathan's Peter, and two or three outside guests, a Rear-Admiral whose name I forget and a Colonel whose name I never knew. The other children appeared for the dessert and young Horatio, who is at Eton, seems to be all the most critical grandparent could expect. Looking round that room on such a happy occasion, the men so distinguished and proved in battle, the women so well loved and respected, the boys so promising and the girls so pretty, my eyes filled with tears, I don't know why. This, I felt, was what Horatio has fought and worked to achieve. He can feel now that his task is done, his family secure and his country well served and defended by this and by other families like it. And then I wondered whether again it can last and whether the tide of revolution which drowned nearly everything of value in France will some day ruin this country too. This is not a catastrophe, if it should happen, which Horatio and I will live to see.

I should warn you, writing as I do in confidence, that Horatio has suddenly begun to look his age—and he is nearly eighty. He is white-haired, thin, and rather deaf. A change came over him on the day he heard a report, mercifully incorrect, of Richard's death in action. A strange aspect, as you know, of this recent war was the presence in the field of representatives sent by the different newspapers, some quite critical of the Generals' tactics but others, like the *Illustrated London News*, with pictures of the Crimea which I found very interesting indeed. One newspaper sent home a truly horrifying account of our attack on the Redan Fort, stating that 'the wounded Lord Maidstone, who had led the last bayonet charge, was brought back on a stretcher, dying leader of a battalion that had ceased to exist.' For three days Horatio believed that his only son had been killed and I grieved again, as I have grieved so often, that we (he and I) should have been childless. Then the news came that Richard was still alive, although badly wounded. You can picture our relief but the damage had been done and Horatio has not looked the same since.

All here join in wishing you a happy and successful New Year and Horatio urges you against allowing Napoleon III to think that he is Napoleon I!

With kindest regards from

Your affectionate Aunt,
Barbara.

That occasion, at Boxley House, in December, 1855, was the last time that Hornblower saw all the family assembled. He returned to Smallbridge in January, 1856, and never left home again. He was well enough to walk in the garden on fine days, well enough to write letters and well enough to enjoy his glass of port after dinner. He wrote to congratulate Richard on his promotion to Major-General. He even wrote to Lord Cowley, expressing his views on the situation in the Near East and stressing the need for Britain to protect the overland route to India. All this time, however, his strength was steadily failing and Barbara, herself an old lady now, had little hope of his surviving the winter. He rallied a little, however, during the autumn and even talked of visiting Boxley again. No such visit took place, however, and Richard brought his children over to Smallbridge for a day in September, just before young Horatio had to go back to Eton. They were to remember this visit afterwards for it was their last. By the end of the year the old Admiral was only just well enough to have a short talk with Richard,

mainly about property and Barbara's future income. The end
came in January, 1857, when he died quite peacefully on the 12th,
aged eighty. He was not bedridden even then, being found by
Barbara in his study armchair with his eyes closed in sleep and
the last volume of Gibbon's *Decline and Fall of the Roman
Empire* lying, still open, on the floor.

An Admiral of the Fleet might have had a public funeral in
London but Hornblower's will prevented it. His last and typical
wish was to be buried quite simply in Nettlestead Churchyard,
and so it was arranged. The Queen was represented at the funeral
and volleys were fired over the grave by a party of seamen from
the guardship at the Nore. Minute guns were fired simultaneously at Chatham Dockyard and a memorial service was held
at St Paul's Cathedral. There is a commemorative tablet in the
church at Nettlestead and another, more elaborate, in the church
at Boxley. Lady Hornblower herself died in 1861 (also aged
eighty) living long enough to watch Richard take his seat in the
House of Lords. The last word on Horatio Hornblower comes
from her and forms part of another letter written to Lord
Cowley:

Smallbridge
12th January, 1858.

My dear Henry,

It is twelve months to the day since Horatio died and never
have I known the months pass so slowly. There is no Wellesley
left of my own generation and I find myself writing to you as the
one nearest to me in temperament if not in age. It is very quiet
here at Smallbridge, for the servants are old as well as I and even
the sound of the carriage is deadened to-day by the snow.
Winters seem to be colder than they used to be but there is no
wind to-day and the woods are strangely silent. Thinking about
times past—and what else have I to do?—I know that Arthur was
the great man of our time, incomparable in courage and wisdom.
But he began with such advantage from birth that he commanded
a regiment when he was twenty-four. My Horatio had no such
help from his family and friends. He was a penniless orphan and
began from nothing, making his way in the service without
interest of any sort, gaining each step by an entire concentration
on the work to be done, unenvied by those who lacked, and who

knew they lacked, his resolution, his knowledge and his skill. I never knew and will never know more than a part of what he did. He lived through desperate situations and was ruthless, I have been told, when success was in the balance. A man of humble birth cannot afford to make a single mistake and he made none, I suppose, for twenty years. He was never fearless, as some men are, but forgot his fears after battle was joined. He became a legend for saying no more than he needed to say but *I* knew him as he really was, a man of humility, of humour, of kindness and charm. It was not his fate to command in any general engagement but he will always be remembered in the Royal Navy as one of the finest officers of his day. The guns are silent now, his flag is lowered, and all is quiet in the churchyard where he is laid to rest.

Appendices

Appendix 1: ANCESTRY

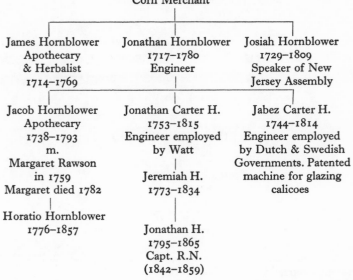

Jeremiah Hornblower
1692–1754
Corn Merchant

James Hornblower
Apothecary
& Herbalist
1714–1769

Jacob Hornblower
Apothecary
1738–1793
m.
Margaret Rawson
in 1759
Margaret died 1782

Horatio Hornblower
1776–1857

Jonathan Hornblower
1717–1780
Engineer

Jonathan Carter H.
1753–1815
Engineer employed
by Watt

Jeremiah H.
1773–1834

Jonathan H.
1795–1865
Capt. R.N.
(1842–1859)

Josiah Hornblower
1729–1809
Speaker of New
Jersey Assembly

Jabez Carter H.
1744–1814
Engineer employed
by Dutch & Swedish
Governments. Patented
machine for glazing
calicoes

William Rawson
Carpenter and Builder

m.

Elizabeth Maynard
y. daughter of the Rev. Samuel
Maynard, Vicar of Brandsby in
Essex

Thomas Rawson
1736–1799
Connected with
East India Company
Shipping
m.
Harriet Stephens
Daughter of Shipbuilder
whose cousin was
Robert Keene,
Captain R.N.
d. 1795

Margaret Rawson
1739–1782
m. in 1759
Died of fever

George Rawson
1742–1787
Lieutenant in the
77th Regiment

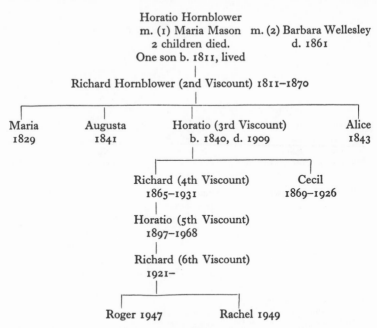

Horatio Hornblower
m. (1) Maria Mason   m. (2) Barbara Wellesley
2 children died.   d. 1861
One son b. 1811, lived

Richard Hornblower (2nd Viscount) 1811–1870

Maria   Augusta   Horatio (3rd Viscount)   Alice
1829   1841   b. 1840, d. 1909   1843

Richard (4th Viscount)   Cecil
1865–1931   1869–1926

Horatio (5th Viscount)
1897–1968

Richard (6th Viscount)
1921–

Roger 1947   Rachel 1949

Richard, Lord Maidstone, the second Viscount, was succeeded by Horatio, who held minor office under the Marquess of Salisbury in 1885 and died in 1909. Richard, fourth Viscount, had joined the Navy in 1878 and, remaining in the service, rose to the rank of Rear-Admiral. He commanded the battleship *Collingwood* at the Battle of Jutland and retired in 1921. Horatio, fifth Viscount, served in the Grenadier Guards, won the M.C. as a subaltern in 1918 and commanded a battalion of his regiment before he retired in 1937. Called back to the service in 1939–45, he was wounded at Dunkirk and confined to staffwork, as Brigadier, for the rest of the war. With fortune much reduced by taxation, he was compelled to sell Boxley House in 1953, retaining only his town residence in Wilton Street, Knightsbridge. When he died in 1968 he was succeeded in the title by Richard, the sixth Viscount, born in 1921, who served in the Royal Navy during World War II, being a sub-lieutenant in the *Achilles* at the Battle of the River Plate and a Lieutenant-Commander on D-Day of the landings in Normandy. He left Britain in 1952 (following his divorce) and has since lived in South Africa.

November, 1852

Dear Sir,

I have directed the Bank to give you this letter on the hundredth anniversary of my death and am confident, therefore, that the events I shall describe are, by the time of your breaking the seal, of merely historical interest and that the men I have occasion to name will have no living children or even grandchildren. The need for this precaution you will presently come to understand, while still wondering perhaps why I should write this letter at all. Will my explanation of one particular event be of interest to my descendants or even to historians? I have no means of knowing what the world will be like in about the year 1960 nor can I foresee at this time whether my professional career will merit by then so much as a line in any compilation made for reference. I write this letter, nevertheless, on the supposition that my name will not be forgotten and that my career will not be wholly unknown. I shall suppose, further, that a certain story about me may have been repeated and that it concerns the *Renown*. When peace came in 1802 I became aware of rumours being repeated without, however, anything being printed or spoken in my presence. At the period to which I refer duels were fought more often than they are to-day and men were more careful of what they said and to whom. It was not likely that I should hear directly what stories might circulate in a Portsmouth coffee house. I knew, however, that singular events give rise to gossip and that gossip may become the substance of biography or history. While recently attending the funeral of a great man I remembered stories that I had heard about him, some true and others false, and I decided then that my descendants, in this one instance, should know the truth and that I would rather they did so than that they should believe, or even deny, a fable. They may suppose that I have no motive now for concealment or distortion, no dread of any possible consequence and no fear of giving offence.

The story I have to tell concerns the 74-gun ship *Renown* in the year 1800, already a half century ago. She sailed from Plymouth in July of that year under the command of Captain David Sawyer. Her Lieutenants were Buckland (First), Roberts, Bush, Smith and (Fifth) myself. The ship sailed under sealed orders but was on a course for the West Indies. It became evident that the Captain was going mad, his insanity inducing in him a conviction that all the officers and young gentlemen were in a plot against him and that only the lower deck men were loyal. His fears were the imaginings of a diseased brain but they underlay his system of command in which all proper discipline was reversed, the officers being treated with unmerited censure, the young gentlemen with unmerited punishment. His most frequent victim was a youngster called Wellard who was repeatedly caned and driven to the point of suicide. As junior lieutenant I was placed on watch and watch. Then Bush and Roberts were ordered to report to the First Lieutenant at hourly intervals during their watch below, they to be properly dressed and he to be properly awake. Still further to undermine discipline the Captain flattered and spoilt the crew as a whole and made favourites of the men he employed to spy on the rest. In the presence of such a captain, anything an officer said could be mutiny while his silence, should he say nothing, might be construed as insolence. I must emphasise, however, that no one deed or word would have sufficed to prove Sawyer insane and that the surgeon would never have dared sign a certificate to that effect. I must also emphasise that the *Renown* was in no state to give battle or even to survive a hurricane.

On her arrival at English harbour or Kingston or at the Admiral's rendezvous elsewhere (our destination was not even known to us) the officers of the *Renown* could apply to the Commander-in-Chief for a Court-Martial on the Captain or else for a medical survey. If they did so the Captain would demand a Court-Martial on *them*. A Court composed of Captains would naturally tend to support one of their number. It would have before it no real proof of his breaking a regulation, nor would a Medical Board have any proof of his insanity. On the other hand, the Captain might employ the worst characters from the lower deck to give evidence of mutiny among the officers; enough to have them cashiered, imprisoned or even hanged. Were the First Lieutenant to declare the Captain ill and confine him to his cabin, it was almost certain that the crew, or enough of them, would rise

on the Captain's behalf. Quite apart, however, from this likelihood, and apart again from Buckland's willingness to act in this
way—much against his character as so far known to me—we had
to consider that the situation, on arrival in the West Indies,
would have been virtually the same. There would be a Medical
Board and a Court Martial or series of Courts Martial, with no
real evidence against the Captain and plenty of testimony on his
behalf. Still more to the point, we had to realise and remind
ourselves that these Courts Martial whatever their verdict, would
mean the professional ruin of all concerned. Lieutenants who had
managed to secure their Captain's removal would never be
promoted or even employed. The whole situation might have
been altered by an encounter with the enemy, which was most
unlikely in mid-ocean, or by the usual incidence of yellow fever,
which was not to be expected before our arrival in the West
Indies; an arrival which would mean disaster for all of us. The
future of the ship and of all its officers depended upon a decision
I should have to take while we were still at sea.

You may wonder a little that I should regard the decision as
mine. I did so because I was, as I knew, the only lieutenant
capable of making it. Nor was it possible for me to discuss the
dilemma which faced us with the other officers, the risk being too
great of our being overheard by those who had been appointed to
spy on us. After careful thought I reached the conclusion that
Sawyer *must not reach port alive*. His death was the only solution
to the problem by which I was faced and it remained to consider
the possibilities open to me, excluding the opportunities which
would be afforded us during an engagement with the enemy.
The alternatives open appeared to be these:

First, I could challenge the Captain to a duel.

Second, I could throw him overboard on a dark night, or

Third, I could arrange a mishap—a musket accidentally fired
or a block or marlin spike dropped from aloft.

The first I had to rule out in the belief that he would not
accept the challenge, and that he could put me under close arrest
for uttering it. The second I had to rule out because the captain
was seldom on deck after dark or before daylight. There remained
only the one method, the accidental death. In making the outline
plan I realised that I had two advantages. I knew, first of all, that
certain men were the captain's informers. It was through them

that I could bring him to a given place at a given time. I also knew that I had a useful ally in Mr Wellard. It was I who had dissuaded him from suicide and I was aware, therefore, that he was willing to take a risk. I had once been situated as he was now and was ready to stake my life on an even chance, a toss of the coin to decide between escape from misery or death. I should need him as a witness to my alibi. Even with such a witness I did not estimate my own chances as better than even.

To arrange an accident without other witnesses I needed darkness and a less frequented part of the ship. That suggested the middle watch and the hatchway from the steerage to the hold, as quiet a place as any in the ship. What accident could happen there? Only one was possible—a fall down the hatchway. And what should bring the Captain there in the middle watch? Obviously, the thing he most wanted (or feared): proof that his officers were plotting against him, a secret meeting in the hold, a meeting at which his enemies could be caught in the act. If he received news of such a conspiracy his first notion would be to go towards the scene by the shortest route, accompanied by a guard. His second notion would be to send a loyal supporter—Mr Hobbs, the acting gunner, for a certainty—to the forward hatchway. With the entrances thus secured, his third notion would be to have the hold searched. I realised that this plan could fail in a number of ways but it was the best I could devise. Wellard was the only person to whom I confided any part of it and he was told no more than he needed to know. Having decided what had to be done, it only remained to arrange for the officers to meet and for the Captain to be told of their meeting. The time I suggested to the others was ten minutes after two bells in the middle watch, the place was to be midships in the hold. It might occur to you to wonder what the meeting could achieve. The answer is that there was nothing useful anyone could say. All that mattered was that the meeting should be held and that the Captain should hear of it. As soon, therefore, as I was relieved on deck by Smith, I spoke of the meeting to Wellard in such a way as to be overheard by Samuels, gunner's mate. I then left Wellard to watch for developments while I made my way to the hold. Present at the meeting were Buckland, Roberts, Bush and myself. There was the sort of futile discussion that might be expected and then Wellard came to give the alarm. Telling the others to go forward, go on deck and scatter, I myself went up the main hatchway to the lower gundeck, followed by Wellard. I ran aft, quietly (I was wearing felt slippers, not shoes) and made for the steerage, the right place at what I hoped would be the right moment.

I have been fortunate on a number of occasions in my life but never more so than on that night. The sequence of events was exactly as I had hoped. Samuels told Mr Hobbs, the acting gunner and Captain's toady, who called another man called Ackworth. These three went aft and Mr Hobbs called the Captain and made his report. The Captain's cabin was secured, as in all ships, by a Corporal and four Marine privates, one sentry on duty at a time and the others within call. Captain Sawyer told Hobbs to go and guard the main hatch after first telling the Corporal to turn out the guard. Both these movements took a little time, Hobbs needing a minute or so to fetch a lantern and the Corporal needing as long perhaps to collect his wits and his men. Once these marines had reported for duty, Captain Sawyer sent two of them forward with orders to guard the fore-hatch, after first telling the rest of the Marines to turn out with muskets, side arms and ball cartridges. The Captain then went down to the steerage, telling the Corporal and the two other men to follow him. When he was thus level with the lower gun deck he sent the Corporal and his men down the ladder, with orders to search the hold. Pistols in hand, the Captain stood peering down the hatchway and shouting to the Corporal to make haste and catch the mutineers before they could escape. Had he descended the ladder himself my plan would have failed. Fortunately for us all he preferred to direct the hunt (as I thought he would) from the hatchway.

At the moment when I ran silently aft with Wellard left behind near the mainmast, the Captain was shouting down the hatchway. I ran straight up to him and kicked him fairly in the back at about waist level. He went over the coaming and head first down into the hold. Without waiting an instant I ran forward to Wellard, wheeled round and began to walk aft again. As I was out of breath I sent Wellard ahead of me, as I might have done in the ordinary way on hearing the commotion. Wellard went part of the way down the ladder and then came up again calling for the ship's surgeon, Mr Clive. Mr Bush arrived at this moment, having passed along the other side of the deck. I sent a midshipman to call the First Lieutenant, who was by this time back in his cabin, and we presently went down together and found the Captain lying unconscious at the foot of the ladder. He was still alive but the surgeon presently announced that he had broken his nose, his collar bone and two ribs and was suffering from concussion. The further effect of the fall was to unhinge his unstable mind and leave him plainly a lunatic and one requiring restraint.

He was evidently unfit for duty and Mr Buckland took command of the ship. My regret, as you may believe, was that Sawyer was still alive, for such a fall could easily have killed him and I had supposed that it probably would do so. The immediate problem was solved, however, and we could now train the crew of the *Renown* for battle. We were in action quite soon afterwards.

You may ask at this point why I should come to be suspected of causing the accident which removed Captain Sawyer from his command. The answer must be that no-one else had the opportunity, the motive and the time. The other officers had gone forward on receiving the news that our plot had been discovered. Buckland and Roberts went up to the main deck by the forehatch, Bush turned aft on the lower gundeck. Only myself and Wellard had gone up the main hatchway, thus coming aft to the after hatchway some minutes before the others could have done. Wellard was there before Bush and my alibi rested on the fact that Wellard and I had been together, each ready to swear that the other had been level with the mainmast when the Captain's fall was heard. The other officers thus knew that I was on the scene before any of them. If it was not an accident I was the only officer that could have done the deed and Wellard the only other possible suspect. As against that, nobody wanted to press the inquiry into what had happened, for that would have brought up the question of where we had all been. So the verdict of misadventure had to be upheld despite any theory which anyone may have formed. Poor Wellard was terrified at first but was happy before long to realise that the truth was unwanted and that he could sleep again at night. He had, of course, seen the 'accident' but had every reason for keeping quiet about it. So far as I am aware he said nothing to anyone.

The sealed orders under which the *Renown* had sailed gave her an operation to complete before her captain had to join the Admiral's flag at Kingston. The actions which followed are not relevant to the subject of this letter but a consequence of their success was the capture of several Spanish vessels for which prize crews had to be found. I was given the command of the largest of these, a ship called the *Gaditana*. Mr Wellard, now midshipman, had been given the command of a smaller vessel called the *Carlos*. Some sixty men, half of them marines, had been spared for this service. A large number of prisoners had to be shipped in the *Renown* herself, the crew of which, depleted by casualties and by detachment to the prizes, was inadequate for the double purpose of working the ship and guarding the prisoners. On the passage to Jamaica Mr Buckland, acting Captain, signalled me to come aboard the *Renown* and told me that Captain Sawyer was on the way to recovery, his talk less inconsequent and his broken bones beginning to heal. It seemed possible that he might be well enough to give evidence before a Court of Inquiry. Buckland asked me whether I had anything further to say about the accident and I replied that I only knew what I had already reported. I doubt whether he was satisfied with this reply or happy, for that matter, about the prospect of a Court of Inquiry, but there was nothing he could do in view of the fact that he too was implicated in the plot which Sawyer was trying to investigate at the time of his fall. We parted and I returned to my duty on board the *Gaditana*.

During the night which followed, I heard two musket shots fired on board the *Renown*. She soon afterwards came up into the wind and I concluded that there was trouble aboard her, probably due to the prisoners attempting to gain their freedom. I collected the prize crews from the other vessels, ordering them first to cut the sheets and halliards, then laid the *Gaditana* alongside the *Renown*, which was by then in the hands of the Spaniards. My boarding party took them by surprise and some of the *Renown*'s crew rallied to our assistance. There was a confused struggle in which the Spaniards were finally overpowered, many of them killed. At my elbow in this conflict was Mr Wellard, who fought with determination and slew at least two of our immediate opponents. As their resistance collapsed I turned to him and said 'Find Sawyer and finish him off'. I did not know at that time whether the Captain was still alive but supposed it possible that the Spaniards might have spared a sick man who was no danger to them. There was no certainty about this because the prisoners who had broken from their place of confinement might not have known that he was sick. He had survived, nevertheless, and Wellard cut his throat, leaving it to be supposed that the Spaniards had done it. None would admit to having killed him but that was hardly matter for surprise. It seemed quite probable, moreover, that his assailants were themselves killed in the subsequent fighting. All the Court of Inquiry could do was to direct that the prisoners should be questioned, which had already been done and was then repeated. They naturally agreed that their ringleaders, or such as were guilty of needless bloodshed, were among the dead. There was no Court Martial and I was promoted to the rank of Master and Commander; a promotion which, owing to the Peace, was not confirmed.

You may ask at this point what I should have done had there been no attempt by the prisoners to capture the *Renown*. I had in fact no settled plan, nor did I know the extent of Sawyer's recovery, but I was still resolved to destroy the man and would have done so by some other means, probably by making it appear that he had taken his own life. This brings me to the last question of all—why was I so ready to commit the crime of murder? You should realise, first of all, that we held life cheap in those days. I had seen bloodshed in action. I had even carried out an execution on board that same ship. I have never been a believer in the doctrines of the Church except, of course, as a necessary part of naval discipline. I did not believe then, nor do I believe now, that lunatics should be kept alive. The money wasted on their maintenance would be far better applied to the training of youngsters for a career at sea. But Sawyer was more than merely a lunatic, he was a danger to the Service and a tyrant to his shipmates, more than useless as an officer and more than despicable as a man. I had no hesitation in killing him nor had I any regret at having done so. My own career, then in the balance, was of importance to the service and to the country. That poor maniac mattered to nobody and even his widow must have been better off without him. I never lost a night's sleep over Sawyer's removal and I don't suppose that Wellard gave it much further thought. He lost his own life soon afterwards, however, being drowned when his jolly boat capsized at Plymouth.

No questions were ever asked nor were any doubts expressed over Sawyer's death. The talk in the wardrooms was rather about the accident which had first deprived him of the command. I suspect that all the rumours could be traced to Mr Smith, the only lieutenant who did not attend our meeting in the *Renown*'s hold. He was officer of the watch at the time but he had been less victimised by Sawyer, perhaps because he spoke with a trace of north country dialect, being thus less socially acceptable and more on Sawyer's level. He could not really believe—nor could the other lieutenants—that an old seaman could fall over a hatch coaming even with a lurch of the ship. But Smith lacked the motive the others had for saying nothing about the incident. He may also have listened to what was said on the lower deck, especially by the creature Hobbs after Buckland disrated him and sent him back to the forecastle. So the legend lingered in the service that I was the man who pushed his captain down the hatchway. I do not think that it proved a hindrance to my career but enough was said to make me a little feared among my contemporaries. On the supposition that the legend is still repeated in any form I owe it to my descendants that they should know the truth. They may reflect, and so may you, that a different sequence of events might have led me to the gallows instead of to the House of Lords. That would be true, however, of half the men who enter the peerage. If they had feared to take risks, if they had allowed obstacles to stand in their way, they would not have been fit to rule.

I am, sir,

your humble and unrepentant ancestor

HORNBLOWER

NOTE BY AUTHOR: There is no documentary evidence that Hornblower's reputation was affected by any story that may have been told about Sawyer and the *Renown*. The fact would seem to be that Hornblower imagined the gossip or most of it, which may suggest that he was more worried by conscience than he cared to admit. He was normally a stern critic of his own conduct and motives. We must remember, however, that his criterion was not the Bible but the good of the service, and no one could suppose that the Navy was the poorer for Sawyer's death.

Appendix 3: WELLESLEY ANCESTRY

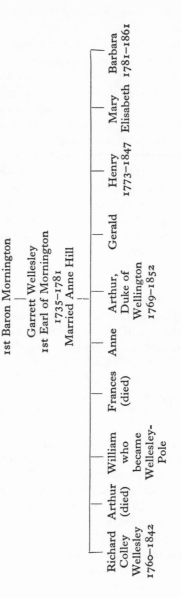

1st Baron Mornington

Garrett Wellesley
1st Earl of Mornington
1735–1781
Married Anne Hill

Richard
Colley
Wellesley
1760–1842

Arthur
(died)

William
who
became
Wellesley-
Pole

Frances
(died)

Anne

Arthur,
Duke of
Wellington
1769–1852

Gerald

Henry
1773–1847

Mary
Elisabeth

Barbara
1781–1861

Appendix 4: SMALLBRIDGE MANOR

We know from living members of the Hornblower family that
Smallbridge Manor was sold soon after the death of Lady Hornblower in 1861. We also know from a newspaper cutting that the
house was accidentally burnt down in 1884 and was never subsequently rebuilt. What is surprising is the fact that its actual
location should have been in doubt, only to be established after
a great deal of patient research. Early confusion had its origin in
a printed account of Lord Hornblower's adventures in 1813.
According to this source, Hornblower was given his orders in
London and asked where his luggage would be. He is then
supposed to have replied 'At Smallbridge, my lord. Almost on the
road to Portsmouth.' Having packed his sea-chest and other gear,
he set off again from Smallbridge 'skirting the autumnal Downs
to Guildford . . . and then down the Portsmouth Road' and so to
embark at Spithead. From these references we should incline to
place Smallbridge in Surrey, only to find that his peerage made
him a Baron of the United Kingdom, Lord Hornblower of
Smallbridge in the County of Kent. There could be no doubt that
Kent was his county. How could Smallbridge be almost on the
road, then between London and Portsmouth? This first problem was, in fact, the easiest to solve. What Hornblower really said
was 'At Smallbridge, my lord, almost on the road to *Chatham.*'
That would at least put him in the right county. It also makes
sense of the reference to Guildford, for a traveller from north
Kent could pass Guildford on the way to Portsmouth.

Our second and far more precise clue to the location of Smallbridge comes in another printed source which describes the
sudden appearance there of the future Emperor, Napoleon III,
on his way to Dover and so to Paris. From that narrative it
appears that the railway line, by 1848, had made its way round
the edge of the park at Smallbridge and that a landslide at that
point had blocked the line to Maidstone, which was eight miles
distant on a fairly easy road. This places Smallbridge on the main

line to Dover, eight miles short of Maidstone by road and some
lesser distance, presumably, by rail. Here again there are difficulties, for the main line from London to Dover, constructed in
1841–44, goes from Redhill to Ashford without even approaching
Maidstone, whereas the branch line to Maidstone from Paddock
Wood, built in 1844, was not a means of reaching Dover at all.
We have seen (page 254) that some of our bewilderment is due to
Prince Louis Bonaparte's mistakes in both language and topog-
raphy, quite natural in a foreigner. If we ignore these excusable
errors we are left with the basic fact, derived from Hornblower
and not from the Prince, that Smallbridge was near the railway
from London to Maidstone and eight miles distant from Maidstone by road. It was therefore, on the branch line from Paddock
Wood at some point between Nettlestead and Wateringbury. It is
evident again, that a place called Smallbridge must be on a river
and at a point where that river is or has been bridged. It should
not be too far remote from another bridge which must be, or must
have been, the larger of the two. The Medway is, in this instance,
the only possible river and Bow Bridge is the only means of
crossing it. There is, however, a minor road from Bowhill which
runs down to the river at a point nearly opposite Nettlestead
Church. This clearly points to the site of a former bridge, smaller
than Bow Bridge because of lesser importance. Smallbridge would
then be the old name for the area round Nettlestead Court. The
position of the church is also significant, suggesting that this rather
than Nettlestead was once the centre of the parish. Where then
was Smallbridge Manor? Could that have been another name for
'The Place'—the old building near the church? This is out of the
question because the Manor was further than that from the railway, the smoke from the passing locomotives being visible only
from the upper windows of the house. This gives us a probable
distance of 500–1,000 yards and brings us to the actual place
where the house used to stand, at the T-junction which ends the
road going nearly westwards from the church; a road which leads
towards the point at which the river was formerly bridged. The
Manor faced down that road and was sited just above the 200-
foot contour. Oakwood was then the home farm and the surrounding park extended to Lone Barn southwards and as far as
the railway line on the east. There is no cutting east of Nettlestead but an embankment and this is where the landslide took

place. No trace of the manor house remains, not even the lodge, but we know from a contemporary engraving that it was a Georgian house of some dignity, facing nearly east like other 18th Century houses and provided with some good neighbours at Mereworth Castle and Roydon Hall.

Appendix 5: BOOKS ON HORNBLOWER

Many chapters in this book relate to phases in Hornblower's career which have already been dealt with in other published works. Readers of this biography who wish to have a more detailed account of his adventures should read these other books in their chronological sequence as listed here. This is not the order in which they were written and published.

Chapter		
1	*Schoolboy*	
2	*Midshipman*	*Mr Midshipman Hornblower*
3	*Lieutenant*	*Hornblower and the Widow McCool*[1]
		Lieutenant Hornblower
4	*Master and Commander*	*Hornblower and the Hotspur*
5	*Secret Agent*	*Hornblower and the Crisis*[1]
		Hornblower and the Atropos
6	*Frigate Captain*	*The Happy Return*
7	*Senior Captain*	*A Ship of the Line*
		Flying Colours
8	*Commodore*	*Flying Colours*
		The Commodore
9	*Peerage*	*Lord Hornblower*
10	*Rear-Admiral*	*The Point and the Edge*[2]
		Hornblower in the West Indies
11	*Admiral*	
12	*Admiral of the Fleet*	*The Last Encounter*[1]

[1] These three stories are included in the one volume entitled *Hornblower and the Crisis*.

[2] This story is outlined in *The Hornblower Companion*, pp. 141-2.

The Hornblower books in order of publication

The Happy Return (or Beat to Quarters, U.S. ed.)	1937
A Ship of the Line	1938
Flying Colours	1939
The Commodore	1945
Lord Hornblower	1948
Mr Midshipman Hornblower	1950
Hornblower and the Atropos	1953
Lieutenant Hornblower	1954
Hornblower in the West Indies	1958
Hornblower and the Hotspur	1962
The Hornblower Companion	1964
Hornblower and the Crisis	1967

All the above are written as novels, with the exception of *The Hornblower Companion* in which C. S. Forester explains how the other books came to be written. The last volume, *Hornblower and the Crisis*, contains a story that the author never lived to complete.

Appendix 6: NOTE ON ILLUSTRATIONS

Frontispiece This portrait, in the possession of the present Viscount Hornblower, was painted by Sir William Beechey, R.A., soon after Hornblower's recapture of the *Witch of Endor* in 1811. The picture was cleaned and restored in 1969, some parts of it even repainted by Miss Stella L. M. Schmolle, who was scrupulously faithful to the original.

Plate 9 In this painting, now in the author's possession, the *Swan V* is shown in pursuit of a smuggling vessel, possibly off Beachy Head. The smugglers have jettisoned their cargo, thus posing a problem to the revenue officers. If they pick up the cargo the lugger will be out of the picture and round the headland before they have finished. If they go after the lugger they will have no proof that she was smuggling. The only solution is to shoot down her masts, which is what they are trying to do.

Plate 13 Portrait of Lady Barbara Leighton from the engraving by Thomas Wright after the oil painting by Sir Thomas Lawrence, R.A., painted in 1810. Its pair was the portrait of Sir Percy Leighton. When Lady Barbara remarried she suggested, from motives of delicacy, that Sir Horatio's portrait should be painted by another artist.

Plate 19 The Battle of Algiers from the coloured aquatint engraved by J. C. Stadler after the oil painting by P. H. Rogers. The defences of Algiers centred upon the Lighthouse Battery, mounting three tiers of heavy cannon. The lighthouse is shown in the centre of the picture with, immediately left, the two-tiered batteries which extended to the head of the breakwater. These less formidable batteries were outflanked by the *Queen Charlotte* while directly engaged by the *Granicus*, *Superb* and *Minden*. Conspicuous in this picture are the high-angled missiles directed against the town by bomb-vessels and rocket-boats.

Plate 20 Boxley House from a recent photograph kindly provided by Mr and Mrs Knowlden, the present owners of the

Boxley House Country Club. The building is little altered since Hornblower's day.

Plate 26   Singapore, visited by Hornblower in 1842–44, was planned by George Coleman of Dublin who laid out the city centre and was himself resident in Coleman Street from 1828 to 1841. Important to the original plan was the Padang or Green, used for playing cricket, round which the Europeans would drive or ride in the cool of the evening. The Padang was painted by John Turnbull Thomson in 1851 and the photograph here reproduced, showing only half of his picture, gives a fair idea of the place which Hornblower visited a decade earlier.

Index

Aberdeen, Lord (4th Earl of), 235
Acapulco, 131
Achilles, H.M. Ship, 161, 163
Ackworth, Mr, 275
Act of Union, The (1800), 208, 210, 226
Ada peninsular, 114
Admiralty, 83, 101–2, 105–6, 108, 110, 124, 126, 138, 145, 175, 182, 186 189, 199, 227–8, 242
Agamemnon, H.M. Ship, 34
Aix-la-Chapelle, 201
Albion, H.M. Ship, 203, 231–2
Alceste, 151–3
Alexander Nevsky (Russian man-of-war), 231
Alexander, Tsar of Russia, 176, 193
Alexandria, 125, 236, 246
Algiers, 116, 239; *see also* Algiers, Battle of
Algiers, Battle of, 199, 201–2, 205, 207, 211–12, 229–30, 233, 243, 262
Alma, Battle of the, 259
Almeira, 119
Alvorado, Don Julian, 127, 129–30, 132
Amager, 176
Amazon, 86
Amelia Jane, 111
Amelie, 145–6, 148, 152
Ancell, Samuel, 25–6
Anderson, Mr, 247
Angoulême, Duc d', 192, 196
Angoulême, Duchesse d', 192, 194
Anson, Admiral George (Baron Anson), 31
Antelope, H.M. Ship, 148
Antigua, 65, 143

Antilles, 223
Apollo, H.M. Ship, 162–3
Apothecaries, The London Society of, 23
Aquila, H.M. Ship, 121
Arcadia, SS, 211
Archimedes, SS (formerly *Karteria*), 239–40
Arens de Mar, 149
Arethusa, H.M. Ship, 48–52, 54, 88
Armitage, Captain, 73, 75–7
Armstrong, Mr, 210
Arnold, Martha, 84
Arnold, Dr Thomas, of Rugby, 84–5
Arnold, William, 84
Artemis, H.M. Ship, 146–8, 150–3
Ashworth, Captain, 247
Asia, H.M. Ship, 231–3, 235
At War with the Smugglers (book by Forster), 84
Atkins, Rev John, 19
Atropos, H.M. Ship, 108–15, 117–122
Auckland, Lord (1st Baron), 84
Austria, Emperor of, 193
Autobiography of Peter Holbrook (book), 30
Aylesford Lodge, 241, 250
Azov, 231

Babet, 51
Bahia de Escosesa, 64, 67–8
Bailey, Mr, 42–3, 45
Balaclava, 260
Ball, Rear-Admiral Sir Alexander, 112, 116
Bantry Bay, 59
Barbary Coast, 115

Barbary States, the, 112, 115–16, 199, 201, 236

Barcelona, 146–7, 149, 151, 153, 155, 157

Barham, Lord, 105

Barnett, Tom, 104, 124, 172–3

Barrow, Sir John, 240

Barton, Captain, 241

Bathurst, Captain, 229, 232

Bay of the Seine, 188, 190

Bayonne, 107–8

Beechey, Sir William, 262

Belfast, 185, 210, 225–6, 234

Bellerophon, H.M. Ship, 195

Bembridge, Isle of Wight, 188

Benbow, Vice-Admiral John, 27

Bentinck, Lord William, 121

Berkeley, Hon. G. Craven, 61

Bernadotte, Marshal Jean Baptiste, King of Sweden, 176

Bessborough, Lady, 132

Bey of Tunis, the, 117–18

Bezzina, family of, 117

Biscay, Battle of, 51, 106

Blackett, Timothy, 41–2, 44, 50, 53–4

Blanche Fleur, 176

Blossom, 218–19

Blue Pigeons Farm, 17, 20, 28

Blue Posts Inn, 38–9, 49, 51

Bolivar, Simon, 227

Bolton, Lord (1st Baron), 84

Bolton, Captain, 143, 145

Bolton, Mrs, 143

Bona, 201

Bonaparte, Joseph (King of Spain), 130, 147, 180

Bonaparte, Prince Louis (*later* Napoleon III), 250–5, 258, 263, 281–2

Bonaparte, Napoleon, 79–81, 92, 101, 106, 110, 121, 126, 130, 147, 164, 168–9, 171, 175, 178–81, 185–6, 189, 191–5, 215–16, 232, 234, 250, 258, 263

Bonaparte, Pauline (*later* Leclerc), 81

Bonham, Sir Samuel George, 247

Bonne Celestine, 191

Boringdon, Lord, 133

Boswell, James, 26

Bouchier, Lady, 235

Boulton & Watt Co, 211

Bowhill, 173

Boxley, 212, 240, 264

Boxley House, 12, 212–13, 224–5, 241, 244, 249, 261, 263

Boyer, General Jean-Pierre, 82

Boyne, Battle of the, 211

Boyne, H.M. Ship, 202

Brace, Captain, 200

Braganza, SS, 249

Brandon, Lord, 133

Brennan, Mr, 210

Breslaw (French man-of-war), 231

Brest, Port of, 59, 64, 88–91, 93

Briare, 168

Bride of Abydos, H.M. Ship, 220–1

Bridgnorth, 172–3

Bridport, Viscount (Alexander Hood), 56, 58–63

Brindley, J., 25

Brisbane, Captain, 200

Bristol, 227

Britannia (book by Camden), 25

Brooke, James (*later* Sir James, of Sarawak), 248

Brown, Mr, 165, 167–8, 170, 194–195, 251, 253–4

Buckland, Mr, 58, 61, 66–9, 71–6, 78–9, 272–4, 276–7, 279

Buckler, H.M. Ship, 73, 77

Bulwark, H.M. Ship, 141

Bunbury, Miss, 142

Burdett, Sir Francis, 209

Bush, Mr, 64–6, 68–9, 71–8, 85–7, 89–90, 94–5, 100, 124, 129, 138, 141, 148, 160, 165–9, 175–6, 180, 191, 272, 274–6

Cabellas, 149

Cadiz, 55, 98, 101, 105–8, 246

Caillard, Colonel Jean-Baptiste, 165, 167

Calais, 252–3

Caldecott, Captain, 108

Calder, Admiral Sir Robert, 105
Caligula, H.M. Ship, 144–6, 157, 160, 162–3
Cambronne, Count, 215–16
Camden, William, 25
Camilla, H.M. Ship, 191
Campbell, Captain George, 61
Canning, George, 125
Canterbury, 34
Canton, SS, 249
Cape of St Vincent, Battle of, 55, 60, 200
Cape Creux, 146, 155, 157, 162
Cape de Verde Islands, 128
Cape Haitien, 82
Cape Horn, 127–8, 131, 134, 136–7
Cape of Good Hope, 246
Cape Perro, 111, 119
Cape San Sebastian, 146
Cape Sicie, 147
Cape Tiburon, 81
Caracas, 221
Carberry, Captain, 73
Cardigan, 7th Earl of, 259
Carleton, Mr, 247
Carlos, H.M. Ship, 277
Carthagena, 101, 119–20
Cassandra, H.M. Ship, 157–8
Castilla, 120, 122, 124
Castlereagh, Lord (2nd Marquis of Londonderry), 202
Catalans, the, 147–8
Cerberus, H.M. Ship, 190
Cette, 146
Chadwick, Mr, 188, 190–1
Champerico, 134
Channel Fleet, 34, 56, 59–60, 62–5, 87–8, 98, 102, 169, 189, 236, 241
Channel Islands, 52, 138
Charlesworth, Dick, 45–6
Charette, M. de, 54
Chatham, 103, 108, 110–11, 123–5, 179, 212–13, 225, 240–3, 250, 264, 281
Chauvelin, Marquis de, 34
Christophe, General Henry, 80, 82
Clam, H.M. Ship, 178
Claros, Colonel Juan, 154, 165

Clarence, Duke of (*later* King William IV), 230, 243
Claudius, Dr, 106
Clausen, General, 194
Cleopatre, 34
Clerk, John, 60
Clive, Mr, 65, 68, 71–2, 75, 275
Clorinda, H.M. Ship, 214, 217, 219, 221
Clorinde, 90
Clyde, 185, 210–11, 225–6
Cochrane, Lord (10th Earl of Dundonald), 92, 138, 230, 232–3
Cockayne, Mr, 210
Codrington, Admiral Sir Edward, 229–31, 235–6
Cogshill, James, 73, 77
Coiba, 136
Collingwood, Vice-Admiral Lord, 111, 119–21, 156, 208
Comet, SS, 185, 211
Conant, Rev. John, 29–30, 32
Conception, 137
Concorde, H.M. Ship, 50–1
Congreve, Sir William, 202, 229
Cook, Captain James, 128
Cook, Mr, 43-5
Cooke, Captain Frederick, 157
Copenhagen, Battle of, 203
Corfu, 235, 246
Corinth, Gulf of, 233
Cornwallis, Admiral Sir William, 50, 87–92, 98
Corunna, 55
Cotard, Mr, 89–90
Cotton, Admiral Sir Charles, 61, 160–1
Cowes, 84
Cowley, 2nd Baron (Henry Richard Wellesley), 261–5
Cowper, Earl, 19
Crab, H.M. Ship, 215
Crabtree, General, 212
Creevey Papers, 134
Crespo, Don Cristobal de, 134–5
Crimean War, 258–9, 263
Crystal, Mr, 124, 141, 150
Cunard, Samuel, 211

Daly, Mr Justice, 208–9
Daly, Richard, 243
Dangan Castle, 208–9
Danzig, 177–8
Daring, 215–16
Dartmouth, H.M. Ship, 241
Daugavgriva, 178–9
Deal, 17–18, 22, 26–30, 32, 38, 111, 175–6
Deal Mercury, 22
de Chauvelin, Marquis, 34
Decline and Fall of the Roman Empire (book by Gibbon), 264
Decrès, Admiral, 106–7
Denny & Co, William, 211
Desgareaux, Commodore, 51
Desperate, H.M. Ship, 221
Dessalines, General, 80
Dey of Algiers, the, 201–3
Diana, H.M. Ship, 247
Dido, H.M. Ship, 248
Didon, 158–9, 163
Digby, Vice-Admiral Sir Henry, 242
Dinford, Mr, 106
Dockyard and Victualling Board the, 64
Dolphin, H.M. Ship, 65
Doris, H.M. Ship, 90
Dover, 32, 34, 252–4, 281–2
Dragon, H.M. Ship, 61, 63
Dreadnought, H.M. Ship, 89
Dresden, 186
Druid, H.M. Ship, 77
Drumcliff Castle, 182–5, 199, 207–8
Dublin, 182, 184–5, 198–9, 226–7
Dublin and London Steam Packet Co., 227
Dumbarton, 211
Dvina, 178

East India Company, the Honourable, 20, 31, 33, 111, 174
Eastlake, Lord, 145
Eccles, Mr, 52
Eendracht (later *Sutherland*, H.M. Ship), 141
Eissenbeiss, Dr, 110, 112
Elizabeth, H.M. Ship, 64

Elizabeth, *SS*, 185
Elliott, Captain Harry, 142–3
Elliott, Judith, 142–4
Engageante, 51
Engravers In England (book by Horace Walpole), 19
Entreprenante, 57
Ericsson, John, 242
Esperance, 58
Essay On Naval Tactics (book by John Clerk), 60
Essen, General, 178
Essex, H.M. Ship, 40
Estero Real, 127
Estrella del Sur, 217–18, 224
Eugenia, 52
Evening Press, the, 210
Excellent, H.M. Ship, 242
Exmouth, Lord (1st Viscount, *formerly* Sir Edward Pellew, *cf*), 192, 199, 201–4, 230, 233–4
Exmouth Papers, the, 76
Ezekiel, 231

Falkland Islands, 128
Falmouth, 48, 50, 57, 246
Fancourt, Margaret, 183–5
Fanshaw, Lady, 142
Fanshaw, Lord, 142
Fanshaw, Rev. Stephen, 142
Farrier's Cottage, 22–3
Faversham, Kent, 102
Fawcett & Preston Co., 227
Félicité, 98
Fell, Sir Thomas, 217–18, 221
Ferdinand, King of Sicily, 120–1, 130
Ferris, William, 84–5
Ferrol, 55, 101, 105
Finch, Captain William, 41, 43, 47, 49
Finisterre, 145
Fitzgerald, Lord Edward, 210
Fitzgerald, W., 182
Fitzmorris, Gertrude (*later* Hornblower), 241
Fitzmorris, Rear-Admiral Hugh, 241

Fitzwilliam, 3rd Earl, 183
Flame, H.M. Ship, 188–91
Fletcher, Mr Justice, 183
Flora, H.M. Ship, 50–1
Floriana, in Malta, 238
Fonseca, Gulf of, 126–9, 134
Force, Piganiol de la, 32
Ford, Captain, 120–2
Ford, Sir Richard, 243
Forester, C. S. (author), 11–12, 285
Forrest, Thomas, 25
Forster, Rear-Admiral D. Arnold, 84
Fort St Angelo, 238
Fort St Elmo, 237
Fort Samaná, 67–9
Freeman, Lieutenant, 190–1
French Revolution, the, 31–2, 79, 92, 168, 256
Frere, Hookham, 171
Frisches Haff, 177–8

Gaditana, La (later *Retribution*, H.M. Ship), 71–3, 75, 277
Galbraith, Mr, 136
Gallois, Rear-Admiral, 158
Gambier, Admiral Lord (1st Baron), 137–8, 169
Gammon, Tom, 27, 31
Gargoute, 231
Garrett, Rev. M., 19
Gazette, the, 89, 121–3
Gely, Mr, 84
Genoa, H.M. Ship, 229, 231–2, 234, 237
George III, King of England, 33–4, 86, 110, 117, 120, 130, 144, 243
George Inn, the, at Portsmouth, 38, 53–4, 87, 204
Gerard, Lieutenant, 124, 141
Gibraltar, 28, 55, 94, 111, 115, 117, 119, 147–9, 169, 200, 203, 246
Glenmore, H.M. Ship, 190
Glenshiel, Earl of, 244
Glorious First of June, Battle of the, 40, 60, 129, 229
Gloucester, 108–9
Gomez, Captain, 217–18

Goodwin Sands, 26
Gortschakoff, Prince, 261
Gosse, Philip, 216
Goulet, 89–90, 93, 95, 100
Graçay, Comte de, 167, 193–5
Graçay, Marcel de, 168
Graçay, Marie de, 168, 170, 193–5, 197, 205, 224
Grafton, H.M. Ship, 40, 46, 52
Graham, Sir James, 240
Granada, 126
Granville, Lord (1st Earl), 132
Grey, Sir George, 62
Griffith, Captain Owen, 125
Guernsey, 51
'Guichard, Dr', 106–7
Guilford, Earl of, 19

Haiti, 64, 69, 76, 79–82, 86
Hambledon, Lord, 140
Hammond, Hon. Archibald, 197–198
Hamoaze, 64
Hanbury Castle, H.M. Ship, 137
Hannibal, H.M. Ship, 39, 170
Hano Bay, 179
Harcourt, Captain, 215
Hardy, Sir Charles (the younger), 57
Hardy, Sir Thomas Masterman, 169
Hargreaves, Captain, 47
Harvey, H.M. Ship, 175–6, 178
Hasted, 19
Hastings, Thomas, 242
Havana, 217
Hawke, Admiral Sir Edward, 27, 31
Heiden, Rear-Admiral Count de, 231
Helmond, 221
Helvicus, Christopher, 25
Hertford, 2nd Marquis of, 183
Hewson, Samuel, 22
Higgins, Francis, 210
Hill, Anne (later Wellesley), 132
Hindustan, SS, 246, 248
Hispaniola, 79–80, 82

Histoire des Aventuriers Flibustiers qui se sont signalés dans les Indes (book by Oexmelin), 32

Historical and Chronological Theatre (book by Helvicus), 25

History of Deal (book by Laker), 22

History of Merchant Shipping (book by Lindsay), 242

History of the Long Captivity and Adventures of Thomas Pellow in South-Barbary, The (book), 25

Hobbs, Mr, 66, 272, 275, 279

Hodge, Mr, 12, 104, 124, 172

Hodge, Winthrop, Knightley & Hay, 12

Hogan, John, 235, 241–2

Holbrook, Peter, 29–30

Holland, Captain, 215

Hollis, Captain, 161

Holyhead, 227

Hong Kong, 247–8

Hood, Lord (1st Viscount), 34

Hooper, Sir Augustus, 219

Hornblower, Alice, 244

Hornblower, Augusta, 244

Hornblower, Lady Barbara (*formerly* Wellesley, Leighton, *cf*), 174, 180, 182–6, 190, 192–3, 195–200, 204–7, 209, 211–12, 214, 220, 222–5, 235–7, 244, 247–8, 250–1, 253, 255–6, 261–4, 281

Hornblower, Gertrude (*formerly* Fitzmorris, *cf*), 241, 250, 262

Hornblower, Lady Harriet (*formerly* Mountstuart, *cf*) (*later* Maidstone, *cf*), 244, 249–50

Hornblower, Horatio:

and childhood:
    birth, 18, 23; choice of name, 18, 30–1; death of mother, 20–3; birth place, 22–3; reading, 24–6, 32; hears stories from sailors, 27–8, 38; school, 28–33; learns French, 32; death of father, 33; midshipman post secured for by Thomas Rawson, 33–7

and naval career:
    serves as midshipman, 38–56: on *Justinian*, 39–40; on *Modeste*, 40–9; on *Arethusa*, 49–52; scarred, 51; taken prisoner on *Pique*, 52; on *Royalist*, 52; on *Grafton*, 52; makes use of French, 54, 80, 102, 106; on *Indefatigable*, 54; taken prisoner in Ferrol, 55; learns Spanish, 55; on *Renown*, 55–6

    serves as lieutenant, 57–78: on *Renown*, 57–8; Battle of Fort Samaná, 67–73; use of Spanish, 69, 80, 102, 106, 127, 148; given command of *Retribution*, 75, 77

    serves as master and commander, 79–99: on *Retribution*, 79–93; commands *Swan V*, 84–5; becomes professional card player while out of work, 85; commands *Hotspur*, 86–98; captain in Sea Fencibles, 102–3

    serves as secret agent, 105–23: receives command of *Atropos*, 108; commands *Atropos*, 111–123; receives command of *Lydia*, 123

    serves as frigate captain, 124–140: commands *Lydia*, 124–39

    serves as senior captain, 140–166: on *Sutherland*, 141, 144, 162; taken prisoner at Rosas, 160; condemned to death, 164; escape, 167–9

    serves as commodore, 167–87: knighted, 171; on *Nonsuch* in Baltic, 175–9; commands *Northumberland*, 190–1; given peerage, 192; appointed captain of the fleet, 199–200; Battle of Algiers, 200–4; promoted to rear-admiral, 214

    serves as rear-admiral, 214–225: commander-in-chief in West Indies, 214–20; awarded

Knight Grand Cross of the Order of the Bath, 222; promoted to vice-admiral, 224, 229 serves as vice-admiral, 229–49: governorship of Malta, 235–240; commander-in-chief at Chatham, 240–2; promoted to full admiral, 249

promoted admiral of the fleet, 249; awarded Chevalier of the Legion of Honour, 255; made Viscount, 255; death of, 264

and Maria Mason:

marriage, 87; birth of son Horatio, 90; birth of daughter Maria, 110; deaths of son Horatio and daughter Maria, 123; birth of son Richard, 169; death of wife Maria, 169–70

and Lady Barbara Wellesley (*later* Leighton):

early friendship with, 130–4, 136–7, 139–40; re-meets after death of Maria, 171; marriage, 174; split in relationship, 193–200; re-union, 204

and Marie de Graçay:

affair with, 168, 170, 193–4, 205, 224; death of, 194–5

and residences:

first sees Smallbridge Manor, 103–5; buys Smallbridge Manor, 173; buys Boxley House, 212–13; moves to Boxley House, 224; return to Smallbridge Manor, 244

and steam ships:

interest shown, 185, 210, 225–228, 239, 241–2; joins board of Dublin and London Steam Packet Co, 227; joins board of Willcox and Anderson, 227; on board of Peninsular and Oriental Steam Navigation Co., 227, 235, 242; works for P. & O., 246–9

Hornblower, Horatio, (son), 90–1, 101, 111, 122–3, 143

Hornblower, Horatio, 3rd Viscount (son of Richard Hornblower), 244, 249, 262–3

Hornblower, Jabez Carter, 18, 21–2, 33, 36, 92, 156

Hornblower, Jacob, 17–24, 31–3, 92, 103

Hornblower, James, 18, 92

Hornblower, Jeremiah, 18, 103

Hornblower, Jeremiah (son of Jonathan Carter Hornblower), 109, 155, 160, 202–3, 225, 234, 241

Hornblower, Mrs Jeremiah, 155–6, 162, 203, 225, 241

Hornblower, Jonathan, 18, 21

Hornblower, Jonathan (son of Jeremiah, grandson of Jonathan Carter), 109, 141, 150, 154–6, 160–2, 180, 202–3, 214, 225, 229, 231–4, 236–9, 241, 250, 255–8, 260, 262

Hornblower, Jonathan Carter, 18, 21–2, 33, 36, 83, 92, 108–9, 156, 203

Hornblower, Josiah, 18

Hornblower, Margaret (*formerly* Rawson), 19–20, 22–4

Hornblower, Maria (*formerly* Mason), 87–8, 90–1, 98, 101–2, 104, 108–11, 122–5, 139–43, 168–70

Hornblower, Maria (daughter), 110–11, 122–3, 143

Hornblower, Maria (daughter of Richard Hornblower), 244, 262

Hornblower, Martha, 109

Hornblower Papers (edited by Parker), 228

Hornblower, Peter, 262

Hornblower, Richard Arthur Horatio, 2nd Viscount (*later* Lord Maidstone of Boxley *cf*), 169–72, 174, 182, 184, 190, 193, 195, 198, 204, 207, 214, 225, 239–41, 244, 249

Hornblower, SS, 249

Hornblower, 4th Viscount, 11

Hornblower, 5th Viscount, 11
Hornblower, 6th Viscount, 11–13, 213
Horneblowe, Nicolas, 17–18
Hotspur, H.M. Ship, 86–98, 100, 141
Hough, Mr, 218
Houghton, Vice-Admiral Sir Josiah, 47–8, 53–4
Houghton, Rev. Mark, 47
Howe, Admiral Richard (2nd Earl), 28, 34, 39, 91, 188, 257
Huggins, Mr, 58, 64, 122
Hughes, Admiral Sir Edward, 39
Hunt, Edward, 86
Huskisson, Mr, 255

Iberia, 249
Ibrahim, 118
Ile de Rhé, 93
Illustrated London News, the, 263
Impetueux, H.M. Ship, 57
Impregnable, H.M. Ship, 200, 203–204, 212
Indefatigable, H.M. Ship, 40, 42, 48–9, 53–5, 88, 181
Inshore Squadron, the, 88–9, 95
Irish Rebellion, the, 208
Isthmus 125, 127

Jackson, Rev. William, 210
Jamaica, 64, 66, 79–81, 214, 218–220, 224, 277
James, Mr, 119
James Watt, *SS*, 211
Jamestown, 137, 216
Java Head, 247
Jersey, Lord (5th Earl), 133
Jervis, Vice-Admiral Sir John (Earl St Vincent *cf*), 42
Johnson, Mr, 219
Johnson, Dr Samuel, 26
Jones, Mr, 110
Jordan, Dorothea, 243
Journal of the late and important Blockade and Siege of Gibraltar (book by Ancell), 25–6
Julia, H.M. Ship, 216

Justinian, H.M. Ship, 34–5, 39, 45

Kaia Rock, 114
Karteria (later *Archimedes*, *SS*, cf), 233–4, 238
Keats, Admiral Sir Richard, 243, 256
Keene, Captain Robert, 20, 34–6, 39–41
Keppel, Captain Henry, 248
Kent Herbal, A (book by Jacob Hornblower), 19, 21
Kentish Companion, The (book), 27
King, Captain, 181
King's School, Canterbury, 33, 35
Kingston, Jamaica, 64, 69, 71–3, 76, 80–1, 214, 219–20, 222–3, 272, 276
Knowlden, T. J., 213
Knox, Mr, 42
Knyvett, Captain, 222–3
Königsberg, 176–7
Kronstadt, 176

Lady Mary Wood, *SS*, 249
Lagoon de Vic, 146
La Guaira, 221
Laird, Major, 154
Laker, John, 22
La Libertad, 129–30, 134
Lamartine, M. de, 250
Lambert, Vice-Admiral Sir Richard, 64, 66, 73, 76–80, 82, 86
Lampedusa, 118–19
Laporte, Gustave, 32
Larpent, Sir John, 246
Lawrence, Thomas, 144
Leander, H.M. Ship, 203
Leclerc, General, 81
Leclerc, Pauline (*formerly* Bonaparte), 81
'Legros, Mr', 106–7
Le Havre, 101, 188–92, 194, 196, 198
Leighton, Lady Barbara (*formerly* Wellesley, *cf*) (*later* Hornblower, *cf*), 139–40, 142–4, 168, 170–2
Leighton, Rear-Admiral Sir Percy,

139–40, 142–6, 152–4, 157–8, 160–2, 164, 169–72, 224
Leipzig, Battle of, 191
Letters of Lord Granville, 133
Life and Letters of a Diplomat (book by Hammond), 197
Lindsay, W. S., 242
Lions, Gulf of, 146, 157
Lisbon, 144, 246
Liverpool, 226–7
Liverpool, Lord (2nd Earl), 220
Loire, 88–9
Longueville, Viscount, 208
'Lopez, Martin', 106
Lotus, H.M. Ship, 175
Louis XVI, King of France, 34
Louis XVIII, King of France, 191–4
L'Ouverture, Toussaint, 71, 79–82
Lucan, 3rd Earl of, 259
Lucus, Richard, 122
Lydia, H.M. Ship, 123–32, 134–9, 141

McCool, Barry, 58–9, 183
McCullum, William, 111–14
McDermott, Mr, 184
Macfarlane, Captain Sir Andrew, 59–60
McTaggart, Commodore James, 41, 43, 47–8
Madeira, 127
Madrid, 98, 106–8
Maggie Jones, H.M. Ship, 176
Maidstone, 11–12, 17–18, 102–5, 124, 172–3, 212, 244, 251, 253–4, 282
Maidstone, Lady Harriet (*formerly* Hornblower), 261–2
Maidstone, Lord (*formerly* Hornblower), 255–6, 259–62, 264
Maitland, Rear-Admiral Sir Frederick, 195
Malaga, 119
Malakoff Fort, 260–1
Malcolm, Admiral Sir Pulteney, 235–6
Malgret, 146, 149, 164

Malta, 86, 111, 115, 117–19, 124–5, 233, 235–50, 243–4, 246, 249, 261
Managua, 125, 127
Manners, Lord, 182
Manningtree, Earl and Countess of, 137
Maracribo, 220
Marie Galante, 52
Marlborough, H.M. Ship, 89, 97
Marmorice Bay, 111–14
Mason, Maria (*later* Hornblower, cf), 84–5, 87
Mason, Richard, 84
Mason, Mrs Richard, 84–5, 87, 91, 98, 111
Marquand, Mr, 94–7
Marr-Johnson, Mr, 213
Mars, H.M. Ship, 61
Marsden, Mr, 101–2
Martin, Rear-Admiral Sir George, 161–2
Martin, Admiral Sir Thomas Byam, 199
Mast and Sail in Europe and Asia (book by Smyth), 26–7
Matson, Charles, 17, 19–20, 23
Maynard, Elizabeth (*later* Rawson), 20
Maynard, Samuel, 20
Meadows, Captain James Percival, 100
Meanguera Island, 129
Mediterranean Fleet, the, 34, 55, 62–3, 115, 150, 181, 201, 229, 234, 236
Méduse, 158–9, 163
Mejidieh, 114–15
Melampus, H.M. Ship, 50–1
Melville, Lord (2nd Viscount), 202
Memoir of the Life of Admiral Sir Edward Codrington (book by Bouchier), 235
Merrick, Mr, 73
Metternich of Austria, Prince, 250
Milne, Rear-Admiral David, (*later* Sir David), 200, 204, 212
Minden, H.M. Ship, 203

Minerva, H.M. Ship, 50
Minorca, 120, 155
'Miranda, Jose', 106-7
Mitchell, Sophia, 197
Modeste, H.M. Ship, 40-4, 46, 48-50, 54
Mona Passage, the, 64, 224
Moniteur, newspaper, the, 167, 189
Montagu, Rear-Admiral Sir George, 40
Montague, Hon. William, 27-8
Montego Bay, 219
Montevideo, 128
Moore, Captain Graham, 98
Morning Chronicle, 169
Moscow, 178-9
Moth, H.M. Bomb ketch, 175
Motril, 119
Mountstuart, Lady Harriet (*later* Hornblower, *cf*), 244
Mudir, 113-14
Murray, Captain, 50

Naiad, H.M. Ship, 90
Nantes, 168
Napier Co., 249
Naples, 107, 121
Napoleon, *see* Bonaparte, Napoleon
Napoleon III, *see* Bonaparte, Prince Louis
National Maritime Museum, 11
Natividad, 127, 129-31, 134-8, 143
Nautilus, H.M. Ship, 108
Naval Chronicle, The, 123
Naval Miscellany, Vol. IV, 160
Navarino, 230-1
Navarino, Battle of, 230-3, 235-6, 258
Navy Board, the, 49, 53-4
Negapatam, Battle of, 39
Nelson, Viscount Horatio, 31, 34, 39, 92, 102, 105, 107-8, 110, 125, 145, 155, 182, 185, 187, 256-7
Neptune, H.M. Ship, 237
Nettlestead, 173, 253, 264, 282
Nevers, 166-8, 194, 196
Neufchateau, Vice-Admiral Bouvet de, 158

Nicaragua, 125-7, 134, 136
Nightingale, H.M. Ship, 120-2
Nile, Battle of the, 60, 200
Nisbet, Rev. M., 19
Noirmoutier, 168-9
Nonsuch, H.M. Ship, 175-6, 179, 191
North Sea Fleet, 102
Northumberland, H.M. Ship, 190-1
Northumberland, Duke of, 77
'*Nouvelle Description des Châteaux et Parcs de Versailles et de Marly*' (book by de la Force), 32
Nymphe, H.M. Ship, 34, 50-1

O'Connor, Fergus, 209
O'Connor, Roger, 208-10, 216
Oexmelin, Alexandre-Olivier, 32
Olot, 153
Oporto, 246
Oran, 115, 201
Orpheus, H.M. Ship, 57-8
Ostend, 101
Owens, Mr, 209

Paddock Wood, 244, 251, 253-4
Palamos Point, 144, 146
Palermo, 116, 120
Panama, 125-6, 131, 134, 136, 138
Panama, Gulf of, 130
Papillon, 52
Paris, 106, 157, 165, 167, 195, 198, 250, 252, 261, 281
Parker, Rear-Admiral Sir George, 90-1, 93
Parker, Nathaniel, 228
Parry, Admiral Lord, 86
Pasha, Ibrahim, 230
Passage Island, 114-15
Patriotic Fund, 122
Peace of Amiens, 83
Peacock, Zachary, 25
Peel, Sir Robert, 182
Peggy, 185-6
Pellew, Sir Edward (*later* Lord Exmouth, *cf*), 34, 48-50, 52-4, 56, 76-7, 88-90, 92, 181-2, 192, 256

Pembroke, H.M. Ship, 148–50, 152, 157

Penang, 248–9

Peninsular and Oriental Steam Navigation Co., 227, 235, 242, 246–9, 263

Peninsular Co., 227

Peninsular War, 259

Peninsular War, The (book by Whitehead), 154

Pennant, Thomas, 25–6

Pennington, Rev. Thomas, 17, 19, 21, 24

Pennington, Mrs Thomas, 19, 24

Penrose, Admiral Sir Charles, 199–200, 203

Perrin, Major, 173–4

Peterhof, 176

Phoebe, H.M. Ship, 214

Pillau, 177–8

Pique, 52

Pluto, H.M. Ship, 144, 146, 153, 157–8, 160–4

Plymouth, 55, 61, 64–5, 82, 90, 98, 100–2, 108, 110, 141–3, 145, 214, 240, 271, 278

Point Llansa, 145, 148, 164

Point Morant, 81

Pomone, 51

Popham, Sir Home Riggs, 128

Port-au-Prince, 80–1

Port Mahon, 144, 146–7, 152–4, 162

Port of Spain, 216

Port Vendres, 146

Porta Coeli, H.M. Sloop, 190–1

Porto Bello, 27, 130–1

Portsmouth, 36, 38–40, 44, 47–8, 51–2, 55, 83–5, 87–8, 121–6, 137–8, 140, 170–1, 190, 193–4, 200, 202–3, 211, 224, 240, 261, 271, 281

Pretty Jane, 222–4

Princess, 100–1

Pritchard, Mr, 22

Prosperine (French man-of-war), 97

Prouse, Mr, 86, 100

Prussia, King of, 193

Puerto Cabello, 221

Puerto Rico, 217, 223

Queen Charlotte (canal boat), 109

Queen Charlotte, H.M. Ship, 200, 202–3

Raglan, Lord (1st Baron), 259–60

Ramillies, H.M. Ship, 39

Ramsbottom, Charles, 220–1

Ramsgate, 27, 32, 111

Ransome, Rear-Admiral Henry, 220, 222

Rattler, SS, 242

Raven, H.M. Ship, 175

Rawson, Harriet, 33–6, 51

Rawson, George, 20–1, 23–4, 31

Rawson, Margaret (*later* Hornblower), 18, 20

Rawson, Thomas, 20–1, 23–4, 31, 33–6, 51, 83

Rayner, Mr, 141, 149

Redan Fort, the, 260, 263

Regency Rakes (book by Warburton), 85

Regent, Prince (*later* King George IV), 171, 189, 226

Reigate, Lord, 197

Reminiscences of Vice-Admiral Sir Josiah Houghton (book by Mark Houghton), 47–8, 53–4

Renown, H.M. Ship, 55–9, 61–73, 75–6, 78–9, 271–2, 276–9

Repulse, H.M. Ship, 161, 163

Resolve, 51

Retribution, H.M. Ship (formerly *Gaditana*, cf), 75–7, 79, 82–3, 86

Le Rêve, 55

Riga, 178–80, 184, 186

Rigney, Rear-Admiral de, 231

Rio de Janeiro, 128

River Plate, 128

Roberts, Mr, 58, 66, 68, 272, 274, 276

Rochefort, 101

Rodney, Admiral George Brydges (1st Baron), 28, 31, 60, 91, 156

Rodney, H.M. Ship, 160–3

Roebuck, H.M. Ship, 214
Romney, Lord, 212
Rosas, 153–5, 160–2
Rosas, Battle of, 144
Rosas Bay, 158
Rosily, Vice-Admiral, 107–8
Roume, Commissioner, 81
Rovira, General, 153–4, 165
Royal George, H.M. Ship, 59
Royal Naval College, 11
Royal William, H.M. Ship, 43, 45–7
Royal Yacht Squadron, 220
Royalist, H.M. Schooner, 52
Rügen, 176
Rule, Sir William, 124
Russell, Lord John, 255

St Helena, 137, 215
St Helena (book by Gosse), 216
St Petersburg, 176, 178–9
St Vincent, Earl (*formerly* Sir John Jarvis, *cf*), 61–5, 72–3, 188, 257
Sta Maria, 137,
Sainte-Croix, Marquis de, 85
Saints, Battle of the, 28, 60
Sally Port, 122, 204–5
Salthola, 176
Samaná Bay, 64, 67–9, 71, 73, 75–6, 78–9
Samaná Peninsula, 64, 68
Samaná Point, 67
Samson, SS, 211
Samuels, Mr, 272–3
San Gennaro, 161–3
San Josef, H.M. Ship, 181
San Juan, 126–7, 217, 223–4
San Pedro, 137
San Salvador, 130, 134
San Sebastian, 107
Sandwich, 17, 22, 26, 28–9, 32
Sandwich Grammar School, 28–9, 33
Sankey, Dr, 77
Sansculotte, French privateer, 34
Santa Barbara, 150–1
Santo Domingo *see* Haiti

Sari Point, 114–15
Saumarez, Admiral Sir James (*later* 1st Baron), 137, 175–6, 178–82, 193, 243
Sauvage, Fréderic, 242
Sawyer, Captain David, 56–8, 61–68, 71–6, 78–9, 272–9
Scarlett, Hon. Sir James, 259
Schank, Captain John, 42, 49–50, 53–4
Scipion, 231
Scourge, H.M. Ship, 34
Sea Fencibles, 102–3, 105
Seahorse, H.M. Ship, 224
Sealion, H.M. Ship, 260–1
Sebastopol, 258–61
Seitz-Bunau, HRR the Prince of, 110, 112, 119–21
Selva de Mar, 153–4, 157
Selyard, Lady, 212
Seymour, Lord Hugh, 80, 82
Shipwreck and Merciful Preservation of Zachary Peacock, The (book by Peacock), 25
Sicily, 121
Sidmouth, Lord (1st Viscount), 202, 225
Simon's Bay, 247
Simpson, John, 40
Singapore, 247–9
Sir Roger Manwood's School, 28–9, 33
Sirene (French man-of-war), 231
Sitges, 149
Slade, Sir Thomas, 39
Smallbridge Manor, 12, 103–4, 124, 153, 172–4, 180, 184, 186, 193, 195, 198, 212, 224, 244, 249–50, 254–5, 258, 263–4, 281–2
Smedley, Josiah, 42
Smiley, Mr, 119
Smith, Caleb, 227
Smith, Mr, 58, 65, 72, 272, 274, 279
Smith, Sir Sidney, 181
Smith, Thomas Pettit, 242
Smyth, H. Warrington, 26
Sneller, John, 33

Society for the Improvement of Naval Architecture, 53
South Eastern Railway Co., 241, 244, 253
Spain, King of, *see* Bonaparte, Joseph
Speedwell, 111
Spencer, 2nd Earl, 62, 64, 73, 79
Spendlove, Mr, 218–20
Sphinx, *SS*, 212
Spithead, 39, 44, 62, 201–2, 204, 281
Stanfield, Clarkson, 262
Stile, Mr, 119
Stockholm, 176
Strachan, Admiral Sir Richard, 50
Straits of Sunda, 246
Styles, Mr, 212–13
Suez, 125, 246, 248, 257
Suffisante, H.M. Ship, 94, 96–7
Superb, H.M. Ship, 203
Sutherland H.M. Ship (formerly *Eendracht*), 141, 144–6, 148, 151, 154–5, 157–64, 170
Swan V, 84–5
Sweeney, Francis, 148
Sweet, Nathaniel, 190–1
Sweet River, the, 218
Swift, H.M. Ship, 28
Synopsis of Quadrupeds (book by Pennant), 24–6
Syrtis, H.M. Ship, 55

Tarragona, 149
Tehuamtepec, Gulf of, 134
Tetuan, 115
Texel, 101, 141
Thames and Severn Canal, 109
Theatre of the Present War in the Netherlands, The (book by Brindley), 25
Theseus, H.M. Ship, 39
Thomas, Rev. William, 19
Thunderer, H.M. Ship, 39
Times, The, 17, 250
Tobago Channel, 215
Tonnant, H.M. Ship, 88
Torbay, 56, 62, 90

Toulinget Passage, 89
Toulon, 101, 106, 147–8, 154, 157, 161, 181
Trafalgar, Battle of, 108, 119, 200, 229, 257
Treaty of Amiens, 81, 86
Treaty of Nanking, 248
Treaty of Paris, 261
Trident, 231
Trim, 208
Tripoli, 201
Triton, H.M. Ship, 222
Triumph, H.M. Ship, 169
Troubridge, Rear-Admiral Sir Thomas, 62–3
Tug, SS, 211
Tunbridge, 103, 172, 174
Tunis, 116–19, 201, 239–40
Turenne (French man-of-war), 158–60, 162–3
Turner, George, 111, 119

Ushant, 62–3, 87–8, 91, 98, 145
Ushant, Battle of, 57–9

Valdivia, 137
Valletta, 112, 116–17, 235–8
Van de Capellan, Vice-Admiral Baron, 203
Vengeance, 111
Vernon, Admiral Sir Edward, 27
Vicary, Thomas, 212
Victoria, Queen, 243–4, 246, 249, 255, 264
Vickery, Captain, 178
Victory, H.M. Ship, 110, 169–71
Vigo, 105
Villeneuve, Commandant, 69, 71, 102, 105–8
Ville de Bordeaux, 158–60, 163
Ville de Paris, H.M. Ship, 62
Vittoria, Battle of, 184
Volos, 238
von Neffzer, Baron Franz Alexander, 198, 205
Voyage to New Guinea and the Moluccas from Balambangan, A (book by Forrest), 25

Waghorn Mr, 246–7
Walker, Mr, 43, 45–8
Walmer, 27
Walpole, Horace (4th Earl of Orford), 18–19
War of American Independence, 28, 91, 243
Warburton, H. R., 85
Ward, John, 84
Warren, Admiral Sir John Borlase, 50–1, 58
Warspite, H.M. Ship, 40, 46
Wateringbury, 282
Waterloo, Battle of, 194, 197, 205, 215, 257, 259
Watkin, Mr, 94
Watterton, Mr, 42–4
Wellard, Midshipman, 66–7, 272–274, 276–8
Wellesley, Anne, 132, 185
Wellesley, Arthur, 132
Wellesley, Arthur (*later* Duke of Wellington), 92, 132–4, 142, 147, 170, 174, 180, 184, 186, 192–3, 197–8, 205, 207–8, 226, 235, 240, 255–9, 261–2, 264
Wellesley, Lady Barbara (*later* Leighton, *cf*) (*later* Hornblower, *cf*), 130–4, 136–7, 139–40
Wellesley, Francis, 132
Wellesley, Garrett (1st Earl of Mornington), 132, 186
Wellesley, Gerald, 132
Wellesley, Henry (1st Baron Cowley), 132–4, 174

Wellesley, Mary Elizabeth, 132
Wellesley Papers, The, 196
Wellesley, Richard (2nd Earl and 1st Marquess), 170, 174, 186, 196, 209–10, 226, 244, 255
Wellesley, William, 132
Wells, Captain, 50
Whitehead, R., 154
Whiting, Captain, 73
Whitworth, Lord (1st Earl), 182
'Wicks, Mr', 106–7
Wilberforce, Bishop, 220
Willcox and Anderson Co., 227
Willcox, Mr, 247
William Fawcett, SS, 227
William IV, King of England, 243
Willoughby, Beatrice, 134
Willwood, 216
Wilson, Robert, 242
Wingo Sound, 176, 178
Witch of Endor, H.M. Ship, 168–170
Withinshaw, John, 125–6
Wodsworth, Rev. William, 30
Wood, John jr, 211
Wood, John sr, 211
Woolwich, 124
Worth (*also* Word, Worde), 17–19, 22–3, 26, 28, 111
Wyatt, Edwin, 212
Wyatt, Francis, 212
Wyatt, Richard, 212
Wyatt, Sir Thomas, 212
Wyatt (*or* Wiat) Sir Thomas, 212